HOW TO ROB THE BANK OF ENGLAND

HOW TO ROB THE BANK OF ENGLAND

THE TRUE STORY OF BRITAIN'S BIGGEST EVER ROBBERY

CLIFFORD THURLOW

ICON

Published in the UK in 2024 by
Icon Books Ltd, Omnibus Business Centre,
39–41 North Road, London N7 9DP
email: info@iconbooks.com
www.iconbooks.com

ISBN: 978-183773-135-0
eBook: 978-183773-137-4

Text copyright © 2024 Clifford Thurlow
The author has asserted his moral rights.

Every effort has been made to contact the copyright holders of the material reproduced in this book. If any have been inadvertently overlooked, the publisher will be pleased to make acknowledgement on future editions if notified.

No part of this book may be reproduced in any form, or by any means, without prior permission in writing from the publisher.

Typeset by SJmagic DESIGN SERVICES, India

Printed and bound in the UK

CONTENTS

Prologue — vii

1. Bird's Eye View — 1
2. The Mugging — 5
3. Trustworthy with Criminal Intentions — 11
4. Smurfing — 21
5. Life Lessons — 25
6. The Sweeney — 29
7. Victimless Crime — 35
8. The Great Unknown — 43
9. The Spider's Web — 49
10. The Dutch Connection — 57
11. Betrayal — 63
12. Good Ole Boys — 73
13. Defying Gravity — 85
14. Murder in the Park — 97
15. Above the Law — 105
16. An Offer You Can't Refuse — 113
17. The Sting — 119
18. The Crooked Sixpence — 127
19. Everybody's At It — 133
20. The Big Fish — 141
21. The Old Bailey — 149
22. The Irish Curse — 157

23. They're Always Watching	161
24. The Darkest Hour	169
25. On Remand	175
26. Dymchurch	181
27. On the Run	191
28. Funny Bone	199
29. '£290m Clue to Headless Corpse'	207
30. The Bengal Lancers	213
31. Fake News	225
32. Señor Dinero	233
33. The Untouchables	239
34. America	245
35. A Crime Against Money	253
36. Con Air	259
37. End Game	269
Epilogue	273
Acknowledgements	277

PROLOGUE

I am sitting beside the blue waters of the swimming pool with an open notebook and the hills of Anatolia rolling away in the distance. Keith Cheeseman is smoking a Montecristo. He flicks ash in a ceramic vase with patches of ancient glaze.

'Roman,' he says. 'Even older than me.'

His wife Sarah appears with a tray holding a pot of coffee and two cups. She wears a pale green summer dress, a shade lighter than her eyes that sparkle and miss nothing.

'Fancy a proper drink?' Keith asks, and I glance at my watch.

'It's not even ten yet.'

'When you do time, you don't think about time.'

He looks back at Sarah with a slight shrug that she reads without asking. She strolls back into the villa and returns with a bottle of raki. She pours two shots and adds water. It turns the liquor milky. Keith takes a sip.

'Now then, sunshine, where shall we start?'

I hit the record button on my phone.

'Let's start at the beginning.'

'Once upon a time in a land bloody far away from here,' he says and laughs.

He wets his lips and pauses for a moment. His expression grows serious and as he thinks back his eyes become as cloudy as the raki in his glass.

How to Rob the Bank of England

It all began on 2 May 1990. It was 9.30am when a courier left the Bank of England and two minutes later was robbed at knifepoint of a briefcase containing 292 bearer bonds worth £291.9 million.

It was the biggest heist in history. It made the Brink's-Mat gold bullion haul of £26 million look like peanuts and the Great Train Robbery of £2.6 million seem like child's play.

The robbery was so big it drew in an international network of criminals, arms dealers and terrorists, including the Mafia, the Provisional IRA and Colombian drugs king Pablo Escobar. It was the kind of money that can start wars and unseat governments. It changed the way banks made loans and hastened the pace of digital banking.

The theft by a young Jamaican wielding a knife appeared opportunistic. That was what the clandestine crime syndicate that planned the robbery wanted the police to believe. They needed to launder the bonds quickly and called in the well-known fraudster Keith Cheeseman to organise distribution.

During the next eighteen months, bonds hidden in ingenious ways were recovered in different places across the world. First, three men with links to the IRA were found with bonds in their luggage, in what the police described as a random search at Heathrow. Two telephone books with bonds between the pages posted to Escobar were found in Miami by US Customs. The FBI, posing as the Mafia, retrieved bonds in New York sent by London gangster Ray Ketteridge and carried by his solicitor Jeffrey Kershaw, who claimed he was a British police informer and went on the run.

Two gangland figures were murdered – both shot in the head.

Eighty people were arrested internationally, yet few were charged and those brought to court mysteriously walked free because prosecution 'was not in the public interest'.

Shortly before Christmas 1991, British police announced that they had recovered all but two of the 292 stolen bonds.

Keith takes a long draw on his cigar and lets out a cloud of smoke.

Prologue

'This is where it gets interesting.'
I gulp down my raki.

The police spokesman on the six o'clock news reported that the sum stolen in bonds was £292 million, rounding up the loose change. The thing is, on the night of the robbery, Keith Cheeseman and a Swiss banker counted 450 bonds, worth £427 million.

What happened to the missing millions? Why the deceit, the cover up? Why did the IRA men and gangsters walk out of court with the charges dropped? And who was the informer who led the police and FBI to track down the bonds so quickly?

Only one man went to jail for the robbery and only one man knows the true story: Keith Cheeseman.

Now comfortably retired to his villa in Turkey, he has pieced together the complex puzzle of the biggest theft in British history and reveals its secrets for the first time.

Some of the dialogue has been fictionalised for the purposes of dramatisation, and some of the names have been changed to protect the guilty as well as the innocent. Not Keith Cheeseman. He has done his time.

He refills the glasses.
This is his story.

Clifford Thurlow
Turkey, May 2023

1. BIRD'S EYE VIEW

It was a warm May morning in 1990, with the sun polishing the steel and glass walls of the NatWest building that rose over the cluster of City banks, insurance offices and, hidden from view, the Bank of England, with its Greek columns and the Union Jack fluttering above the roof as if to say all was well in the world.

And it was.

At least for Keith Cheeseman.

He moved away from the window. Keith hated the NatWest. In fact, his dislike of banks was such that he would have taken one down every day of the week if he'd had the chance. But there was something specifically irritating about the National Westminster, the way it blocked his view like a raised finger. He smiled.

I'll have you one of these days.

He glanced around. An Englishman's home is his castle. This was his, the penthouse at the Barbican, London, with fresh flowers in tall blue vases and Persian rugs neatly placed over shiny oakwood floors. Mrs Primrose, the cleaning lady, kept everything immaculate, the way he liked it. He had learned in the army there is a place for everything, and everyone has their place. He'd signed on at eighteen with the Royal Artillery in 1961 and did six years – an unlucky number intoned twice in his life by judges as they cracked their gavels down on the bench.

At 24 he entered civvy street with a vague plan to become richer than his rich brother. Keith didn't find it hard making a living in business, but crime made him feel alive. It filled the empty spaces inside him, the sense of boredom, of repeating yourself. When you are on a job, you step out on the highwire. There's no safety net. Every second is packed with life, that feeling that one slip and you're dead. It is all-consuming. Aside from the money, he thought of robbing banks as a counterbalance to banks robbing everyone else, with their insatiable greed for profits that filter up to the shareholders and executives.

Was he going to charge into the NatWest with a sawn-off shotgun and a getaway driver outside with the motor running?

No.

Keith was a fraudster, a con man, the last of the old-time villains, men with pride in their craft, a certain honour among thieves who say fair cop when they're collared, never carry a weapon and never grass. He thought of himself more as Robin Hood or Dick Turpin, looting banks, not to give to the poor exactly, but to spend lavishly and tip heavily. Trickle down, Mrs Thatcher called it. Defrauding banks is clean. If you dip into someone's account, the bank is duty bound to repay the money. No one gets hurt – except the banks.

He strode down the hall in carpet slippers and put the kettle on. He took a grip on the roll of flesh over his waist then went up on his toes to stretch his shoulders. He was a big man, still fit from athletics and football – he could have gone pro, and had trials for Everton and Birmingham, but back in the day Stanley Matthews, the most famous player in the country, was only earning £23 a week. How could you live on that?

That's the downside of the good life. You eat too much. You get addicted to the faint waft of the Caribbean every time you light a Montecristo. When you open a bottle of 1968 Château Lafite, you're not going to leave half.

He poured hot water into a mug and settled it down on the coffee table in the living room. A shaft of light lit the volumes in his bookcase. He liked hardbacks, solid books with a leathery smell, made to last. He'd worked in a library once and discovered that reading takes a certain amount of skill. You have to come at

Bird's Eye View

a novel like you've met a stranger on an empty railway platform and you don't know what's going to come out of it. Life was like that. Every day was a new page.

On the table was a copy of *War Plan UK*, a book given to him by Martin Newman, a former fellow resident at Wormwood Scrubs. Duncan Campbell, the author, had a dire warning that Britain was unprepared for a nuclear strike. Not that Martin, with his Mick Jagger looks and starlet girlfriends, was worried about Reds under the bed. What interested him was the chapter describing the secret Ministry of Defence narrow-gauge railways, below the streets of London, being used to shuttle bags of cash between banks. Martin had got hold of a key and they had gone down for a recce. Robbing the train would need a six-man crew to pull it off. It had potential, but Keith didn't like getting his hands dirty like a criminal.

He opened the book and read a few lines but couldn't concentrate. Dust motes danced in the beam of light. His temple pulsed, a tell when you're playing poker. He had a feeling, an intuition, that something was going to happen. Something massive, world changing. He took a sip of coffee.

That's when the phone rang.

Keith glanced at his Rolex as he reached for the receiver. It had just gone 10am.

'Hello.'

'Morning, darling, you're up early. What are you up to?' Henry Nunn's voice was posh, effete and confident.

'You know, minding my own business,' Keith answered.

'That'll be the day. Your nose is always in someone's business.'

'Yes, but only my nose.'

Nunn chuckled as Keith's gaze fell on the Antonio Canova Venus on the shelf. The Capodimonte figurine – one of his favourites – was worth more than his new Jag in the car park below the building.

Henry was a disbarred lawyer, as bent as a paper clip and as much at home with the villains who ruled London as he was in the royal box at Ascot with the Duke of Edinburgh. Once upon a time, he sold the Duke a set of Irish flintlock pistols, not because he needed the money, but because it was 'amusing' to know there were firearms of ambiguous provenance in the palace. Henry had helped him furnish the apartment with dodgy *objets d'art*. As Keith liked to tell friends, he once had hanging over his bed a 'Monet worth a lot of monet'.

He did a deal to put it back in the National Gallery where everyone could enjoy it and popped in for a nostalgic peek when Henry had tickets for a new exhibition. He liked Henry. He was a cross between Machiavelli and the Marquis de Sade – perverse, capricious, never dull.

'Alright, Henry, what are you selling?'

'*Pas une chose*. Not a thing, dear. I wondered if you'd like to come over this evening at about seven for *une omelette française*. Some of my chickens have come home to roost.'

'Have they now?'

Henry's tone changed. 'Last time we met, I suggested you smooch some of your people …'

He left the sentence hanging.

'That you did and that I did.'

'Perhaps another little powwow is in order. We might be talking big numbers.'

'There's big and there's *big*?'

'Let's say tons.'

'Very nice, Henry. Two eggs for me …'

'Sorry?'

'In the omelette, dear boy.'

'You mind your cholesterol.' The voice went back to camp. 'By the way, what happened to that gorgeous friend of yours?'

'He's not your type, mate.'

'Don't be so sure. See you at seven.'

2. THE MUGGING

Forty minutes before, at 9.30am, John Goddard buckled his briefcase and walked smartly down the steps from the Bank of England into Threadneedle Street. Goddard was a courier for Sheppards Moneybrokers, a man of 58, fit and sturdy in a grey suit and polished shoes.

He couldn't help smiling. The sun does that. All the grey City men forever looking down at the rainswept pavements had straightened their backs and were marching along as if war had just been declared. He passed a girl in a blue-and-white dress.

'Morning,' she said.

'Morning,' he replied.

She was pretty.

In the briefcase he carried bearer bonds, to what value, he had no idea. It was not his position to know such things. His job was to make sure the package inside the briefcase safely reached its destination.

It was extraordinary – in fact, Keith Cheeseman found it hard to believe – that every working day, Monday to Friday, Goddard and scores of couriers like him walked up to £30 billion in bearer bonds back and forth across the Square Mile. No guards. No guns. Just men with good leather shoes, a steady pace, a look of quiet determination and a stout, if unpretentious, briefcase.

The bonds they transported were government treasury bills or certificates of credit supplied by commercial banks. Known collectively as bearer bonds, they carry huge numbers – £1 million was not unusual – and differ little from bank notes in that they 'promise to pay the bearer' the sum on the certificate. 'On demand'.

It was through these bonds that banks lent and borrowed money short term and John Goddard felt that, in some small way, his role as a courier was the grease on the wheels that kept the money markets turning. He took a deep breath.

Was he getting older, or were the girls getting prettier?

He smiled to himself as he turned into Nicholas Lane, a narrow passage shaded by high Regency buildings.

Then ...

... he really wasn't sure what happened. How it happened. The sequence. The speed of it all.

A man stepped from the shadows and pressed a knife to his throat.

Time froze. He wasn't afraid. There was no time to be afraid. It was like a dream. He saw himself as if from across the road looking at a stranger.

Then the man spoke, breaking the spell.

'Don't be a fucking hero. It ain't your money.'

'What ...?'

The man wrested the briefcase from Goddard's grip and sprinted off through the maze of City streets.

It was all over in five seconds.

The thief was Patrick Thomas, a petty crook of Jamaican descent, who kept running until he arrived breathless at Charlie's Bar, where his friend Jimmy Tippett Junior was eating an egg and bacon sandwich. Tippett, then nineteen, was the son of *the* Jimmy Tippett, a prize fighter from South London who sometimes crossed the river for a few rounds at Repton Boxing Club. The former bath house in Bethnal Green, East London, was where the Kray Twins, Ronnie and Reggie, began their career of mayhem and murder.

The Mugging

Tippett was an enforcer, a dangerous man with imagination. One time, he was responsible for collecting a £100,000 gambling debt for the gangster Terry Coombs, at £10,000 a week. After three payments, the subject closed his wallet. Tippett went to the mortuary and came out with a bag containing a bloody arm that he hung on the debtor's front door in Lewisham. The geezer, as he said, paid up with an extra £10,000 for taking liberties.

Writing in his autobiography, *Born Gangster*, young Tippett recalled his dad arriving home when he was a boy of six and tipping out carrier bags full of bank notes onto the bed. It was the life he wanted, the life he was born into, and it came as no surprise that Pat Thomas wanted to impress him. The Tippetts were crime royalty. Pat was a foot soldier without connections trying to make a name for himself – and easy to take advantage of.

Thomas had been told to deliver the briefcase without opening it. But criminals have big egos, and big mouths they can't help putting their feet into. He couldn't resist showing off the haul and had to wait until Tippett had finished his sandwich.

'Alright, you got me,' Tippett said, wiping his lips and lighting a king-sized. 'What's in the case?'

'Let's go in the toilets and have a look.'

'Whoa, steady on. You're not going all Boy George on me …'

'Once you go black …'

They laughed and puffed on their Rothmans. They squeezed into a toilet cubicle and Thomas unbuckled the briefcase. If he was expecting to find diamond rings and strings of pearls, he would have been disappointed. Inside the case were a dozen folders in different colours. Each folder contained certificates that Tippett recalled 'looked like the kind of thing you get at school for swimming ten lengths' – except these certificates were embossed with the names of various high street banks, the Alliance and Leicester, Nationwide, Abbey National and the National Westminster. Printed in fancy lettering were very large sums – up to £1 million.

'Fuck me.'

'Let's have a couple,' Tippett said. 'Nobody'll miss 'em.'

'You having a laugh? They're numbered, look. I just wanted to see what it was for myself.'

'You didn't know? Fuck me. Who set this up, then?'

'Some poofter. I got a call, didn't I ...'

'You got a call? Who are you, James fucking Bond?' Tippet flicked through the certificates in one of the files. 'There's millions here.' He looked up at Thomas. 'This is too big for you, mate. This is 25 years.'

Thomas's face broke into the sort of smile men have when their horse comes in at 20–1.

'It's the big time, innit.'

Thomas resealed the briefcase and the last Jimmy Tippett saw of him that day was 'swaggering out of Charlie's Bar'.

···◆•————•◆···

John Goddard was rigid with shock but unharmed. He shook himself, took a breath, and ran back to the Bank of England.

Banks give the impression that their venerable institutions, housed in buildings that look like churches and temples, are slow and ponderous, that bankers are priests there to serve the public good. Like much in the banking world, this is false. Banks are always ahead of the curve when it comes to technology and move when the need arises like hares, not tortoises.

During the twenty minutes Pat Thomas spent with Jimmy Tippett in Charlie's Bar, bankers with nice accents were screaming down telephones and the serial numbers of the stolen bonds were gliding over computer terminals in banks across the globe.

Executives from Sheppards sprinted fast as express trains to Lloyds of London, the world's most famous insurance company, with its boast: 'Proud to take on any type of risk.' They sat down with the insurance brokers and senior police officers, good chaps in tailor-made suits, acquainted with each other through public school and gentlemen's clubs.

The Mugging

The moneybrokers revealed that the briefcase carried by John Goddard had contained 292 bearer bonds worth in total just under £292 million.

'Say that again,' said one of the policemen.

'£292 million.'

'In a briefcase?'

'It would have needed a Transit van to carry it in cash.'

They sighed and shook their heads. A woman dressed in black with a white apron brought in tea in porcelain cups and plates of biscuits, the English way, and they got down to business.

From Goddard's description of a knife-carrying young black man, police profilers reasoned that the robbery had been random, a one-in-a-million happenstance. Detective Chief Superintendent (DCS) Tom Dickinson, in charge of the investigation, believed the mugger would find what to him looked like worthless certificates and throw them away.

'I expect we'll have the case solved in a matter of days,' he boasted.

Sheppards had minimal insurance against the bonds being stolen – it had never happened before – but needed to up the premium in case they were never recovered. Lloyds set the increase at £750,000, which the moneybrokers agreed to pay.

DCS Dickinson glanced across the table at the broker from Sheppards as if it were his fault. 'This was a crime waiting to happen,' he added, and the good chaps nodded their heads and stirred their tea.

What the men gathered in that room did not know was that the police hypothesis, that the mugging was opportunistic, was exactly what those behind the robbery had anticipated and planned for.

What they had not planned for was the lost twenty minutes Thomas had spent at Charlie's Bar with Jimmy Tippett, giving the Bank of England time to circulate the serial numbers of the stolen bonds.

The delay cost the criminals millions of pounds and would cost Patrick Thomas his life.

3. TRUSTWORTHY WITH CRIMINAL INTENTIONS

Keith Cheeseman had been anticipating a bonds heist since January, when a courier working for Rowe & Pitman had forgotten to secure the straps on his briefcase and dropped £4 million in certificates of deposit on his way to the Bank of England.

A young surveyor found the bonds outside the Stock Exchange on Throgmorton Street and marched straight into the lobby to hand them in. He was rewarded with a magnum of Laurent-Perrier champagne and enjoyed fifteen minutes of fame being photographed by the newspapers.

The coverage did not go unnoticed.

Two weeks before the robbery, Cheeseman had met Martin Newman for coffee at the Café Royal in Regent Street. That's when Martin had given him the copy of *War Plan UK* that he'd bought – or lifted – that morning at Foyles, Keith's favourite bookshop, on Charing Cross Road. As they were leaving, they bumped into Henry Nunn in his tight-fitting pinstripes with a rosebud in the buttonhole. Keith introduced them.

'Martin, my old mate Henry. Watch yourself, he's the king of the shirt-lifters.'

They shook hands. Henry fluttered his eyelashes as he sized up Martin. With his long hair and black leather jacket he was not within the dress code for the Café Royal, but the maître d' turned a blind eye for those who brought style. Under his jacket, Martin wore a scoop-necked red vest revealing a lush carpet of chest hair.

'Honestly, I prefer those who have already abandoned their shirts,' Henry remarked. His tone changed as he turned to Cheeseman, with lines deepening on his brow. 'Are you still in touch with your friend in Indonesia?'

'Lovely chap. Wife's got a new poodle.'

'Jolly good.' Henry turned back to Martin with a smile. 'So nice to have met you.'

He climbed the stairs and waved as someone came down to meet him.

The robbery was all over the BBC at 6pm and it occurred to Keith that news is always a mixture of truths, half-truths and bollocks. The DCS in his shiny suit kept a straight face as he told the British public that a thief working alone had nicked bearer bonds worth £292 million and 'wouldn't be able to spend a penny' because the serial numbers had been circulated 'to every bank in the world'.

Detective Chief Superintendent Dickinson knew that the statement was untrue. Once minted, bearer bonds have the same versatility as uncut diamonds, whether the serial numbers are known or not. Using bearer bonds to hide and move assets may not be cheap, but it is easy. There are law firms and chartered accountants in the City that don't display brass plaques, and behind their closed doors all your financial needs will be met with no questions asked. As there is no record of who the seller is or who is buying the bonds, you can move money in high denominations and store it in fiscal paradises, where the sun always shines on fishermen casting their nets in picturesque bays and *omertà* is a way of life.

Terrorists and criminals trade stolen bonds as collateral in arms deals, drug deals, terror plots and property speculation. Bonds washed through private banks in tax havens finance wars and overthrow governments. When Colonel Oliver North

Trustworthy with Criminal Intentions

diverted cash from weapons sales to Iran in 1985 to fund the American-backed Contras plotting to oust the socialist government in Nicaragua, they used bearer bonds as security.

Keith remembered watching the movie *Die Hard* at the Odeon Leicester Square. Alan Rickman, playing the lead bad guy, swipes bonds worth $640 million in a couple of duffel bags and tells his gang that by the time the authorities know they've gone 'they'll be sitting on a beach earning 20 per cent'. Keith felt as if he were standing in Rickman's shoes all the way to the final fist fight when Bruce Willis as a New York detective foils the plot.

And now in other news ...

... while police search for the bond robber, poll tax rioters continue to occupy Trafalgar Square ...

Keith turned off the TV and poured himself a gin with a lot of tonic.

He had made *that* call after lunch. His conversation with Abyasa Tjay – TJ to his mates, lasted 90 seconds.

'TJ ...'

'The answer is yes,' he said the moment he heard Keith's voice.

'You can't have heard already?'

'You forget, my friend, we are always ahead of you in London – by six hours.'

'Still ...'

TJ was in.

Big time.

The bubbles from the tonic went up Keith's nose and made him laugh. For some reason, what came into his mind was the night at the Waldorf Astoria in New York in June the previous year when he first met TJ. Vice President George Bush happened to be there at the same time, visiting the long-time Indonesian President Suharto who, like Picasso, was generally known by a solitary name. The Astoria was the watering hole for those in the pink, in the know and on the make.

Keith had forgotten his wallet and was in the lift ready to go up to his suite when a secret service man in a black suit caught the doors before they closed. George Bush entered with an escort of aides.

'I do apologise for holding you up,' he said.

'That's alright. Got all the time in the world,' Keith replied.

'Oh, you're English.'

'Keith Cheeseman.'

'I'm George.'

'I know, sir, the vice president.'

'For my sins. Lovely country, England. Always a pleasure to visit.'

'Except for the bloody rain.'

George laughed.

They stepped out on the top floor. Keith collected his wallet and went back to Peacock Alley, the lobby bar, to join Rocky Graziano; the one-time middleweight boxing champion of the world was looking for partners to buy a vineyard in Napa Valley. They were still there when George Bush passed through with his men in black.

'Hi there, Champ. Hi, Keith,' he called.

After this fleeting acknowledgement from the vice president, Keith always got the best table in the restaurant and was treated as a VIP by all the staff in the hotel.

Later that evening, he was having a drink with Ben Blessing, an American based in Holland. Blessing was an icon, a mythical figure, the man little boys who dreamed of scamming banks wanted to be when they grew up. His reputation had earned him the sobriquet Mr Big.

A group of Indonesian women dripping in gold and wearing sparkling dresses passed through the lobby like a flock of chattering parrots. TJ was following them but peeled off when he saw Blessing and headed towards the two men. Ben introduced them. TJ had a firm grip when they shook hands and looked Keith in the eye as if he were taking an X-ray. He was related by marriage to the old butcher Suharto, but probably had bigger ambitions.

'Are you here on business, Mr Cheeseman?'

'I am.'

'And what is your business, if you don't mind my asking?'

'I rob banks.'

'With a fountain pen,' Blessing added.

TJ didn't laugh. He glanced at Blessing, then lowered his voice. 'It is the only way to live,' he said. 'Do excuse me, I must take care of the concubines …'

Keith met TJ again later that year, in Florida with Mark Lee Osborne, a disqualified bond trader from Texas. Keith had some JC Penney bonds with mixed values of $10,000 and $20,000 he wanted to cash in. TJ glanced at the bonds and shook his head. The sums were too small for him to deal with.

'May I tell you a story I was told by my father?' he said and sipped his drink. 'There are two bulls in a field above a meadow with a herd of cows. The young bull says: let's rush down there, cross the fence and fuck a cow. The old bull is silent for a moment, then he says to his young friend: no, let's go down there slowly, cross the fence and fuck them all.'

'Hey, that's funny,' Mark Osborne said.

'It is not a joke, Mark.'

They went out to eat at an Indonesian restaurant. TJ introduced Keith to *nasi goreng*, the national dish, and he introduced TJ to the Silver Oak Cabernet Sauvignon from California at $60 a bottle. They bonded over their love of bonds and Keith returned home confident that he had a good contact when the right deal came along. He flew back to the UK on Concorde, always a good place to meet people, and searches were cursory, if they happened at all.

He straightened his dark-blue-and-plum-red-striped tie and slipped on his suit jacket. The lift took him down to the car park in the basement where his green 2.4-litre Jag was as shiny as an emerald in the half-light. Rodney Miller, the doorman, was waiting to go up.

'Evening, governor,' he said.

'You been polishing my car again?'

'Lovely motor. Going somewhere nice?'

'Who's asking? You working for MI6?'

'That's my secret, Mr Cheeseman.' He lit a rollup. 'You hear about that robbery? Millions some bloke got away with.'

'Hope he enjoys spending it, that's what I say.' They laughed and Keith tucked a tenner in Miller's top pocket.

'I don't want that,' he said.

'Easy come. Easy go. One of my chickens came home to roost.'

'Nice one. Don't get that bloody motor dirty.'

Keith climbed in the car. The big engine roared like a 747 and it wasn't easy sticking to the speed limit driving to Mayfair. The roads were empty. Everyone was either rioting over Maggie's poll tax or staying at home to avoid it. He parked in a meter slot and locked up. It was warm still. The sun had turned the windows orange along the length of Seymour Place with its red-brick mansion blocks and houses with marble steps and columns.

He crossed the road to Henry's place, an Aladdin's cave crammed with high-ticket antiques and paintings by old masters. There was a Goya in the kitchen, a row of Dalí prints in the hall and the front door wasn't locked. He closed it with a bang so Henry knew he'd arrived. It was 7.10pm. A champagne cork popped as he entered the living room and Henry filled six glasses.

'A toast,' he said. 'To us.' They clinked their crystal flutes.

They were, Keith thought, an odd bunch. Henry with his fleshy pink face, grey eyes sharp as flint and the permanent look of vague disdain that comes to those who have seen and done it all – at least twice. At his side stood Roger, his 'assistant', whom Keith had met before. Feminine, amenable, forgettable, he sipped from his glass and stole into the shadows.

There was a big Irishman named Houlihan in a donkey jacket who looked as if he had just strolled in from a building site. He pulled a sour face drinking the champagne, but apart from that his expression never changed. He watched and listened, the eyes and ears of someone higher up the food chain.

Henry introduced Keith to John Bowman. He was English, tall with pale-blue eyes and waves of silver hair, a banker based in Switzerland with a young Swiss wife and two sons at Charterhouse. He wore a signet ring with a crest on the pinkie finger of his left hand, and Keith could tell from his Armani suit and bench-made Oxfords that he had the expensive tastes of someone always two quid short of a fiver.

'So nice to meet you finally,' he said.

'Finally?'

'Henry has filled me in.'

'He's going to get himself filled in one of these days.'

Ray Ketteridge had crossed the room and lifted a briefcase on to a round mahogany table.

'Here we are, Keif, come and take a butcher's.'

He squared up in a boxer's pose as Keith approached. Keith raised his fists in response.

'What do you reckon?' Ray said. 'Think you can take me?'

'As long as you've got one arm tied behind your back.'

'You still wouldn't have a chance.'

'Unless I kick you in the bollocks.'

'That ain't Queensberry, is it?'

Ray straightened his shoulders and gave Keith what he thought of as a friendly slap on one cheek, which Keith didn't like but let it go.

'How're you keeping, son?' Ray asked.

'You know. Can't complain.'

'This time next week, you won't have anything to complain about.'

'You don't know my wife.'

He laughed. 'You're a bloody comedian, Keif, you know that.'

Ray Ketteridge was a hard man inside a Savile Row suit who must have seen Michael Caine in Neil Jordan's movie *Mona Lisa* and styled himself on the actor. To be fair, he did look like Caine, broad, handsome, his quiff of fair hair bronzed by the sun on the Costa del Crime, as the tabloids called the Spanish coast.

This was the second time Keith and Ray had met. The first had taken place after a last-minute invite from Henry Nunn to meet at Tramp, the nightclub in Jermyn Street. When Keith arrived, Nunn and Ketteridge were at a corner table with a plump chap with the dishevelled look of those who wear shirts with frayed collars to show they went to the best schools. He stood immediately, with a broad smile, and spoke with a lisp.

'So you are K-K-Keith Cheeseman,' he said, before they were introduced.

'And you are?'

'N-n-nobody. N-n-nobody who matters.' He waved over his shoulder as he left. 'Have a p-pleasant evening.'

Ketteridge snapped his fingers and the waitress came running over.

'Who's that then?' Keith asked.

'We were at Gordonstoun,' Nunn answered. 'Best shot in England, so he tells anyone who will listen. So glad you could join us.'

The previous year, Ketteridge had been implicated in a £32-million bank fraud in France. After spending nine months on remand, Nunn had pulled strings to get him out of jail. It's a cliché to say it's who you know, but clichés are usually spot on. Nunn managed to get the charges dropped and Cheeseman had a funny feeling that it involved the man with the frayed shirt and stammer. 'No names, no pack drill, as we used to say in the army.'

They drank whisky and ate nuts from bowls the waitress kept filling. There was dance music. Nobody danced. It was too early. When Princess Margaret appeared in a cloud of smoke and hangers-on it was never before midnight. Keith had been at the club one night when the owner, Johnny Gold, chucked out a couple of Georges for being too drunk – his mate George Best and singer George Michael. On another occasion, Keith watched Prince Andrew on his first date with the actress Koo Stark and, later, Andy was often on the dance floor clutching

Sarah Ferguson like a drowning man to a lifeline. That was before they married in 1986.

Henry Nunn crossed one well-pressed trouser leg over the other and gazed about him with the relaxed smile of someone who has just found the answer to a difficult clue in a crossword. He was a spider at the centre of a web of aristocrats and gangsters and had come to see that these two groups, who at first glance appear to be opposites, had in common a love of the good life, ambiguous morals and an unconscionable fear of boredom. An introduction from Henry Nunn said you were trustworthy with criminal intentions.

Villains are like washerwomen; they love to gossip. Who's in jail. Who just got out. Who nicked what and who fenced it. How their sister once dated Reggie Kray and they went three rounds with Frank Bruno. Getting involved in, and escaping scot-free, from the French job gave Ray Ketteridge his bona fides. He was a player in the same game as Keith Cheeseman.

Keith had become renowned in criminal circles when his story went public at the Old Bailey and his name was splashed across the tabloids. In partnership with Lord Angus Montagu, he had bought non-league Dunstable Town Football Club and persuaded soccer legend George Best to come out of retirement to play for the team. Keith opened dozens of accounts in fictitious names and made £300,000 taking out false loans at the Beneficial Bank. He was arrested with Lord Montagu when the fraud was discovered. In the High Court Keith was convicted and served almost four years of a six-year sentence. Angus Montagu had pleaded not guilty and was acquitted.

'One law for them, one law for us,' Ray remarked.

'As it should be,' Nunn added.

They both looked at Nunn and looked back at each other, aware that what was meant to sound funny wasn't funny at all.

4. SMURFING

The ormolu clock on the mantel chimed the half hour as Keith watched Ketteridge unbuckle the briefcase. From it he removed twelve different coloured files. He made two stacks, six files in each.

'Keif, Jonny. Let's see what we've got.'

Keith unpacked the bonds and kept them in six piles around one side of the table. He went through each pile, counting in his head. Bowman did the same. They stood back, the table decorated like a handless clock.

'I make it £210 million,' Keith said.

Bowman looked back at him as if he'd just been stung by a wasp. 'Mine's £217 million.'

'What's that make?' Ketteridge asked.

Bowman stroked his wave of hair. 'It comes to £427 million.'

'Now that is a surprise,' Ketteridge said, and Keith registered no surprise in his voice at all.

Keith and Bowman counted the opposite piles and reached the same total. The six men stood there in silence. On the polished mahogany table in Henry Nunn's living room, they were not looking at 292 bonds worth £292 million, as DCS Dickinson had reported on the six o'clock news. What they had was a little less than a ream of A4 paper, weighing about five pounds, consisting of 427 bonds worth £427 million.

'What lucky boys we are,' Henry said, breaking the silence. His expression in the dimming light showed no change.

Keith lit a cigar and glanced through the smoke from Ketteridge to Nunn and back again. Ray had thrust his hands in his trouser pockets and looked like a huge crow about to take flight. £427 million – with a buying power of more than £10 billion in 2023 – was head turning, mind blowing, unrealistic. Had it been 26 million, like the Brink's-Mat robbery, they would have shifted the bonds in a fortnight and all had a nice pay day. £427 million was an ocean, and he could see them all drowning in it if they weren't careful.

'What do you reckon, Jonny?' Ray asked, and Keith noticed Bowman's hands were shaking.

'We can restructure a portion,' he replied.

'Smurfing,' Keith added.

Ray looked back at Bowman. 'You explain it to me as if I'm a monkey.'

'Restructuring is breaking up large transactions into smaller ones so as to avoid detection. As a debt security, bearer bonds are not registered. It's a loophole built into the system for investors who want to remain anonymous.'

'The stinking rich,' Ray said.

'That means whoever holds the paper is presumed to be the owner.'

Ray shook his head. 'What's this about smurfing then?'

'Just slang,' Keith replied. 'You know those little blue cartoon characters called Smurfs? They divide up tasks the same way funds have to be divided before they're invested.'

Bowman continued. 'The international banking system is like a river. We open shell companies using individual bonds as capital and slip them into the flow. As we shift the capital through different companies and different banks, the original deposit is washed away and the cash is laundered.'

'How long's that going to take?'

Keith blew out smoke. 'For this lot? About 100 years.'

'You have other ideas, Keith?' asked Nunn, knowing that he did.

'I do, as it happens. I spoke to my contact today in Indonesia.' Ray had been pacing about. Now he stopped to listen. 'He said he'll take £200 million ...'

There was an inward rush of air as they all took a breath. Even Houlihan's dead eyes came to life.

Smurfing

'At 25 per cent.'

'What's that, £50 million?' Ray said. 'You must be fucking joking.'

'No, Ray, I am not joking. It's a good rate.'

'Fucking 25 cent. Who is this geezer, anyway? I don't even know where bloody Indonesia is.'

'Far East. You know, Philippines, Korea. Next to Australia. Our bloke's related to President Suharto. He has a position in the Treasury.'

'I dunno, Keif. I don't trust foreigners. How do we know he'll pay up?'

'That's not a problem. The money'll go in escrow.'

He glanced at Bowman. 'What's that, then, Jonny?'

'We would engage an escrow agent who works as a neutral third party. They hold the bonds offshore for us and the cash offshore for the buyer. They make the exchange when the two parties come together.'

'And charge for it?'

'A relatively small sum.'

'I still don't trust bloody foreigners. Or banks.'

It struck Keith that Ray Ketteridge saw a £1-million bearer bond as being worth £1 million, its face value, which it is if it's legit. Twenty-five per cent on £200 million for hot bonds was the best deal they were going to get. Ray didn't seem to know that.

'What do you think, Henry?' Keith asked.

'Not my decision, dear boy.'

'It might not be your decision, but what do you think?' Keith persisted. 'We're not talking about five grand, are we? We're talking about 50 mil.'

Henry glanced at Ray. Ray was out of his depth and Keith couldn't work out why Henry wasn't pulling him out of the water. Why had the police reported that 292 bonds had been stolen when there were 427 on the table? Who had set up the robbery and who stood to gain from the 135 unrecorded bonds worth £135 million at face value? What did Ray Ketteridge and Henry Nunn know that the police didn't?

There were a lot of questions Keith Cheeseman wanted to ask, but this was not the appropriate time. It was actually the time to bow out gracefully. But, then, when you're standing next to almost half-a-billion quid in bonds freshly nicked from the Bank of England, your toes tingle and there's an adrenaline rush that hits the brain like a Class A drug. *Fuck it*, he thought, *I'm in for the ride*.

'I don't want to press you, Ray, I'll just say it once more. Twenty-five per cent on 200 mil is a very good rate. My man will fly out to Panama or wherever and have the money sitting in the bank. We'll shift our bonds there and the escrow dealer will put us together. The going rate for the dealer is 2 per cent. That's a million on 50 mil. We come home with £49 million in offshore deposits and a suntan.'

'You may be right, Keif. It's a good rate if we can't get better,' he replied and shoved his hands back in his pockets. 'The fing is, how's this foreign geezer reckon he's going to shift that kind of number?'

'I don't know, Ray. I don't know how the engine in my Jag works. I just turn the key and drive it. Banks in the Far East run by their own rules. He'll probably slip it into the Treasury on some bogus oil deal and clean it through shell companies and trusts – smurfing big time.'

They were silent again. The room had grown dark. Roger switched on the lights. Ray paced, smoking, and stopped to stub his fag out.

'This is early days,' Henry Nunn said. 'We don't have to do anything definitive tonight.'

Ray glanced at Keith. 'See, a word from the wise,' he said. 'Keep the doors open. Let's think about this.' He counted out five bonds and gave them to Bowman. 'See what you can do with these.'

He counted out another five and gave them to Keith. 'Talking about 25 per cent, Keif, that's your piece. See what you can get.'

Houlihan watched as Keith folded the five bonds neatly in three and slid them into his inside jacket pocket.

5. LIFE LESSONS

For Keith, banks were poison and bankers shady shysters who care about nothing but personal bonuses and shareholder profits. His disdain began in 1972 when his building company – W.W. Parrish West Midlands – had £7-million worth of work on the books and Barclays and the local branch of the Bank of Ireland both cancelled his overdraft facility for no apparent reason. He borrowed money from mates and had to pay it back at high interest.

When banks crash, the government dips into the Treasury to bail them out. When businesses crash it's like a glass dropping on a stone floor, they smash into a million pieces. The lesson Keith learned was that if you are in the building game, the way to get ahead is to get local government contracts with their guaranteed finance. To get through that barred and bolted door, it's not what you know ...

All business, as in all things in life, begins with connections. Connections are links in a chain that grow stronger as you forge new links. You take a local councillor to a swanky hotel for dinner and you don't try to charm him. You charm his wife. Then your wife and his wife have lunch. If you don't have a wife, that's alright, there are thousands of young actresses happy to earn a few bob playing the role.

Next, you invent a wedding anniversary or a special birthday and invite lots of guests to a reception. That's when people start talking about you and that's when you get to meet the chairman of the planning committee – another link in the chain. He's going to ask his fellow councillor what you're like and he'll say you're a lovely bloke – not on the make, just bidding for the occasional job. It takes time. It costs money.

And that's an important lesson: it takes money to make money.

For the charm offensive, Keith had the perfect partner in his wife Dawn – Mrs Cheeseman II – whom he'd met in the first-class lounge at Heathrow. Like taking a suite in Claridge's or the Waldorf Astoria, a seat in first class is a statement of intent, like the Rolex and custom-made shoes, every detail is a projection of who you are and what you expect from life. With her dark eyes and dark curls, Dawn was tall, willowy and kitted out in Paris and Milan couture. She had trained as a barrister before setting up Central Appointments, a temp agency with eight offices in London and an eye on the continent.

Along the way, they met John Stonehouse, the local Member of Parliament. He invited Keith to the House of Commons where a drink with fixer George Brown led to lunch on the terrace with Labour leader Harold Wilson and Marcia Faulkender, a woman for all seasons. This was during the 1974 general election campaign and Wilson was flying all over the country on a helicopter loaned to him by Eric Miller, a director of Fulham Football Club, a mate of Keith and the bon vivant owner of the Peachy Property Corporation.

Keith mentioned that he also leased a helicopter through his building company and would make it available if it ever became necessary. He had learned that generosity is like a boomerang, the harder you throw it out, the faster it comes back to you. Tip well. Don't forget the little people. The maid who makes the beds in a first-class hotel gets a second-class wage packet at the end of the week. Leave a fiver on the bedside cabinet.

Two days after meeting John Stonehouse, Miller's chopper was grounded up north in bad weather when Wilson had a conference to attend in Devon. Keith got the call from George Brown.

'No problem, mate, I'll have my pilot in the air in ten minutes. It's parked up in Battersea.'

'That's marvellous, old chap. You'll be in line for a medal at this rate,' he said, half joking, and paused for a chuckle. 'What do you fancy?'

'I don't know, an OBE might be nice.'

'We'll have to go through Marcia for that. It'll cost.'

'What doesn't these days? What are we looking at?'

'Hard to say. I'll get back to you.'

Keith got the whisper that it would cost an £8,000 donation to the Labour Party to get his chest pinned with an OBE – the Most Excellent Order of the British Empire, an award for chivalry, charity and contributions to the arts and sciences. It all made sense to Keith, politics was a dark art and a devious science. He came up with the £8,000. He gave it to George in a brown envelope and George told him the next day he had passed it on to Marcia.

After Labour's victory in the election, Wilson moved into Downing Street and Eric Miller bent a knee to receive a knighthood. Keith was curious to know how much he had paid for it but never pushed the matter with Marcia, 'Rasputin in a red dress,' as John Stonehouse once said.

As for Sir Eric, he committed suicide shortly after by shooting himself in the head – twice.

John Stonehouse was a rising star in the Labour Party when, on 20 November 1974, he left a pile of clothes on a beach in Miami and faked his death – by drowning or a shark attack. He travelled in secret to Australia, where he used numerous false identities to transfer money between banks but was spotted by a teller in New South Wales who called the cops. Stonehouse was returned to Britain where he faced 21 charges of fraud, theft and conspiracy. He was sentenced to seven years.

On arriving in HM Prison Blundeston in Suffolk, he spent the night in a holding cell and was relieved the following morning when he walked into the garden and bumped into Keith Cheeseman picking strawberries.

'Hello, son, I thought I'd see you here one of these days,' Keith said.

'I shouldn't even be here.'

'They all say that. Make the best of it, John.'

Keith never got his OBE. He got what he calls an OOBE – Ordered Out of the British Empire. Marcia became Lady Faulkender. George Brown starting globe-trotting as foreign secretary before donning ermine robes in the House of Lords, and Keith took this as one more lesson: politicians are criminals in masks lacking that quality of honesty and loyalty bona fide criminals have; well, most of them. When you make a deal, you shake hands, look one another in the eye and keep your word. Your word is your reputation. It's what keeps you safe. If you're caught, you eat your porridge. You never grass. Grass is the green stuff on a football pitch.

6. THE SWEENEY

Keith played soccer for the army and had always fancied going pro. After being demobbed in 1967, he went for a trial at Dunstable Town Football Club. He played for the reserves but didn't make it into the squad. Six years later, when he was past his football-playing prime, the club came up for sale and in 1973 he raised the money to buy it with Lord Angus Montagu, a man who enjoyed a good supper and whose name added glamour on the club letterhead.

Signing the legendary ex-Manchester United star George Best put the club on the map and Cheeseman under the spotlight, so much so that the satirical magazine *Private Eye* raged about him in its Knacker of the Yard column: 'How come the owner of Dunstable Town FC drives a Lamborghini?'

The answer was simple. Keith was opening false accounts and taking out £1,000 loans. In part to maintain his lifestyle, but more because both his building firm and football club were suffering cash-flow problems. While the banks in the seventies were laying off staff and reporting billions in profits, small firms with confirmed work booked in were being denied loans. Keith had every intention of servicing the debt, but before the profits rolled in the crime was uncovered when David Beatty, manager of the local branch of the Beneficial Bank and finance director of Dunstable Town FC, decided to use players' names and addresses for the false accounts, rather than names from the phone book.

Keith was duly charged with fraud and stood in the dock at the Old Bailey with his partner Lord Angus, who pleaded not guilty. The judge considered Angus too dim to be a fraudster. 'On a business scale of one to ten, the duke is one or less, and even that flatters him,' he told the court. Angus walked out with a clean sheet while Keith walked downstairs to a damp cell that stank of dirty underwear.

Was Angus Montagu in on the fraud? Keith Cheeseman never said and the two men remained friends.

In 1985, after the death of his brother Kim, the 11th Duke of Manchester, Angus had become the 12th Duke of Manchester. He was praised after his three-minute maiden speech in the House of Lords for its brevity. The duke became the chairman of the famous Tampa Bay Lightning ice hockey team with a pledge to raise funds. The money didn't come sliding in, it went skimming out. The debts mounted and in 1991 Angus was charged with fraud. He applied the same defence. According to his lawyer, he was too 'gullible, vain and foolish' to be a confidence trickster. The judge obviously didn't think much of British titles and the duke served two years in a sweltering Florida prison before being deported back to Blighty.

···◆–●————●–◆···

Shortly after Keith was charged with the Dunstable bank job, when he was on bail, he was offered a way out by an inspector he knew in the Sweeney – the Flying Squad. They met in a pub, obviously.

'If you want to get off this, there is a way,' he said.

'I'm all ears, Tony.'

'I'll charge you with possession of a gun ...'

'You having a laugh?'

'Hold on a tick, hear me out. If I charge you with keeping a firearm, that's a more serious offence. It takes precedence over the fraud. That way, the Sweeney will take over the investigation, and we can drop the charge. There'll be some money in it as well.'

'Now you are having a laugh.'

'Twenty-five grand suit you?'

'Would you need a receipt?'

He laughed. 'We'll need something.'

That something was intelligence on His Grace Angus Montagu, on his mates in the Lords, on the people Keith drank with and dined with, on anyone and everyone who may or may not have been involved in bank fraud or any kind of criminal activity. He was offering Keith Cheeseman a job.

'Listen, Tony, I don't want to fall out with you. It's a bloody good offer, but you know me, and it ain't me.'

'Yeah, that's what I thought. Worth a try, Keith.'

···◆─●────●◆···

Six years in the army had been good grounding for prison life. Keith didn't feel the need to buck the system and learned how to play it to his advantage. He didn't blame anyone else for getting collared – you have to weigh that into the balance when you take up crime; it's part of the risk and, in a funny way, part of the thrill. You have to make friends and do favours inside, the same as you need contacts outside. With friends in high places, like the garden or the kitchen, you get the best grub and easiest assignments.

Keith abhorred violence, but he quickly learned that it is vital to project an aura of menace, an implied willingness to use violence. This was even more so the case in American prisons, as he would learn later in life. Everybody has to be aware that you cannot be intimidated. You're a doormat if you allow that to happen.

With bent screws – which most are – and a bit of cash to draw on, you live relatively well. Keith had his regular hamper from Fortnum & Mason, his Harrods Christmas pudding, a case of wine for the screws and the odd bottle left in his cell.

John Stonehouse's worry was his girlfriend, Sheila Buckley. She was broke, so Keith's wife Dawn gave her a job with Central Appointments and they drove out to Blundeston together in the convertible Jenson Interceptor Keith had bought as a company car for W.W. Parrish. The girls had big hair and wore tight skirts.

The prisoners would rush to the cell windows just to see them clip-clopping in on their stilettos.

One of the old lags asked him, 'Which one's yours?'

'We mix and match,' Keith said. Untrue, but it was worth it just to see the look on his face.

'Blimey, I wish I had your life, Keith.'

'So do I.'

Keith didn't try to be flashy, but he was outgoing with a big personality. He moved between jobs in the garden and the library. He was chatty, a storyteller. He liked people. Prisoners came to him for advice. Everyone had problems: a wife at home having it off with the plumber, their mum dying and they couldn't get a temporary release to go to the funeral, a lack of fags, a lack of money, a debt to someone who had threatened to cut their thumb off. There seems to be winners and losers in life and they take that with them into prison.

Keith was living better behind bars than most people on the outside. In fact, one of the broadsheets ran a feature on him in the lifestyle section that led to Questions being asked in Parliament and a cartoon by JAK – Raymond Jackson – in the *Evening Standard*, showing six waiters with steaming tureens lining up outside Keith's cell.

Why, when Keith operated a successful building business and was usually at the best table at the best restaurants with celebrities and royalty, did he feel the need to scam and swindle banks?

It is not an easy question to answer. It was the buzz, the craic, the pleasure of cheating a system he believed was designed to cheat the people who trusted that system. You only get one life and you don't know how long it is going to last. You can get a job, work for 40 years, pay into a pension and retire to a nice little bungalow in Margate. That is a good life. A life well lived.

But what if the poor bugger dies in a car accident or gets some life-changing disease at 50? Thirty years with your nose at the grindstone and what have you got to look forward to? We see on our death bed, not our whole life flashing before us – as with a drowning man – but an endless sequence of all the things we wanted to do and never did.

Keith was born on 10 June 1942 during the Blitz. The Luftwaffe attacks in what was called the 'Baedeker' raids, after the German travel guides, saw bombs falling on London and cities all over Britain. His dad owned a TV rental shop in Luton and he went to the local secondary modern. Rationing didn't end until 1954, when Keith was twelve and the country was still a bombsite. Conscripted into the army aged eighteen, he signed on for six years with the Royal Artillery and walked out into the Swinging Sixties with one desire: to enjoy life and live it to the full.

In Blundeston, encouraged by John Stonehouse, he read *The Outsider* by Albert Camus. The writer seemed to have spent his whole life pondering the purpose of human existence and concluded that man's search for the meaning of life is absurd in a world devoid of eternal truths or values. So, Keith concluded, if nothing means anything, you might just as well get on with life and enjoy it.

That's what he did in Blundeston, until he crossed the Governor, and his dog days came to an end. The Governor didn't like John Stonehouse with his posh accent and probably thought he was looking down on him. When John was reported by one of the grasses for some minor misdemeanour, the Governor made him clean the toilets by hand.

Keith complained to the Governor on John's behalf and before the end of the week he was transferred in a paddy wagon, first to HMP Albany, then that little piece of hell on earth they call Parkhurst – begging the question that lingers still in Keith's mind. Why send someone convicted of non-violent fraud to serve out his sentence among the most violent offenders in the country: murderers, terrorists, gun runners, child molesters, rapists?

Parkhurst had housed Moors murderer Ian Brady and the Yorkshire Ripper Peter Sutcliffe. Ronnie and Reggie, the infamous

Kray twins, tabloid stars, kings of London crime, had their eyes on Keith Cheeseman the moment he strolled into the exercise yard with his bobbing walk and big smile.

Now, there's a challenge, Keith thought. What can I do for them so they don't do for me?

What Keith's tour through the prison system had done was give him a reputation as someone who didn't grass, and who knew a thing or two about robbing banks. Hence the meeting with Ray Ketteridge and Henry Nunn in Tramp, the fleeting introduction to the jolly toff in the worn-out shirt and the corollary, John Goddard meeting his fate 200 yards from the Bank of England.

7. VICTIMLESS CRIME

Twenty-four hours had passed since the robbery, twelve hours since Keith had left Henry Nunn's Mayfair pad with the five bonds worth 5 million now fanned out on the kitchen counter. He padded down the corridor in his blue silk dressing gown and retrieved his copy of *The Times* left outside the door by Rodney Miller, the doorman. He made a cup of coffee and two slices of toast, which he buttered and spread with thick-cut Oxford marmalade.

He set them down on the counter and sat on the stool because it was there and that's where you were meant to sit in a modern kitchen, though try as he may he'd never found it very comfortable. The sun poured in the windows and at just after nine o'clock that Thursday morning the streets of London were abuzz outside with the millions going about their daily lives, emerging sweaty and harassed from the Tube, running for buses, hurrying to jobs in offices and shops and the last of the small factories being pulled down to make way for high rises and more offices.

He was going to have to call TJ and tell him the 200-mil deal was off the table – at least for the time being. Keith had his contact in Holland, Ben Blessing, Mr Big, but the heist was so high profile, the bonds weren't just hot, you could feel the heat warming up the kitchen. He unfolded *The Times*.

The headline ran 'The Biggest Robbery in British History' and described how 'a lone thief had escaped with £292 million in bearer bonds, not a penny of which he will ever be able to spend'. DCS Tom Dickinson, in charge of the case, told *The Times* that the 'mugging was a disaster waiting to happen and a significant threat to the nation's financial institutions'. He added that as the serial numbers had already been circulated, the bonds were just worthless scraps of paper.

Of course, that wasn't true. As, indeed, the number of bonds stolen and their value reported in the press was likewise untrue.

All very interesting.

Keith picked up one of the five bonds and waved it under his nose. There was a whiff of fish from the ink, oil from the printing press, the sweet aroma of all the things a man could do with unlimited money. *I dunno about buying Dunstable, Manchester United is more like it.*

He made another cup of coffee and called Henry Nunn.

'I was expecting your call.'

'I bet you were.'

'I've got so much to do today, you can't imagine. We could have a cup of tea at the Royal. Half past ten?'

'Look forward to it.'

He went back to the bedroom and peered into his closet with its row of suits for all seasons that Mrs Primrose sponged and pressed and took to the cleaners. The warm weather called for a blazer, fawn trousers, ox-blood brogues, a white shirt and paisley tie.

Keith and Dawn divorced shortly after he came out of Parkhurst and, in a whirlwind romance, he had married Kerry Dedman, a fiery, feisty, blue-eyed blonde with the glamourous looks of an actress, which she would have liked to have been, and ran her own escort agency with an office in Soho. Keith had promised to go straight and said as much in a speech to the wedding party packed with celebrities and aristocrats on a rainy spring day in 1981. There was a round of applause, they raised

Victimless Crime

their glasses and Martin Newman, his old mate from Wormwood Scrubs, stepped up on the stage.

'Hold your horses,' he said. 'Telegram just arrived; thought I'd read it out. Are you listening?' He tapped a glass and waited for quiet. 'Best wishes for Keith and Kerry on 28 April. Long and prosperous future to you both, signed,' he paused ... 'Jerry, Dick, Tony and Karen from the Fraud Squad.'

Keith promised to go straight. He did try. W.W. Parrish had gone down the drain, Dunstable Town FC had gone into receivership and George Best was propping up the bar in the Phene Arms in the backstreets of Old Chelsea. Having joined Dawn on the board of Central Appointments, Keith owed HM Revenue & Customs a king's ransom in back taxes now the agency was defunct.

He had served three years and nine months on his six-year sentence and come out with a few grand tucked down the back of the sofa. Keith's first business at the age of 26 was dealing in scrap metal. He knew the game and started up again. It paid the bills and Kerry's twice-a-week appointments with the hairdresser. She liked clothes, pubs and felt most at home in the East End where, as luck would have it, she had been staying with her mum when Patrick Thomas relieved John Goddard of his satchel full of bonds.

Keith had been looking round for a more lucrative enterprise when the phone rang one morning and it was Martin Newman with a small problem.

'I need help opening a few false bank accounts,' he said. 'You wouldn't happen to know anyone who could help?'

It was like Blackpool midwinter under a black sky and suddenly someone had turned on all the lights. The organ grinder revved up. He could hear the murmur of the carousel spinning. Keith heard someone laughing and realised it was him.

'You're not going to believe this, Martin. I was sitting here looking at the phone and dreaming of someone calling up and asking if I knew anyone who could open a few false bank accounts.'

'They call that synchronicity.'

'What a lovely name. If I have a daughter that's what I'm going to call her.'

Keith had met Martin when they were housed at the Wormwood Scrubs hostel, where prisoners are put on the day release scheme to prepare them for life back in the real world. Martin had done four years for drug offences. He looked like a rock star and had been earning a living with his rock star mates who enjoyed a line or two. Before he had become obsessed with robbing the trains carrying cash between banks underground, he devised a scheme that relied on his boundless charm and sex appeal.

He started dating modest girls who worked in banks. They were easy prey for Martin to seduce and he could persuade them to transfer money from well-heeled accounts into bogus accounts Keith opened with false names and addresses. *It's a victimless crime*, he told them. No one gets hurt. No one loses any money – except the banks who are duty bound to put the missing money back in their customers' accounts.

The girls were happy to be seen around town on the arm of a Mick Jagger lookalike and Keith, flush with fresh funds, bought his apartment at the Barbican from Johnny Lloyd, who had acquired the property with money linked to the Brink's-Mat gold bullion robbery out in Heathrow in 1983. Keith paid a cash deposit and a dodgy lawyer arranged a mortgage through the Halifax.

It was like living on top of the world. The Barbican had its cinemas, concert halls, bars, a bank, even a police station. His penthouse in Willoughby House shared a floor with nice neighbours – Lord (Master of the Rolls) and Lady Donaldson, the Bishop of London, Major Ferguson and the Australian writer and performer Clive James, with his bitter tongue and brilliant mind.

The actor Charles Dance lived in Shakespeare House, the adjacent building, and when they had a drink together in the Shakespeare, the pub on the corner, Charles would always have his bottled lager served in an ice bucket. On the floor below

Victimless Crime

Keith in Willoughby House, Arthur Scargill, the leader of the National Union of Mineworkers, occupied an apartment bought and paid for by the NUM. Maggie Thatcher won the battle to close the mines, sell up the utilities and turn the country into what she called a share-owning Shangri-la. The miners were crying in their soup, but Arthur came out with a nice view and a book deal.

Between wives, Keith dated Fiona Richmond, the actress renowned for getting her kit off in a string of B-movies. She wrote a column for the monthly magazine *Men Only* and, before Keith, was the girlfriend of Paul Raymond – Mr Soho – the owner of the Windmill and Raymond's Review Bar. Once when Keith had to appear in the Magistrates Court on a charge that was dropped, she loaned him her car to drive to the hearing. It was a yellow E-type Jag with the number plate FU2. She later sold the plate for £500,000.

Keith tucked *The Times* under his arm, locked up, strode down to the lift and found Clive James standing there with a long face like a lost Labrador. On the elevator door was a hand-written note: Out of Order, signed by Rodney Miller.

'It's that Rodney Miller who's out of order,' Clive said.

'Mechanical things always let you down in the end.'

'Just like people.'

'You're a right bloody cynic, you know that.'

'Got to make a living somehow.'

They had a good chuckle as they made their way down 300 steps and Keith drove Clive into the West End where he had a meeting at BAFTA in Piccadilly. He parked behind Jermyn Street, where there was always a place for him in the yard at the back of his shirtmaker's shop. Keith cut through Air Street to Regent Street and found Henry Nunn at a table in the Café Royal, looking as bright and as devious as a gargoyle.

The seats seemed to be entirely filled with Americans hoping to catch a glimpse of the ghost of Oscar Wilde, who had frequented the venue with his poet boyfriend Bosie Douglas, ordering the most expensive wines and sending them back as corked. Keith had read Oscar's *The Ballad of Reading Gaol* in Blundeston and felt an empathy for the man sentenced to two years' hard labour for a victimless crime no longer on the books.

'Morning, dear, you don't fancy a Gauguin by any chance?'

'What?'

'Paul Gauguin, one of his Polynesian pieces.'

'You can stick your Gauguin, Henry, what the hell's going on?'

'Oh dear, who's got out on the wrong side of the bed this morning? Earl Grey?'

'Yeah, why not.'

Henry poured a cup. 'No milk, darling, it spoils the bergamot flavour.'

'Well, thanks very much for the tea lesson, Henry. You do know you let the best deal in your life slip through your fingers last night?'

Nunn sat back and pressed his palms together as if in prayer. 'I am just the nexus, Keith, the coordinator. This is Ray's deal.'

'We're walking away from 50 mil, Henry. You know what they say about a bird in the hand? Not that you've ever had a bird in your hand …'

'Now who's giving their granny lessons?' he replied. 'I can't tell Ray what to do.'

'Are you frightened of him?'

'Keith, I am not afraid of anyone.'

'Then why the fuck didn't you say something, put him right? Ray seems to think a million-pound bond's worth a million pounds.'

'When he finds out it is not, you can get in touch with your man.'

'What if it's too late?'

'He's a businessman. He'll wait.'

Keith ate a chocolate digestive and pushed his copy of *The Times* across the table.

'Another thing, Henry, how come it says here a thief came away with 292 bonds, same on the news last night, when you and I know it was a lot more than that?'

'I have absolutely no idea.'

'Really?'

'Keith, would I lie to you?'

'Course you bloody would.'

'Yes, but not on this occasion.' He paused. 'Everything has its time. For now, it's a waiting game.' He drank his tea and put the gold-rimmed cup back on the saucer. 'Now, what about that Gauguin?'

8. THE GREAT UNKNOWN

Villains like spending time together. They tend to be regulars in the same pubs – a mistake, really, as the Old Bill quickly learns when something's going down from bar flies who earn their drinking money whispering snippets of overheard conversation. Snitches sometimes end up in dark alleyways wearing what Pablo Escobar called a Colombian necktie, slitting some poor bugger's throat and pulling his tongue through the cut – not an amusement, but a warning.

In the meantime, DCS Dickinson at the City of London police headquarters in Bishopsgate was not a happy man. He had promised to solve the bonds robbery in days. More than a week had gone by and the cork board in his office that he'd envisioned being filled with photos and Post-its scrawled with clues and telephone numbers remained an empty landscape except for one item: a photofit of the mugger, a man of Jamaican appearance in a hood.

Dickinson had brought in every snitch, grass, nark and blabbermouth from every manor the length and breadth of London. Nada. Whoever it was who had planned the robbery seemed to have made sure that the members of his crew didn't know each other or the essential details of the plot. What they did expect was the biggest payday in their criminal lives, and that required patience and keeping shtum.

Keith doubted that Ray Ketteridge and Henry Nunn had waited until the champagne cork popped before looking inside John Goddard's briefcase. The temptation was far too great. They must have known there were 427 bonds not 292 – worth £439 million not £292 million. Why the discrepancy, the subterfuge? Sheppards had circulated the serial numbers of 292 bonds, leaving £135-million worth of bonds not accounted for.

That could only mean it was an inside job. If you want to know how to rob the Bank of England, you either go in with guns blazing and a bag of gelignite to blow the safe or shuffle the numbers through myriad accounts until a new configuration obscures the loss. If scores of couriers walk £30 billion in bonds across the City each day, the £135 million unnoted and unmentioned by the bank is less than half a per cent of that. It you've got £100 and you lose 50p, you're not going to lie awake at night worrying about it.

The fraud was a puzzle with pieces Keith would put together as new clues presented themselves. For now, he slipped his bonds between the pages of *Smiley's People* and relied on John le Carré to look after them. He imagined John Bowman would wait a few months before pushing his bonds out like little boats into that flowing river of capital, as he had explained poetically to Ray Ketteridge. How, when and exactly how much Ray was going to get had not been settled and it occurred to Keith that he and Bowman were the canaries in the cage set up to test the climate.

----•——•----

The first glimpse of the stolen bonds came ten days after the mugging, when a photocopy of a £1-million bond from a source in Northern Ireland chattered out of the fax machine at the office of a London broker with a note saying that the original was available. Bearing in mind that bonds 'promise to pay the bearer' the sum on the certificate, finding a broker willing to stretch to 30 or 40 per cent on a dodgy bond would not normally have been a tough call. You can never underestimate the power of greed.

Keith imagined brokers in red braces with houses on mortgages in Esher and Weybridge sitting around a table in Ropemaker Street studying the fax while they discussed the implications of handling a bond from the big heist and deciding that in this case honesty was the best policy. They duly contacted DCS Dickinson with the news and went home on the 6.10 from Waterloo with that feeling you get when you have done the right thing for the wrong reasons.

The 'alleged' 292 bonds had not been destroyed, as the super had promised on the BBC. They were out there like a virus threatening to unsettle the scales of global finance.

Two days after the fax emerged, a man strolled into the National Westminster in Glasgow and placed a £1-million bond on the counter in front of a young teller. She must have welcomed a break in what was another routine day, while being terrified that the certificate might be accompanied by a deadly weapon.

Tellers do not carry £1 million in cash in the drawers under their desk; it would rarely be more than a few thousand pounds. Bank insurance premiums are high not because of bank robbers, but because of the risk of those at tills and behind desks having wandering hands and an eye for opportunity.

'I won't be a moment, sir. This must be checked by my manager.'

Off she went while the man stood there waiting for his million quid. Did he have a bag? Was he aware that the weight in notes would have been up to 100 pounds? Not that it mattered. The manager called the police and a fleet of vehicles were racing down Sauchiehall Street in minutes. The million-pound man was Irish, from the Republic. He was questioned by police in Scotland and again by Special Branch. He was deemed an innocent dupe and never charged.

Henry Nunn called Keith the following day. He had tickets to see a show of work by Damien Hirst, one of the leading figures in a group called the YBA: Young British Artists. They studied Hirst's shark in formaldehyde, the paintings of spots and the flies buzzing around in a glass cube called *A Hundred Years*, revealing, the card said, that flies die when exposed to public light.

'Did you know, Van Gough died 100 years ago, in 1890?' Nunn said. 'Shot himself.'

'In the foot?'

Nunn laughed. 'You should invest in Hirst. He's the new Warhol.'

'I don't know that Mrs Primrose would approve. She hates flies.'

They left the Newport Street Gallery and strolled down the road to the Black Dog, an old-fashioned pub in Spring Gardens.

'What do you fancy?'

'I think it calls for a whiskey,' said Henry.

'Irish?'

'You read my mind.'

Keith brought glasses to the table beside the window. Two weeks had gone by since the robbery and the weather was still holding. Henry wore a fawn linen suit, his Oxford tie and a boater that he removed and placed on the chair next to him. At the gallery, Henry had mentioned the Irishman trying to pass off a bond in Glasgow. Keith had waited to learn more.

'So the Irishman walked out with a clean bill of health?' Keith began.

'Here's the thing with the Irish, they always seem thick, even when they are geniuses. They act the fool and it comes over as charming. They get away with murder.'

'That's what I worry about.'

'You worry too much.'

'Don't make a blind bit of sense to me. They've got some face with a bond that belongs to the Bank of England, dupe or not. He must have got it from somewhere. And the police let him go.'

'Perhaps they have a tail on him. You know, little fish and big fish.'

'There's certainly a big fish and it's not your mate Ray Ketteridge.'

He laughed and made no comment.

'Irish *eejit* walking the streets. That's normal. Irish gorilla in your living room watching the stash. Looks like a pattern to me.'

Henry took another sip from his glass, nodded slowly and passed judgment. 'Very good,' he said.

'Well, am I right? Or am I right?'

'Time will tell. Mr Dickinson has formed a task force, by all accounts. Operation Starling, they've called it. Forty agents. He's even brought in someone from Special Branch who specialises in Irish terrorism.'

'There we are, just what I said.' Keith finished his drink. 'That Goya you've got, didn't that come from Ireland?'

'That's a long story, my dear …'

'I'll get another round. I'm not in any hurry.'

'I'll get them …'

'No, no, no, you stay there, make sure no one nicks your hat.'

Keith returned to the bar and they settled back with their tumblers, no ice, so as not to ruin the taste. Henry crossed one leg over the other and took a sip from his Dunville's single malt.

'It was four years ago, in 1986,' he began. 'The IRA lifted some old masters from Sir Alfred Beit's estate in County Wicklow. Russborough House, all quite lovely, but too remote to be safe, in my opinion.'

'Isn't Beit the diamond dealer?'

Henry nodded. 'He has a wonderful collection, a Vermeer and a Goya among them. Well, he did. The paintings were worth £20 million at least. The IRA had no problem taking them, but no clue how to move them.' He took another drink from his glass. 'They went to the UDA, the Ulster Defence Association.'

'Aren't they the other side?'

'They are indeed. Prods and Provos. God save the Queen and off with the Queen's head. But you know how it is with terrorists, idealists on paper, not in their wallet.'

'And they came to you?'

'I didn't say that,' he replied. 'Do you know Jeffrey Kershaw?'

'Doesn't ring a bell.'

'He's a young solicitor, *very* attractive, very capable. You'll meet him, I'm sure. Anyway, he got everyone to put down their Armalites for five minutes and they all walked away happy.'

'Except the diamond dealer. Did he get his paintings back?'

'Yes, I think so, one or two. The rest,' he said and blew invisible dust from his fingers, 'are out there in the great unknown.'

'In your kitchen you mean.'

Keith glanced out of the window. Outside, there was a bench under a tree. At one end, a cat with its legs in the air was licking its privates. A couple at the other end were kissing like there was no tomorrow. The scene seemed to represent something – perhaps something Damien Hirst would have understood. But the meaning was lost on Keith. He emptied his glass.

'I'm going to try again, Henry, it's been bothering me. Who was that Houlihan fella?'

'A nasty piece of work. That's all I know. Something to do with Ray.'

'He's a mug, you know that. Ray, I mean.'

'That's neither here nor there, not for the moment.' He rolled out his long white hands. 'We must wait and watch as things unfold.'

His stood and put his hat on.

'Very nice, Henry. Where'd you get that hat?'

'Not in Ilkley Moor. It was made for me. In Panama.'

9. THE SPIDER'S WEB

One thing Henry Nunn did not mention to Keith Cheeseman that day at the Black Dog was his relationship with Thomas Coyle, described by a judge and reported in the *Irish Times* on 20 September 2000 as 'the biggest criminal fence ever to operate in the Republic'. A fence of such distinction dealing in artworks would require distribution across the Irish Sea and, by any rationale, he would be in bed with Henry.

It was Coyle, according to the same article by Elaine Keogh and Jim Cusack, who had 'handled the multi-million-pound haul of paintings stolen from the home of Sir Alfred Beit'. If what Henry had told Keith was true, Coyle would have worked with Jeffrey Kershaw in uniting the IRA and UDA to distribute the stolen paintings – most of which, it would turn out, were recovered in Istanbul.

Three weeks after The Big One, as one of the tabloids headlined the heist, Coyle returned to the newspaper columns when he was arrested in what British customs alleged was a random search at Heathrow Airport. The canny Irishman, who had served time as a fence, had flown in from Dublin with £77 million in bearer bonds hidden in a suitcase and two suit bags.

That is: £77 *million*.

The luggage was not all his. He carried two of the pieces for two associates, his brother-in-law Anthony Rooney and Edward Dunne. They arrived on a later flight and were immediately arrested. The three men claimed that they were on their way to Miami, Florida, to buy a racehorse and the bonds must have been planted. They had never seen them before, they didn't know what bonds were and had no idea, said the master fence, how they could be sold, laundered or fenced.

While they remained in custody, DCS Dickinson's task force established that after acquiring the bonds, Coyle had recruited John Gilligan and Jim 'Danger' Beirne to help sell them. Gilligan was a celebrity gangster with a long record who would later be given a 28-year sentence for trafficking cannabis. Beirne was a former Roscommon footballer with a right boot that could cause life-changing injuries to any player in a different coloured shirt. He had been jailed in 1983 for three years after obtaining 353 gold Krugerrand coins worth £96,000 from a Jersey bank using a forged bank draft.

The £77 million in bonds would have achieved a good £20 million on the black market, meaning there was plenty of dough to spread around. Coyle was smart enough to know they needed a higher level of expertise and had brought in Gilligan and Beirne because of their personal links to a man by the name of John Francis Conlon. Coyle and his associates weren't bicycle thieves and petty hoodlums, they handled big scores like the Alfred Beit robbery, but they were not threaded into the spider's web of international criminals, terrorists and state actors who could use £77 million in treasury bonds to write a new page in the *Encyclopædia Britannica*.

John Francis Conlon moved in those circles. He had good relations with Mafia families in the United States, as well as security agencies and arms dealers. He was a regular guest at the hilltop villa on the Costa del Sol where Monzer al-Kassar lived with his wife Raghdaa and their four children. Always immaculately dressed with perfect manners, the so-called Prince of Marbella was the source of some of the biggest crimes of the post-Cold War era, including the illicit arming of right-wing rebels in Nicaragua and the *Achille Lauro* hijacking on 7 October 1985.

The Spider's Web

That morning, four terrorists from the PLF, the Palestine Liberation Front – a splinter group from the PLO, the Palestinian Liberation Organization – took control of the Italian cruise ship *Achille Lauro* off the coast of Egypt, as she was sailing from Alexandria to Ashdod in Israel. They threatened to kill the eleven Americans on board unless 50 Palestinian militants were freed from Israeli prisons.

To show they meant business, the gunmen shot and killed Leon Klinghoffer, a 69-year-old Jewish-American, and pushed him overboard in his wheelchair. The ship sailed on to Port Said. After negotiations with Palestinian and Egyptian officials, the hijackers freed the hostages and surrendered in exchange for the promise of safe passage to an undisclosed destination.

On the afternoon of 10 October, the four hijackers boarded an Egypt Air Boeing 737 that took off for Tunisia with several members of the negotiation team. As they crossed the Mediterranean, on the orders of President Reagan the plane was joined mid-air by two US Tomcat F-14 fighters based in Crete. They trailed the Boeing as it requested permission to land at both Athens and Tunis. The requests were turned down and the Tomcats flew wing-to-wing with the 747, something fighter pilots are trained for, but terrifying for the Egyptian at the controls of his commercial airliner. The pilot was ordered to land and immediately descended to the runway on a NATO air base in Sicily. The hijackers were arrested and jailed for up to 30 years.

Monzer al-Kassar had armed the Palestinian gunmen, as he famously partnered US army Colonel Oliver North in what became known as the Iran–Contra Affair. In 1985, the same year as the *Achille Lauro* hijacking, the Prince of Marbella arranged the deal where US officials covertly sold arms to their sworn enemy Iran, to use the unlogged hoard of cash to fund the radical right Contras in their struggle to overthrow the elected government in Nicaragua. The affair had been underwritten using bearer bonds.

International terror plots, arms and drugs deals, property speculation by Mafia bosses and runaway oligarchs with assets to hide and secrets to sell bring together parties that are unpredictable and do not trust each other. Bonds sleeping in shell companies in obscure zero-tax atolls from the North Sea to the Caribbean loosely guarantee that the exchange agreed upon will in fact take place.

At the core of the spider web are facilitators like Monzer al-Kassar, who remain untouchable all the time governments need dirty work done and the politicians who give the orders through back channels want to appear to have clean hands. These playboy outlaws move freely around the globe, but they are being watched by security agents who monitor their associates and conspirators. When they are locked up, the process starts again as a new lord of crime fills their shoes.

Monzer al-Kassar, the son of Syria's one-time ambassador to Canada and India, started out as a small-time thief with his first arrest recorded by Interpol in Trieste, Italy, in 1973. According to a 2009 report by the United States Congress, through his long career, al-Kassar fixed deals to supply arms and military equipment to rebel groups in Nicaragua, Brazil, Cyprus, Bosnia, Croatia, Somalia, Iran and Iraq. His luck ran out arming FARC, the Revolutionary Armed Forces of Colombia, and he was jailed for 30 years in 2009. John Francis Conlon had less time in the sun. He began a ten-year sentence in 1992 for his part in a £500,000 cocaine deal.

The treasure acquired by crime syndicates through arms, drugs and secrets has to be laundered somewhere, and that somewhere in most cases requires the services of Good Chaps with pink cheeks who personify English exceptionalism and broker these nefarious deals from offices smelling of polished wood in the City of London. With cut-glass accents, outward modesty and a certain silliness easily confused with integrity, they make drug czars and mass murderers feel vaguely ill at ease being served malty tea in antique bone china with hallmarked silver spoons they may be tempted to slip in their pockets.

It's commonly believed that the English invented offshore trusts. This is not strictly true. The concept existed in Ancient

The Spider's Web

Rome when legionnaires who grabbed land, resources and slaves were reluctant to surrender their plunder to Caesar. The system of trusts introduced by the Romans became fully developed under English trust law in the Middle Ages during the time of the eleventh- and twelfth-century crusades, when rape and pillage were back in fashion.

A trust is a legally binding arrangement that enables you to transfer property, cash or assets, like diamonds and bonds, to another person or legal entity for the benefit of a third party. That third party can be a company in name only, which you own and which makes, buys and trades nothing, an empty shell. That company with a click on a keyboard can shift cash and bonds to another shell company and another, from one jurisdiction to the next until the assets vanish like morning mist over the turquoise blue waters of the West Indies. Offshore trusts set up in London provide absolute secrecy and are structured in such a way that no name has to appear on the company register, no tax returns are required and thus no tax is paid.

When £292 million in bonds is reported as being nicked at knifepoint from a courier leaving the Bank of England, every trust manager and serious criminal in the world takes notice, as do the Feds. In very little time, a Global Research Unit was set up by the Federal Bureau of Investigation, allowing them to work closely with Tom Dickinson and Operation Starling.

None of this was good news to Keith Cheeseman and John Bowman. Aside from the £77 million recovered by UK Customs, Keith was sure Ray Ketteridge would by now have distributed bonds to other third parties, and it was unlikely that £200 million in certificates even remained to transfer to Abyasa Tjay. Would TJ accept a smaller amount? Before contacting him, Keith and Bowman drove out in the green Jag to Ray's country house on the outskirts of London.

They sat beneath the shade of laburnum trees with their lanterns of yellow blossom. The garden was well laid out with rose bushes climbing the latticework fence and banks of plants coming into flower. The house, Keith noted, was tastefully furnished with some landscapes typical of Henry Nunn's refined taste. Ray and John drank beers from the bottle. Keith had a glass of wine and the bees buzzed around the laburnum blossom.

'You must have green fingers, Ray,' Keith said. 'Do you do it all yourself?'

'Mostly I do. Can't trust anyone who never gets dirt beneath their nails. You do a bit of gardening, Keith?'

'I've got a window box.'

Ray looked at Bowman. 'Fucking riot, this bloke.' He stretched out his legs clad in khaki shorts and open-toed sandals, the combination oddly more menacing than Ray Ketteridge in a suit and tie. 'So, what are we doing here? You bringing me some good news?'

'You said you didn't trust the Indonesian mate of mine. John's got an idea that might work,' Keith said.

'Come on, then, let's hear it.'

Bowman slipped his glasses on as if they helped him think.

'I can set up a trust for you in Panama, actually with a cousin of mine,' he began. 'We can transfer some bonds to a shell company with you as the beneficiary and exchange them for assets in a company owned by the Indonesian.'

'Abyasa Tjay,' Keith inserted.

'Fuck me. You're not still going on about that £200 million, Keif?'

'We could try a smaller amount. I haven't spoken to TJ. Thought I'd speak to you first. We could try 50 mil?'

John leaned forward. 'At 25 per cent, less the fees, you'll have £12 million in Panama,' he explained. 'With a reasonable commission, say ten per cent between Keith and me, you'll have more than £10 million free and clear.'

'Don't work out though, does it, Jonny? You go into a casino with 50 mil and come out with 10 you ain't exactly a winner.'

'You are if you've gone in with 50 mil in counterfeits and come out with a stack of used fivers and tenners,' Keith said.

Ray stood and paced about in his sandals. He looked like a man who had failed his O-Level maths and all these numbers

The Spider's Web

were coming at him like a migraine. With the innate confidence that comes from good looks, broad shoulders and two strong fists he didn't mind using, Ray Ketteridge had risen through the crime ranks to a position beyond his own abilities, the Peter Principle they called it. He wasn't the lead player in the bond's job, but a walk-on character in someone else's theatre. The puppet, not the master.

A maid with lisping Spanglish appeared with salmon and cucumber sandwiches and another round of drinks. They pulled up chairs to a garden table with a Union Jack parasol for shade.

'*Muchos gracias*, darling,' Keith said.

Ray bit into his sandwich and talked as he chewed. 'The fing is, Keif, now we've gone an' pissed 77 mil down the khazi, I'm under pressure to get bigger amounts for the bonds, not smaller. If it was a score, we might have something to talk about. But ten out of 50, that's taking the piss.'

Keith was circumspect. 'Maybe you're right, Ray,' he said, moving on, stroking his ego. 'How come the Irish managed to get their hands on all that dosh?'

'Don't fucking ask. Wasn't up to me.' Ray ran his palm over his Michael Caine hair. He took another bite from the salmon and cucumber. 'There's a lot going on you don't know about. A lot I don't fucking know about.'

'It's just amazing they were caught in a random search.'

'What's that supposed to mean?'

'It was in the paper. Customs are pretty pleased with themselves. They do this, you know, psychological training. They spot people who are trying to hide something just by the way they walk, the way their eyes dart about. Stuff like that.'

'Yeah, whatever. I like you coming up with ideas, but this one don't float,' Ray said and took ten flicks with his Colibri to light a fag.

Keith pushed his luck. 'They must have been connected to, what's his name, Houlihan? He didn't do the mugging by any chance?'

'You sound like Peter Sissons on bloody *Question Time*. You know damn well it weren't Houlihan.'

'I only know what I've been told. Or I've read in the newspapers.'

'How old are you, Keif? Don't you know you can't believe everything you read in the fucking newspapers?'

Two streams of smoke poured from Ray's nose like spectral tusks and in his blue eyes was a look of total bewilderment.

10. THE DUTCH CONNECTION

While Keith was nearing the end of his sentence for the 1977 Beneficial Bank robbery, he was moved to the adjacent hostel in Wormwood Scrubs where he first met Martin Newman. After prison breakfast each morning, they went out on day release to jobs in the community.

Keith was on the books of a jeweller friend in Hatton Garden who 'required' him to make overnight visits to the Midlands, where Keith was in fact looking for business opportunities for when he was finally out. The payslips from the jeweller showing return train fares for trips between London and Birmingham gave him a certain amount of leeway with the 6pm curfew and most days – the Scrubs being located at Du Cane Road in West London – he had a late lunch or an early dinner with Martin at Trader Vic's in the Park Lane Hilton, or Tiddy Dols Eating House with its rock-star clientele and waiters in velvet tunics.

Now, over a decade later, Keith and Martin got together once a month or so and reminisced on the good old days at Trader Vic's. On a warm July Friday evening, two months after the bonds robbery, Martin told Keith he was making a road trip to Holland and Belgium.

'You dealing again?' Keith asked him.

'Nah, I'm doing promo work for a new band. Lot of money in music.'

'Best news I've had all week. You can pick up the tab now you're rolling in it.'

'Hardly. I just lost 140 grand in a suitcase. Bloody cops getting it wrong again came stamping up my stairs at three in the morning. I threw the case out the window into some bushes. When I went to pick it up, some bastard had pinched it.'

'That's how trickle down works. Some bloke's out there walking through the bushes at night wondering how he is going to feed his wife and eight children, stumbles on a suitcase and all his dreams are answered.'

Keith had tossed his tie over his shoulder so it didn't get splashed and opened the shells of his mussels cooked with shallots and garlic. Martin sipped his water like it was wine and drank down his wine like it was water.

'Did you read, the Germans have started taking down the Berlin Wall,' he said.

'And?'

'I don't know, must be something in it.'

'Second-hand bricks.' Keith had a thought. 'When are you leaving on this trip, then?'

'Monday.'

'I might just come along for the ride. I'll call a mate of mine.'

The call was to Ben Blessing, one man who probably disagreed with the maxim never shit on your own doorstep. He lived on the Gouden Bocht, or Golden Curve, the prettiest canal in Amsterdam, where property was so expensive that, except for a museum and the Goethe Institute, most of the stuccoed palaces had been bought up by the mega-rich banks Ben had been defrauding for years, £100,000 here, £100,000 there, never greedy, never getting caught.

When Ben set out on his life of fraud in the United States, he discovered that banks stored bonds as security on mortgages until they were paid off. While the bonds were in the bank safe,

The Dutch Connection

it was relatively easy for tellers to remove a few from different files and sell them on for a percentage to the likes of Mr Blessing. They knew that the loss would not be noticed until the mortgage was redeemed, by which time the pilferer would have moved on or died or risen to new heights and new rackets in the bank. Just as law enforcement attracts men who are often bullies, banking attracts those who are innately devious.

Ben agreed to take three bonds – £3 million – from Keith at a generous 40 per cent and must have seen it as a loss leader. There was a lot more out there, he knew that, and Ben Blessing more than anyone knew the price would come down. This was the first time they had done business after meeting with TJ at the Waldorf Astoria, and the sums worked out very nice indeed. At 40 per cent, Keith would pick up £1.2 million. Ketteridge had said his share would be 25 per cent of what he could get for the bonds. That gave him a sweet £300,000: the mortgage at the Barbican paid off and a holiday with Kerry, maybe one of those Scandinavian cruises to see the Northern Lights riding over the midnight sun.

Martin picked Keith up in his black Beemer early Monday morning, and they drove down to Harwich. There they joined the line of cars waiting to board the ferry, the *Koningin Beatrix*, before crossing the Channel to the Hook of Holland.

Keith's overnight Louis Vuitton bag was in the boot with a change of clothes and the blue silk pyjamas Kerry had bought for him in Harrods at Christmas. He would spend the night with Ben Blessing on the Gouden Bocht and no doubt enjoy a stroll through De Wallen, the red-light district with its hash bars and girls exposing their curves from behind shop windows. Not that Keith was a participant. He didn't do drugs, and he took his wedding vows seriously, but he did appreciate the sheer bravado of those near-naked hookers with their air of whimsy and nihilism. You couldn't beat London for style, elegance, fashion – anything,

How to Rob the Bank of England

really, but Amsterdam did have its charms. The car gained another few yards.

'Look,' Martin said, 'they've pulled a BMW out of the line.'

Keith leaned across him to see. 'A black BMW,' he added.

Four customs officers were all over the vehicle, opening doors, the boot, taking stuff out, looking under mats. The driver was led away to a hut.

As Martin let out the clutch and moved forward, Keith felt a burning sensation on the left side of his chest. His pulse raced. For a moment he thought he was having a heart attack. He slid his hand into his inside jacket pocket and removed £3 million in three hot bonds still smelling of the mint.

'I wonder if it's these they're looking for,' he said.

'Does anyone know you're carrying them?'

'Ray does. I told him.'

'Anyone else?'

'Not unless he shared it. Then, why would he?'

'A bit of a coincidence …'

'It is now,' said Keith. He pointed. Another black BMW had been pulled from the line. He waved the three bonds under his nose like a fan.

Martin pointed at the barrier. 'I can give it a go, Keith. Always fancied a car chase. Your call,' he said.

The lane of vehicles was hemmed in by low cement ridges. To Keith's left was an exit lane leading to a roundabout and the road into Harwich.

'The Beemer's in your name?'

'Yeah, all legit.'

'Spend your winnings. Cut your losses,' Keith said. 'No one will believe this.'

Martin watched as Keith ripped the bonds in half and half again. He ripped the halves into smaller and smaller pieces until £3 million in green inked certificates became wedding confetti that he shoved in an empty Styrofoam coffee cup. He kept three slivers from the bonds, each with a serial number on it, and pushed them up inside his tie. He got out of the car and dropped the cup in a bin. He lit a cigar and glanced again at the *Koningin Beatrix*. I could have bought that with 3 mil, he thought.

When their turn came, the car was ransacked and they were led into the hut for a thorough body search, down to their underwear. Jail time teaches you not to worry about those things. It occurred to Keith as he put his trousers back on that with a cigar tube he could have rolled the bonds small enough to shove up his arse as Dustin Hoffman had done as Louis Degas in the movie *Papillon*, but he was glad he hadn't.

11. BETRAYAL

Ben Blessing was philosophical. Robbery, he said, is not an exact science. They had a night out in Amsterdam, the scraps of bonds were washed away in the Channel and Keith, with a £3 million headache, took a weekend break with Kerry in Dymchurch on the edge of Romney Marsh, where he kept an Elddis Tornado caravan in a false name.

Beneath the insulated floor, he had stashed his 'on the run' cache of cash, a box of Montecristo No. 4s and changes of clothes – a gas fitter, an army officer, a tweed suit, knitted tie, green cords and a deerstalker hat that gave Keith the look of a famous Victorian detective.

This strip of the south coast where the sheltered coves provided a safe harbour from the mutinous seas was popular with pirates during the seventeenth century, and during a spell running the library at Blundeston, Keith had read the Russell Thorndike smuggling novels set on the Marsh. Reading releases you from the limits of yourself. John Stonehouse had said that once and it had stayed with him.

They drove out Saturday morning, Keith with the same overnight bag he had packed for Amsterdam. Kerry got out of the car in her four-inch white stilettos and sank into the mud. She took a grip on her two hips.

'Oh, no, we're not staying here, are we?'

'You're getting such a bloody snob, Kerry. Didn't you grow up in a caravan?'

'You know damn well I didn't.'

'And no, we're not staying here. I just wanted to take a look. We've got the suite at Charlie's place.'

'Oh my Gawd, you are pushing the boat out.'

Charlie Gray was an old mate from the East End who had made his stash and gone straight, opening a hotel with sea views and a two-star Michelin restaurant that served fish and chips on greaseproof paper printed with tabloid cuttings about the Krays and the Great Train Robbery. The fish was cooked the old-fashioned way, in beef dripping, the chips blanched in boiling water before being plunged in hot oil, the process providing a creamy interior with a crunchy coating, as Charlie, half in jest, described his first wife.

Outside the hotel, parked ostentatiously next to the entrance, was Charlie's signature yellow Rolls-Royce.

They checked in. A lad in a white shirt ran the cases upstairs. Charlie was behind the bar polishing a glass when Keith walked in.

'How's crime these days, Keith?' he called.

'Full of bloody criminals. I'd go straight if I had your money.'

'If you had my money you'd be polishing glasses. Fancy a drink?'

'Never say no to a drink.'

Kerry appeared from reception with the key as he was speaking. 'No, thank you, Charlie, he's going out for a walk,' she said. 'Keith's not a man who has one drink.'

Charlie laughed. 'How are you, darling? Nice to see you.'

'And you, sweetheart. I'm going for a swim.'

'Be careful, there're sharks out there.'

'Don't have to worry about me. I know how to deal with sharks.'

'Never a truer word,' added Keith.

Kerry was a survivor, a player. She was the archetype East End 'bird' in designer outfits with a weakness for the slinky black dresses made by Frank Usher. She was related through some distant uncle named O'Shea to Ron and Reggie Kray. This gave her a sense of criminal *noblesse oblige*. She liked the idea of being a 'gangster's moll' and had seen the film *Get Carter* so many times she could quote chunks of the script.

Get Carter was based on a Ted Lewis novel and directed by Mike Hodges, with Michael Caine as an underworld figure out for revenge after the unexplained death of his brother. Caine was sharp, moody with a restrained air of violence and totally believable as a villain. What grabbed Kerry was the role of Anna, played by Britt Ekland, whom she vaguely resembled. Anna, the girlfriend of the gang's boss, was having it off with Jack, the Caine character. After one more job, they planned to run off together to South America like Ronnie Biggs after the Great Train Robbery. Villains are often a cliché. Kerry was always asking 'Who's that?' and 'What does he do?' She liked being the centre of attention and Keith knew her secret dream was to be in the movies.

Keith had first met Kerry when he was in Wormwood Scrubs, at a time when the prison was chock-a-block with violent men like 'Mad' Frankie Fraser, the Richardson's gang enforcer, in for murder, and Kenny Noye, cleared of stabbing a policeman to death and convicted for handling gold from the Brink's-Mat bullion robbery. Kerry was visiting Kenny Jackson, serving time after being sent down on some charge related to a knife fight. After they were introduced, Kerry started sending Keith presents and visiting Keith instead of Kenny.

Kerry ran a 'dating' agency called Aristocats with offices in the same building as the Windmill Theatre in Great Windmill Street. The 'dating' was with girls named Fifi and Mandy, at 50 quid an hour, which meant Kerry was often carrying a lot of cash. When Keith was out, on their first date, he went to meet her in a bar in Greek Street and was surprised when he walked in that she wasn't alone. She was sitting there smoking beside her minder, a bloke named Bishop who didn't know how to mind his own business.

Bishop clearly fancied Kerry himself. He was brash and belligerent in a black suit with a knitted black tie. He made a comment about old lags thinking the world owed them a favour and one thing led to another, as they do. In Parkhurst Keith had shared canteen tables with psychopaths and schizophrenics who think they're Napoleon. You learn to stand your ground, no matter what. Keith still had the prison vibe in his bones. He snapped. He grabbed Bishop by his tie and pulled his head down on the table. Bishop drew a gun from behind his back, but he was at a bad angle and Keith snatched it from him by the barrel. He kept hold of the tie and let Bishop half raise his head.

'Now, you behave yourself, son,' he said and released him. 'Bugger off and leave us to have a quiet drink.'

Keith returned the firearm by the hilt and Bishop stuck it back in his belt.

'I'll fucking get you one of these days,' he swore.

'No you won't. You stay safe and look for another job.'

Keith glanced at Kerry and she turned to Bishop.

'Toodaloo. Off you go,' she said, and waved her fingers.

Kerry clearly enjoyed the exchange. She divorced her taxi-driver husband and married Keith. As a wedding present, Kerry introduced Keith to Ralph Haeems, a double-edged sword as it turned out. Haeems was Mr Fixit for the villain fraternity, known for defending the Kray twins at the Old Bailey in 1969 when they were convicted for the murders of George Cornell and Jack McVitie and imprisoned for 30 years. Haeems lost the case but was acknowledged as the finest defence barrister of his generation.

Keith was a friend of Jim Sutherland, the owner of the Marquis of Cornwallis and the Earl Grey pubs in Bethnal Green. He went to pick him up one evening at the Earl Grey to go and watch Millwall at home to Newcastle United. The moment he arrived, Jim's wife rushed towards him.

'He's been arrested.'

'What?'

'Someone nicked his car last night and it was used in a bank job.'

'A bank job! I don't believe it. Where is he now?'

'I don't know, do I?'

Betrayal

'Where's the phone?'

Keith called Ralph Haeems and explained the situation.

'Don't worry. I'll sort it,' Haeems said.

Keith sat at the bar for more than an hour, reading the *Evening Standard*, waiting until Jim appeared.

'We missed the match, mate. What happened?'

'You! That's what happened. They were letting me go when Ralph Haeems walks in looking like he was ready for a bout of tag wrestling. The police said if I was so bloody innocent, why did I need a top brief to get me out?'

'And?'

'They rearrested me. Asked me all the same bloody questions.'

'What did you tell them?'

'What do you think I told them? You can't squeeze nothing out of an empty toothpaste tube. I didn't do nothing, just lost my new Jag.'

'Moral is, Jim, don't go buying Jaguars. Villains love 'em.'

And this was the double-edged sword. Ralph Haeems got involved in springing Jim to do Keith a favour. The payback was that he wanted Keith to take him to the strip show that had opened upstairs at the Phene Arms, his old stomping ground back in the days when Georgie Best was kicking a ball about in Dunstable.

Undernourished women taking their clothes off wasn't of much interest to Keith, but there was an upside. That night at the Phene, he met a lady who became known in the red tops as the Dusky Maiden, and Keith being Keith, they remained friends. Sometime later, when the Dusky Maiden was having a fling with the manager of the Streatham branch of the NatWest, it was a godsend: the very bank Keith had always wanted to take down.

···◆·•————•◆···

Kerry had packed her black bathing costume for their weekend away in Dymchurch and they set off for a walk along the beach. Keith needed to clear his head. Ripping 3 mil to shreds was like taking a chainsaw to your own arm – well, not exactly, but he felt the phantom pain of the amputation as he watched Kerry wade into the waves.

Families had staked out their territory with towels and umbrellas. Men slept with newspapers over their faces. Mums made sandwiches. Kids ran around screaming and splashing each other. He'd done the same with his brother on the beach in Ilfracombe a lifetime ago. There was an innocence, a decency, a collective feeling of well-being. These were civilians, working people who paid their taxes and did the right thing. He scorned their way of life, the life he was born into, and envied it, too.

When Keith left the army in 1967 aged 24 – the week the Beatles released *Sgt. Pepper's Lonely Hearts Club Band* – he got a job for a couple of years selling water meters for George Kent back in Luton. He did well, he had the patter, but one day is much like the next and the time comes when you realise you are not doing what you want to do or being who you want to be. It is at that moment that you become who you really are. Like the balloon freed from the child's hand, you cut the ties of the past and fly into your own bewildering destiny.

Keith saw an opportunity to go into the scrap iron business – where there's muck there's brass, as they say. He invested in a new suit – a tailor-made Prince of Wales check, six-button, double-breasted jacket with tapered trousers and a wide tie – and resolved never to take orders from anyone ever again.

Except Kerry, of course.

'I'm going for a swim,' she called and dived into the waves.

He stood, digging his toes in the wet sand, and watched as she swam out front crawl, turned and swam breaststroke parallel to the beach.

Three mil.

Three thin sheets of paper smelling like a Sunday roast and a promise.

If British customs officials at Harwich were searching for stolen bonds inside random black BMWs, there had to have been a tip-off. An inside man. He had told Ray he was going to Holland, but no one knew he was going with Martin Newman, in

Newman's black BMW. Had he mentioned it to Ben Blessing? He was sure he hadn't and, even if he had, Blessing would not have told anyone. Why would he?

Did Ray Ketteridge have him followed?

Did Ray Ketteridge tip off Tom Dickinson? Had he been followed by agents from Operation Starling?

It made no sense. Ray wanted to make his fuck-you money out of the bonds and as far as Keith was aware, unless he'd taken a rake off from the 77 mil acquired by the Irishmen, two months had gone by and he hadn't made a penny. It was hard to believe Ray was a snitch. He wasn't some backstreet chancer trying it on. He grew up knowing the game, knowing he was going to be a gangster.

Keith watched a lad running along the beach tossing a kite in the air. His dad jerked the string, the kite hovered, looked like it was going to fly, then plunged back down to earth. The look of despair on the boy's face was just how Keith himself must have looked when he dropped the confetti-filled Styrofoam cup in the rubbish bin. He shook his head, shaking out the memories.

An Irishman walks into a Glasgow bank with a £1-million bond and walks free. No charges. How could that happen?

The likely lads Coyle, Rooney and Dunne, caught with £77 million in bonds at Heathrow, were on remand at Keith's old alma mater Wormwood Scrubs, waiting to come to trial at Knightsbridge Crown Court. From what Henry Nunn had told him, they intended to plead not guilty.

And what about Henry?

He had gone over this in his head many times. When the black kid snatched John Goddard's briefcase, someone high up in the Bank of England knew exactly what it contained – how many bonds and how much they were worth. He was sure Ray Ketteridge did not move in the circles where the wide-boy toffs were protected by class and privilege.

Henry Nunn did.

In that case, what was the Irish connection?

Who was Houlihan?

Why was Ray Ketteridge overseeing the distribution of the bonds, not Henry Nunn?

And why were the police looking for 292 bonds when he had seen with his own eyes and counted with his own fingers 427 bonds?

Kerry came running out of the surf looking fresh and he wrapped her in the towel he'd been carrying.

'You look gorgeous,' he said.

'So do you.'

They ate the two-star fish and chips with a five-star bottle of oaked Chardonnay. A large woman in a green low-cut dress and red hair nattered on in a loud voice to a skinny bloke wearing glasses as thick as wine bottle bases about how rent control was killing their business letting out flats in Croydon.

Charlie Gray came to the table to say hello.

'You remember Roy Dobbs, Charlie?' Keith asked him.

'There was a face for radio! Haven't seen him in donkey's years.'

'Shame. Rumour was he'd take someone out for a ton.'

Charlie lowered his voice. 'You're not looking for a hitman?'

'I most certainly am. That bint in the green dress has ruined my appetite.'

Charlie kept his voice low. 'Good customer. Comes down once a month. Never heard her husband say a dicky bird.' He glanced at Keith's empty plate. 'How was the fish 'n' chips, then?'

'Gourmet, mate. Delicious.'

'On the house, seeing as it's you.'

'There, you see, Kerry, a real gent,' Keith said. 'Fancy a nightcap?'

'No, I'm a bit tired, think I'll go up.'

'Keith?' asked Charlie.

'No, I'm going to pass.'

'There's the man who never says no to a drink saying no to a drink twice.'

'Third time lucky.' Keith rose and stood away from the table. 'One more thing, Charlie,' he said and pointed at the painting hung next to their table. 'Is that a Paul Nash on the wall?'

'Yeah, he lived in Romney Marsh, did you know that? It's called *Sheepfold*. It's a print, of course. I sell them for 50 quid. All numbered.'

'Not for me, son. Only buy originals.'

'Now who's the snob?' Kerry said.

···◆·———·◆···

Kerry did the things women do in the bathroom for twenty minutes before climbing into bed. Keith sat beside the picture window smoking as he stared out into the black night. Charlie was right. Keith believed you should *always* stay for the extra drink. That's when things happen.

You're not yourself, are you, my son?

He flicked ash into the ashtray.

Keith did not suffer from depression. Boredom, irritation from time to time, frustration when people were as thick as bricks, impatience when the lights turned amber and the car in front waited for green. A feeling of unease had settled about him like a hat that's too tight. He took a long draw on his Montecristo and his reflection stared back at him from the window's darkened glass. He wasn't stressed, anxious, what do the French say? Melancholic. He felt betrayed.

12. GOOD OLE BOYS

The name Mark Osborne dropped into his head while he was sleeping. He woke up with the sea breeze wafting through the room and Kerry in the shower singing. It was nice to see her happy. He was the first to admit that he wasn't the easiest bloke in the world to live with.

Keith liked his own space. He liked to ponder the mysteries of existence and the passing of time. He wondered sometimes why he spent so many hours planning to rob banks with a hairclip and a fountain pen, when with the same amount of time and tools he could have made the money just as easily in business. Then he had to remind himself: it wasn't the money, it was the highwire. People think laundering bonds is easy. It could be lucrative, but easy it wasn't – as Ray Ketteridge was finding out.

He opened the curtains. The sky was blue without a cloud, one of those rare days in England when anything seems possible.

Keith had dismissed Mark as a lightweight, a potential disaster area, but why not? He liked him and that was how Keith judged people, a gut instinct, nothing cerebral. The world is made up of good people who imagine they're saints and rarely are, and bad people with the devil in them who know exactly what they are. They're the ones with an elbow on the bar and a twinkle in their eyes.

He had first met Mark in Florida the previous year when he had gone to see TJ with a bunch of $10,000 and $20,000

JC Penney bonds. It was small potatoes for TJ, but Mark had shifted them at 30 per cent, giving Keith a respectable £20,000, the average annual salary for a well-paid plumber in 1990. As a former bond trader banned from trading by the Securities and Exchange Commission (SEC), Mark knew the business from the inside as well as the dark side. He was also a friend of Ben Blessing and that was like being anointed by the Pope.

Two months after eating *nasi goreng* together in Florida, Mark Osborne was in London and Ben suggested Keith show him the sights. He was staying at the Savoy with his girlfriend Alice Walker – wide eyes, short skirts, big hair. Mark was looking for investors in a water purifying product called Aquatest. He met potential partners during the day and when the clock struck 6pm the couple did what they liked doing best, beaming and bragging at the bar of the Earl Grey with Keith and Kerry.

Mark Lee Osborne had a cockiness about him that seemed endearing and people overlooked his loudness and shortcomings. His Texan drawl gave his anecdotes an authenticity and added to the underlying humour. He was small, half Keith's size, and in matching suits they looked like Danny DeVito and Arnold Schwarzenegger in the movie *Twins*. The whole pub went quiet and listened when Mark told that old chestnut about waiting to meet a beautiful girl in a Los Angeles bar when Frank Sinatra walks in.

'So I says to Frank, you don't know me, but I'm waiting for a girl and it would really impress her if you said, "Hi, Mark" as you walk by.'

'I can do that, Mark, sure,' Frank replied.

So the girl arrives and joins Mark in his booth. They order cocktails and a few minutes later Frank Sinatra leaves the bar for the restaurant. He pauses on the way.

'Hi, Mark,' he says. 'How are you doing?'

'Fuck off, Frank, can't you see I'm busy?'

The pub roared with laughter and Alice almost fell off her bar stool. Keith didn't mention it, but he had been at a dinner party in Australia when Dawn was setting up a branch of Central

Appointments in Sydney and, after a concert, Frank Sinatra told the same story about himself.

When Alice, after her third – or was it fourth – gin and tonic, said Mark liked 'to shoot the works', as she put it, Keith arranged a night out at The Vic in Edgware Road, the former Victoria Sporting Club, where in the old days bookmakers met to set prices for horse races. They started playing cards with their winnings – bookies always win – and in the sixties it ended up as a licensed casino. High rollers drove the numbers up through the 1980s, until the The Vic hosted poker games with the highest stakes in the world with pots running into tens of thousands of pounds.

Mark was a roulette man. He played 'the street', any row of three numbers: 1,2,3; 4,5,6; up to 34,35,36. It paid out 11-1 and swallowed chips faster than a greedy pigeon on a Saturday night after the pubs close. Keith was an 'outside' man, playing the table perimeter on reds and blacks. You cannot beat the casino. With its advantage of the 0 slot – the house takes all – every bet gives you less than a 50-50 chance of winning. There is a lot of artistry in poker, but an element of luck with the fall of cards, the same with backgammon and the roll of the dice. Only chess and the Japanese game Go are pure skill. You learn these things on a three-year stretch.

Keith had a strategy that guarantees a good night out at the casino – which usually provides free drinks – without sending you into receivership.

The system requires 31 units of currency, dollars, pounds, Swiss francs, in any multiple: ten, 100, 1,000. You begin by placing a one-unit bet on the red or black option, or the odds and evens option. If you win, you put the £1 to one side and leave the original stake on the red or black. If you lose, you double up with two chips. If you win, you take the winnings and go back to one chip. If you lose again, you double up once more to four chips. You repeat the operation, taking the winnings and returning to one chip, or doubling up if you lose from four to eight to sixteen.

If you lose five times in a row, which is rare – but not that rare – you have gone through your 31 units. You leave your plastic in your wallet, finish your drink and get a taxi home. If you win consistently, you can flutter some of the winnings on individual numbers like your wife's birthday and get the occasional 35–1 return. You can't make a fortune and you don't lose one.

They played for an hour. Keith came away with £300. Kerry was short a ton and Alice watched Mark toss away £2,000 playing as if he had a death wish. For Mark it was a good night.

The following evening Keith booked dinner at Trader Vic's and they ran into Ray Ketteridge, Henry Nunn and Nunn's old chum from Gordonstoun whom Keith had first met at Tramp and was introduced to him this time as Symes – although it could have been Simes, short for Simon, or Simeon. Or Simmons? Or Simpson?

'Do-do-do excuse me. S-s-s someone I haven't s-seen in yonks.'

Symes stuck out his big hand, laughed his big laugh and wandered off to speak to people already seated.

Keith continued the introductions. 'Mark Osborne and Alice Walker, over from Texas,' he said, the men shaking hands, Henry with his tight-lipped smile as he glanced down at shoes and watches, tell-tale signs. 'Ray Ketteridge and Henry Nunn.'

'Here on business, Mark?' Henry asked, as he would.

'I am. And if you know anyone who has an interest in pure water, I have the very product they are looking for.' He gave Henry an Aquatest card.

'I shall bear that in mind. So nice to meet you.' He kissed the back of Alice Walker's hand. So Henry Nunn.

Dinner for Keith was a nightmare. Kerry always wanted to know who everyone was and now he had Mark Osborne revved up about getting investors for Aquatest. Keith lowered his voice and leaned across the table.

'Mark, my son, those two are villains, pure theft, not pure bloody water.'

'They look like men who like to diversify.'

'I'll diversify you in a minute. You going to top up my glass?'

The after-dinner treat was a visit to the Mayfair casino, where Mark drew £10,000 on a credit card – a sum so large even Keith had never seen anyone change up that much money in chips before. He then proceeded to lose half and acted like a winner walking out of the casino at 3am with £5,000 in cash. Of course, the credit card may have been dodgy. Keith didn't ask.

This was the routine repeated every night. Mark would get louder in proportion to the amount he had drunk and every time the croupier raked in his stake he spread more chips on the green baize of the roulette table trying to make up what he had lost. Occasionally he did win and taking home £3,000 one evening seemed to make up for a week shedding up to £5,000 almost every night. After a week, all the croupiers and doormen knew him.

'Evening, Mr Osborne.'
'How are you?'
'Nice to see you.'
Mark loved all that.

Two weeks after Mark and Alice returned to the States for Christmas, Mark invited Keith to visit him in Houston to see the Aquatest factory manufacturing his water-purifying product and to meet business acquaintances with a mutual interest in the financial markets. It was January 1990 – four months before the City bonds job – the dry Texas days a welcome change from the London chill and Mark his usual puckish self.

First stop, the Alamo in San Antonio, the Spanish mission where Davy Crockett and James Bowie died in the 1836 massacre during the Texas Revolution. They drove out in Mark's Cadillac with the registration plate ADIOS. After wandering through the site, they sat in the plaza outside the mission to have a coffee and Keith leapt suddenly from his chair with a burning pain in his ankle. He had been bitten by a Black Widow spider.

Mark needed all his strength to help Keith back into his car. He rushed to the nearest hospital and the immediate treatment to neutralise the venom saved Keith's life. He was discharged into

Mark's care and they returned to what turned out to be the marital home while Keith recovered. Mark kept Alice Walker in a penthouse in downtown Houston and a tolerant wife in the suburbs with a colonial mansion and two stretch limousines in an American garage the size of a basketball court.

Texas is the Lone Star State that fought for its freedom against Mexico and was once an independent republic that retained its own way of doing things. Mark was a 'good ole boy', a respected member of the Cattlemen's Club, founded by FedEx boss Freddie Smith, and the Country Club at Galveston, 50 miles from Houston, where Mark kept another house and probably another girlfriend. Galveston was the second-richest city per capita in the United States. With its thriving banking industry, it had been dubbed the 'Wall Street of the South'.

Good ole boys are white men of a certain background and education who all seemed to skirt the law in some way and admired others who did so. They did not see themselves as criminals, but rebels making a stand against the enduring enemy: the government in Washington misusing their taxes and messing with their laws. Likewise, they did not see themselves as racists sporting bumper stickers with the Confederate flag on their pickups and boasted that the same black family had worked in their kitchens through three generations. This cosy network of Texan powerbrokers gave Mark Osborne connections with bonds and banking all across the state and an endless supply of business opportunities.

He wanted to show off his network to Keith Cheeseman and took him on tour across the state and on into Louisiana, Alabama and Arkansas. Mark spent money like water – not a bad way to become popular, of course – and had a gambling habit that cost $10,000 a day. Everywhere they went, Mark introduced Keith as 'his mate from London', which for some reason impressed the Texans, as if an English accent gave the speaker an elevated air of culture and worldliness.

They stayed at the larger-than-life Peabody Hotel in Memphis where they serve champagne and chocolate-covered strawberries.

Elvis Presley used to buy his shirts from the gentlemen's outfitters and twice a day, at 11am and 5pm, the pet mallards housed on the roof are escorted down in the elevator to the foyer and, to the sound of a trumpet fanfare, are accompanied by a liveried footman across a red carpet to have a swim in the fountain. The Peabody featured in the film *The Firm*, based on the John Grisham novel and starring Tom Cruise in a plot about money laundering; one of Keith's favourites. They say at the Peabody that you always run into someone you know within 24 hours. In Keith's case, it was the director of Peterborough United FC.

Keith left the Peabody with a $4,000 bottle of Louis XIII brandy, a surprise gift from Mark, and they drove to Graceland, the estate in Whitehaven where Elvis had lived and was buried aged 42 beside his parents, for a private tour arranged by Freddie Smith.

They arrived at 11.30am and sat down with Elvis's daughter, Lisa Marie Presley, to a late breakfast consisting of bacon and eggs with hot muffins. It was cooked by Elvis's lively Aunt Delta – sister of Elvis's father Vernon – who had 'spoiled Elvis rotten' and had looked after Lisa Marie since she was a baby. While Lisa Marie kept popping in and out, no doubt bored by more guests at Graceland, Aunt Delta told them not to believe all that stuff in the papers about Elvis having an addictive personality.

'The only addiction I can recall was Elvis loved his banana, peanut butter and jelly sandwiches,' she said. 'He loved those sandwiches so much he would send his jet down to Denver to get one made up at his favourite deli.'

'He sent his jet out for a sandwich?' Mark said.

'He was Elvis, don't forget.'

Texans are generous and Keith left that day with the gift of a red Kansas City Chiefs jacket. 'You know, Elvis gave that painter Salvador Dalí a cowboy shirt and I've got a picture here somewhere with him wearing it.'

It was when they were leaving that Keith noticed the front gate and supporting walls were peppered with bullet holes. The guard explained that their neighbour down the road was Jerry

Lee Lewis and he had let loose with his rifle in a fit of pique when Elvis became more successful.

They returned to Houston and Mark took Keith to meet Sheriff Johnny Klevenhagen. They went out for chicken fried steak with pecan pie, washed down with jugs of Lone Star Original, the best ale in Texas. Johnny Klevenhagen then insisted in the insistent way of policemen that they accompany him back to the precinct.

Keith did wonder for half a moment if this was a set up and the Feds were on their way to arrest him in connection with some past crime he'd forgotten about. But no, on the contrary, Johnny sat at his desk, took a printed parchment-coloured sheet from the drawer and asked Keith for his full name. He unscrewed the top from a fountain pen and, in neat calligraphy, spelled out William Keith Cheeseman on a certificate naming him an Honorary Deputy Sheriff.

'My good friend, this makes you a member of a very exclusive club with only two members. You and your lovely prime minister, Mrs Margaret Thatcher.'

'Blimey, that is an honour. Me and Maggie.'

'You are now an honorary Texan and a Deputy Sheriff.' Johnny Klevenhagen gave Keith a badge and swore: 'You will never be pinched in Harris County, Texas.'

Having been introduced by Mark Osborne, Keith assumed the pledge was part of the good ole boy pact that anything dodgy in the white-collar crime world was of no concern to the law in Texas.

It struck Keith that the tour culminating in a Deputy Sheriff badge was readying him for one last meeting Mark had arranged with a Texas banker. Throughout the trip, he had never mentioned Aquatest. Keith had seen the modest shoebox of a factory with a couple of Mexican alchemists mixing liquids. But Mark's blood didn't warm to the thought of water purifying. He loved bonds.

The meeting took place at the downtown Hilton. They sat at a round table with fresh linen, wildflowers in a vase and a jug of iced lime water. Keith watched a tall cowboy duck his head as he entered the door and amble in a rolling walk towards them.

He was dressed in a black suit with silver buttons and fringes swinging from the sleeves, a belt with a turquoise buckle, Cuban heeled boots with jangling spurs and a ten-gallon hat. He had a pointed silver beard like the Confederate general Robert E. Lee and a bank to sell.

They stood and shook hands.

'Billy Bob Ryder,' he said. He looked down at Mark in his hidden shoe risers, up at Keith, then down again. 'I take it you are Mr Osborne?'

'I am Mark Osborne, and I am happy to make your acquaintance,' Mark said. 'And this is my associate from London, England.'

'Keith Cheeseman.'

'Mr Cheeseman. It is a pleasure. My people hailed from England, a place they call Plymouth. That was going back some. You know what the name Ryder means? It means just that, rider.' He pondered this mystery for a moment, then lowered his voice to confide. 'I got me an oil well and 6,000 acres. What am I doing with a bank at my grand old age?'

They sat. A waitress came.

'Now, darlin', you can bring us a pot of coffee, strong with a jug of cream,' he said and continued where he had left off. 'Seventy-two and a wife not yet seen her 25th birthday to keep my sheets warm. You get but one life and you have to beat out what you can from every second.'

'You are a man after my own heart, Billy Bob.'

'And you, Mr Osborne, are a man after my own bank.'

Mark touched his fist to his heart like a Freemason. 'Which I will cherish as if it were my own dear mother. God bless her soul.'

Billy Bob Ryder turned and glanced across the table. 'And you, sir, are you out here in God's country hunting for a bank?'

'If the opportunity arises, Mr Ryder.'

'Now I may be long in the tooth, but I've still got fire in my belly. You call me Billy Bob and I will, if I may, call you by your Christian name.' His tone deepened. 'I take it you are a Christian?'

'Church of England. Just like the Queen.'

Ryder smiled and Keith could see the gold molars at the back of his mouth. The coffee came and they talked good Christian business.

Banks being for sale in the Lone Star State was not unusual and often comprised of one or two branches with names like the Cattleman's Association Bank or, coined from the street corner where they stood, River Street or Main Street Bank. It seemed as if any good ole boy – if the whim took him – could open a bank simply by raising the regulation sum of cash, excluding what was called immovable assets such as land, buildings, boats and planes. If a bank fell short of capital, it went up for sale and appeared on a state list.

What appealed to Mark Osborne was that the Ryder Bank was well capitalised and he could wrangle up sufficient dubious bonds held by dubious confederates as cash collateral. He had talked about this at meetings across Texas with steak-eating hustlers who spoke with the same slow drawl and gave the same slow nod of the head across wide desks as polished as conkers to confirm they were in for the whole nine yards. It did not require more than a few thousand clients to run a legitimate bank with minimal profits as a front for more lucrative activities in the back office.

Mark had not at any time asked Keith if he wanted to be part of the deal and must have assumed he would jump at the chance. Perhaps that's what the $4,000 bottle of brandy was all about? Keith wasn't sure about the brandy but Mark had been right in his assumption. Some people want to own a racehorse or a private jet. Keith had always fancied a bank.

Before the banks in Britain conglomerated and became giant vacuum cleaners freed from government oversight until they ran into trouble, as they always do and always will, there were discreet pocket-sized banks which used one of the major banks, such as Barclays, as a clearing house and served an elite clientele of a few thousand people in elegant surroundings.

Such was the Chelsea Bank close to London's Carlton Towers hotel in Cadogan Place. During what became known as the secondary bank crisis between 1973 and 1975, many small banks were being driven out of business. Keith got a heads up before the Chelsea Bank came on the market from his friend Paul Whitney, who owned a bank in Aruba, the tiny former Dutch colony in the Caribbean.

Keith had access to bonds and a decent sum in cash but was at that time under investigation for his dealings at the Beneficial Bank. He spoke to Henry Nunn, who set up a meeting over lunch in the oak-panelled dining room at Simpson's in the Strand with Lord Malcolm Selsden, the finance adviser at Midland Bank before it was gobbled up by HSBC. Keith's lawyer, David Goring, had agreed to take a seat on the board and, speaking on Keith's behalf, asked Lord Selsden to participate. He agreed 'for a hefty salary' to act as the ostensible purchaser and future chairman of the board.

The Chelsea Bank was withdrawn from the market at the last minute, but Keith had done his research and learned that once you had control of a bank, you could build a slipway for launching illicit bonds into the gushing tsunami of international capital that passed through the City of London on its way to calmer waters. It was, in a very real sense, a licence to print money.

There was nothing new in this – nothing new under the sun, so the saying goes. The Medici family in fifteenth-century Italy were already fabulously rich with art, land and gold. But it was only when they opened a bank that they became the richest family in Europe with the political power vast fortunes bring.

Mark called in the pledges made by the good ole boy network. The finance and paperwork were in place but the deal collapsed because he had not read the small print, the finer details. He had been disbarred from bond trading and it was highly unlikely, even in Texas, that he would be granted a banking licence. If he thought Keith was a good candidate to head the Ryder Bank, that was another nonstarter. He was English with three years jailtime to his name for bank fraud.

Keith had one last meeting with Billy Bob Ryder to break the news face to face, the decent thing to do. He watched him ride off into the sunset at the wheel of his Cadillac with a Christian curse on his lips, back to the arms of a wife still waiting to reach her 25th birthday.

Bank crime is a serious business. Men like Ben Blessing had a rich life, culturally as well as financially, by playing the game like Bobby Fischer played chess – the American boy wonder Keith had studied in HMP Blundeston. Fischer had learned Russian aged twelve just so he could read Russian chess magazines. He was the American champion aged fourteen and in 1972, at 29, became the World Chess Champion after beating the Russian Boris Spassky in what was billed as the great Cold War confrontation in Reykjavik, Iceland.

Mark Osborne did not have that dedication. He wasn't a player. He was a playboy in a land where villains did not trust each other and their word was not their bond. Keith would become good friends with John Gotti, the 'Dapper Don' who headed the Gambino Mafia family in New York, America's most powerful crime syndicate. He described business between villains this way:

> 'You strip down to your swimming shorts, walk into the sea together, talk out of the side of your mouth and do the deal – then you whack him anyway because he will have changed his mind by the time you both get back to the beach.'

Keith flew back to London on a FedEx jet, courtesy of Freddie Smith.

13. DEFYING GRAVITY

Kerry didn't like living up in the clouds at the Barbican. It gave her vertigo. She felt more at home in Bethnal Green where everyone from the bobbies on the beat to the Pearly Kings and Queens in their splashy costumes was a comedian and she could wander with her mates down Petticoat Lane with its barking costermongers selling goods that had just fallen off the back of a lorry: *Kiss me quick and it's half price for you, darling.*

Keith kept a flat off Hackney Road, a ten-minute walk to the Earl Grey. He rose from his bed with jet lag and set off with Kerry for a drink with Jim Sutherland. Along the way they must have passed a dozen houses behind cages of scaffolding, all being repainted with new roofs and double-glazed windows. The East End had always been run down with narrow terraces and soot-blackened buildings. Now the yuppies were moving in and gentrifying the place.

'How's America?' Jim asked as he poured two Bloody Marys.

'Big,' Keith said. 'Big and hot.'

'Just how I like my women.'

'Don't let your wife hear you say that.'

Keith glanced around the saloon bar as he brought the glasses to the table. Even the Earl Grey had taken on a new vibe with its polished young women in neat suits and accents that belonged three miles up the Thames in Chelsea. East London was spitting distance from the City, the perfect nesting ground for a new generation on the make.

After the Wall Street crash in 1929, the United States Congress created the SEC – the Securities Exchange Commission – and passed reforms that provided oversight to the securities market: the Securities Act in 1933 and the Securities Exchange Act in 1934. Free marketeers Maggie Thatcher and Ronnie Reagan considered these regulations, put in place to prevent property speculation and bank runs, to be dead weights holding back the world economy. With their faith in trickle-down economics – you reduce taxes for the corporations and the rich so that they spend more and the wealth leaks through the cracks to the poor – Thatcher and Reagan took a blowtorch to the rules and regs to make the banks more competitive and open to risk.

Keith Cheeseman liked Maggie and approved of the changes. He knew it would lead to inflation, speculation, crisis and chaos – and where there's chaos there are more opportunities for grifting and fraud.

'You're quiet, babe, still tired?' Kerry asked.

'No, I was just thinking about Gordon Gekko.'

'Who's he when he's at home?'

'He's the character in *Wall Street*, the movie, Michael Douglas. He was the one who said greed is good.'

'My sort of bloke.'

Now that greed had stopped being one of the Seven Deadly Sins and become a virtue, people no longer regarded those who moved bonds and manipulated markets as crooks but as nimble entrepreneurs competing with bankers embezzling their own banks. Brokers at savings and loans associations in the United States were handing out mortgages to what they called NINJAs – people with no income, no job and no assets. It was assumed that house prices would go up in value indefinitely and those who defaulted on the loans would be able to sell the property and come out ahead. It was a bubble that would burst in the greatest debt crisis in history, but mortgage and bank officers had already stashed their commissions and were putting their kids through private school – for the education it provided and the connections that were made.

Keith believed the maxim: every great fortune begins with a great theft. The gravy train had pulled out of the station and he had a ticket.

First class, of course.

Kerry finished her drink. 'Hungry?' she asked.

'Always bloody hungry. That's my problem,' he replied, and she laughed.

'Pie with liquor. That will set you up.'

With new coffee bars opening on every corner, Keith was glad that Kelly's had survived and they dropped in for lunch for old times' sake. S.R. Kelly and Sons was a traditional pie and eel shop with white tiled walls and 'faces' on both sides of the counter. With tea in a half-pint mug and a plate of pie, mash and liquor, Keith was back in his own skin.

Everything about the American trip seemed unreal. He had never spent any time in the Southern states and it really was another country, everything exaggerated, the landscape, the people, the promises. He was disappointed the deal to acquire the Ryder Bank had fallen through, but it was a learning experience. Now he knew that buying a Texas bank was viable, he just had to find the right partners.

···◆·●————●·◆···

Keith returned to the Barbican. The following morning, Henry Nunn called.

'Welcome home.'

'How did you know I was back?'

'A little bird told me. Listen, I have two tickets for *La Bohème* at the Opera House tomorrow. Do you like Puccini?'

'Never met him. I thought opera was Roger's thing.'

'Thursday's his cottaging day. Meet me at the bar at seven. I'll take you to my new club for dinner.'

Keith slipped the receiver back in its cradle and sat back making a spire with his fingers.

Henry Bloody Nunn. What's he after?

This call was eight weeks before John Goddard was relieved of his satchel of bonds in Nicholas Lane, and without knowing it Keith was being groomed as the potential launderer.

He was still finding his ear for opera and wasn't sure whether he liked it or not. What Keith had learned was that ministers, lords, celebrities and money people met at the opera, and it was a good place to be seen.

After the performance they wandered through Covent Garden to Soho. Keith turned up the collar of his coat. There was a chill in the air and a lot of bare young male flesh on show. Just like the gentrification of the East End, Old Compton Street with its grim pubs and grim intellectuals hobbling with walking canes to the French House was suddenly alive at 10.30pm with young lookalikes from Village People: leather and chains, an Apache in full headdress, a few blokes in dresses. Keith half expected the entire throng to break into a rendition of 'Y.M.C.A.'

'Your kind of place,' Keith remarked.

'You think so?' Henry slowed his pace and paused. 'If we were in the stands at a football match surrounded by skinheads in red braces, would they be your kind of people in your kind of place?'

'You're right, Henry, my apologies. No hard feelings?'

'Not between us.'

They turned into Dean Street and entered the Groucho, the club named in honour of Groucho Marx who wittily said he would refuse to join any club that would have him as a member. As they were making their way through the bar to the dining room, a woman stopped them.

'Are you a drummer?' she asked Henry.

'Do I look like a drummer?'

She shook her head angrily and turned to Keith. 'What about you? You look like a drummer.'

'I'm not bad on the fiddle.'

She stormed off. 'Fucking tour and no fucking drummer.'

'Was that Madonna?' Keith asked.

'Probably.'

They ate buttermilk chicken with champagne.

'It's a funny old thing,' Keith remarked. 'I've only been away for a couple of months and everything's changed.'

'You're just seeing the world through new eyes. It's the same dirty old London with money under every mattress.'

'That's what Mimi needed,' Keith said, and Henry wasn't sure what he meant. 'In *La Bohème*.'

'Money? Hardly. It's a love story.'

'Love story my arse. You can't con a con man. Mimi's dying. She needs a decent plate of grub and a doctor. So what does Rudolf do?'

'Rodolfo.'

'Rodolfo scratches out a couple of lines for a poem, then burns his manuscript to stay warm – a show off, in my opinion. He finds out Mimi's dying and just kneels at her bedside weeping and doing sod all. Whatshername, Musetta, she's the one who sells her earrings and buys the medicine. When Rodolfo and Mimi sing their big number, it fools us into thinking it is a love story. It's not. What it tells us is that poets are in love with the idea of love and in love with themselves.'

Henry raised his glass. 'Bravo. I don't know that Puccini would agree, but it's a novel take, I must say.'

'Worst people in the world, poets. Prisons are full of them. Poets and Napoleons.'

He laughed. 'You're on form. There must be something going on I don't know about.'

'If only. Lean time, I don't mind telling you. Fancy buying a bank in Texas?'

Henry put down his knife and fork. 'A bank,' he repeated. His eyes bobbed up and down in their sockets as he thought about that. 'What do you have in mind?'

'If banks in Texas fall below a certain level of capital, they go on the market. There's a couple every week, one or two branches, two or three thousand clients.'

Henry shook his head. 'And the profit?'

'Next to nothing. What you get with a bank is, what's it called, entrance ...?'

'Entrée?'

'That's the word. They're laundromats. You stuff in the grubby securities, press go and they come out clean.'

'I like it, Keith,' he said, and a little smile crossed his thin lips. 'And, you know, we might just have the wherewithal to do it.'

'Really?'

Henry touched the side of his nose in that gesture that says there's a secret and now was not the time to share it.

He changed the subject.

'I ran into Ralph Haeems at Tramp, and he said he missed the good old days of the Dusky Maiden. Whatever happened to her?'

'No idea. Keeping her head down, I imagine.'

'Was it really spanking and bondage going on?'

'You know the story. It was all over the bloody papers.'

'Short-term memory,' he lied and refilled the glasses.

···◆·●————●·◆···

In the summer of 1985, Keith met Diana McCleary, aka the Dusky Maiden, at the Phene Arms with Ralph Haeems, and was surprised to run into her again a week later at Kerry's escort office in Great Windmill Street. What she was doing at Aristocats he didn't ask, but while they were chatting Diana mentioned that her new boyfriend was the manager of the NatWest.

Talk about bells going off ...

'The NatWest?' he echoed.

'In Streatham. Lovely bloke. I was stripping at a stag do at the local football club,' she said and hushed her voice. 'He was all over me, after the show, like, but in a nice way. You know, nothing coarse or nothing.'

'A gentleman?'

'Yeah, what I call disciplined, if you know what I mean.'

Keith mimed spanking the air and she laughed.

'We should do a double date with Kerry?' he said.

'He'd love that.'

Keith's suggestion was tongue in cheek, but Diana McCleary took it to heart and they arranged to meet for dinner. Keith paid, naturally, and James Burrows, NatWest's young branch manager, had the time of his life listening to Keith's story about a pub crawl with Stewart Granger and Georgie Best that ended up in Brick Lane eating salt beef bagels with men on the night shift on their way home from work.

'You know Georgie Best?'

The Hollywood actor had not impressed Mr Burrows. Best was a legend.

Kerry shook her head. 'James, didn't you know, Keith used to own Dunstable Town Football Club,' she explained. 'George came out of retirement to play for the club.'

His mouth fell open. 'Blimey, yes, I remember that. That was you. I'll drink to that.'

They met twice more in the coming weeks. On their third night out a month later, Keith picked up Burrows and the Dusky Maiden in a 1971 Silver Shadow he had bought as a favour to a mate sewing mail bags in Wormwood Scrubs. He drove leisurely through Clapham to Battersea and across the Albert Bridge to the Phene Arms. Angus Montagu, now the Duke of Manchester, was waiting for them with a table upstairs where a dancer was sliding around a greasy pole wearing a pair of tinsel knickers and a bored expression.

'Studying sociology at King's,' Angus said. 'Such a nice *gurl*.'

After the Beneficial Bank debacle, Keith and Angus had remained friends, even though Keith had done his time in prison and Angus had got off scot-free. Keith always called on Angus – meaning his title – to impress the impressionable. Diana McCleary curtsied and James Burrows had that look of a man who always knew he was going to arrive and had finally got there.

Keith had done background checks. Ex-coppers were good at that sort of thing and were always up for earning a few quid. Burrows was married to a woman the informer believed was a born-again Christian and had what the *News of the World* – 27 October 1985 – called a 'Love Brush' with former ice-skating star Sally-Anne Stapleford, a neighbour in Streatham.

Burrows smoked a pipe. That evening when he was lighting the tobacco with a cheap Bic, Keith grabbed it and gave him a black-and-gold Dupont.

'You don't want to be seen with that old rubbish, have this.'

Burrows lit his pipe and slid the lighter into the ticket pocket in his brown chalk-striped suit as if such gifts were normal and expected. He was enjoying the high life, running two households and keeping Diana on the side for extracurricular activities. How a stripper-cum-escort-cum-dominatrix filled in her tax returns Keith had no idea, but Burrows had approved loans for her to buy a car and put a deposit on a flat. Keith was glad. Strippers have a short shelf life with their clothes on.

He stuck a tenner in the pole dancer's sparkly pants and glanced back across the table at James.

'How's business in Streatham, my son?'

'Booming. Doubled our turnover in two years.'

'That's what I like to hear.'

The branch manager of the Streatham NatWest had dug himself in deep with his BDSM sex nights with Diana McCleary, the teatime visits to Sally-Anne's sheets in her modest semi, the Rolls-Royce Silver Shadow slicing through the South London backstreets to take him to extravagant dinners with a duke in Mayfair.

Keith believed an honest man couldn't be corrupted and when he suggested a scam to divert money into 'ghost' accounts, Burrows jumped at the opportunity. In the coming weeks, Keith created twenty accounts in false names and sent his chauffeur to collect loans from £10,000 to £38,000. Angus, the Duke of Manchester, had a fleeting need for £4,000 to see him through a moment of financial difficulty – that moment being much like the last moment and the next – and was granted an unsecured loan.

Burrows and Keith wined and dined. They passed late night hours with anonymous groups of celebrity glitterati, had lunches at Simpson's with the Queen Mother sitting just feet away. But all good things come to an end, as they say, and end it did with His Grace the duke, Burrows the dupe and the Cheesemans, Keith and Kerry, all charged with criminal conspiracy and splashed across the red tops with lurid headlines – 'Bank Manager's Love Sessions with a Stripper', 'Lord Angus Montagu on Plot Charge', 'Ass of a Duke Cleared', 'Nights with the Dusky Maiden'.

They came to trial at the Old Bailey. Burrows said he had been blackmailed into providing loans. No one was listening. He was jailed for two years. Kerry Cheeseman walked free. She hadn't done anything. Lord Angus Montagu played his 'I'm sorry I'm a fool' trump card and was acquitted. Educated at Gordonstoun and a former officer in the Royal Marines, he was described by his counsel as 'a very stupid person, gullible and a bit of an ass'. The judge said he was 'stupid and negligent'.

'You should have known, or someone should have told you, that when you take out a £4,000 loan from a bank, it has to be repaid.'

Keith believed you would always get yourself into more trouble by testifying. He pleaded guilty and Ralph Haeems, in an abacus of complex mathematics, showed that Keith had by some vindictive quirk of bad luck spent more time than he should have done locked up for the Beneficial Bank fraud that, when added to the time he had spent on remand, 'this essentially kind and honest man who has taken the guilt for the NatWest affair upon himself when those with broader shoulders may have done so', had already paid the price for this victimless crime.

The judge, with his rare-beef pink cheeks below a horsehair wig, sat motionless in a moment of silence. Keith and the briefs in black gowns, the reporters with pens poised and the people in the public gallery held their breath until in the still air of the court room he pounded his gavel. He spoke in a voice that was deep and distinguished and announced that William Keith Cheeseman would serve a suspended sentence remitted for time served.

There was a sigh of relief.

A few people cheered and were hushed by the ushers.

Hearing Keith finish telling the story, Henry Nunn clapped his hands then clicked his fingers. Another bottle of Moët & Chandon appeared at the table.

'Wonderful,' he said.

'While it lasted.'

'You must have known it would come to an end?'

Keith sat back nursing his glass. 'Nice club,' he said, looking round. 'Nothing overdone. Nice art on the walls.'

'I'll speak to the membership secretary …'

'Don't think I haven't thought about it,' Keith said, lighting a cigar and picking up Henry's question. 'Imagine you're George Best. You've beaten two defenders, you swerve to your right and put the ball in the back of the net. It's that feeling. That glimpse of heaven. Of perfection. Or completion. Roger Bannister must have felt it when he broke the four-minute mile.'

'Of winning?'

'More than that. I'd phone the bank and ask for a £10,000 loan, then send the driver in the Roller to go and fetch it. In an hour we'd be stacking the money up in used twenties on the kitchen table. It's that feeling of defying gravity. Of overcoming the impossible. You know there's a risk, but there's a risk every time you get on a plane.'

'Without risk, what would life be?'

'A job and a pension.'

Henry shook himself as if a cold chill had slipped down his spine. 'I knew Angus at Gordonstoun. He was a silly ass then and he's a silly ass now,' he remarked. 'He's one of those English public schoolboys proud of how much he can drink and how he can't speak a word in a foreign language.'

'You don't need to if you're a duke.'

'It's the attitude. I've been surrounded by these people all my life.'

'So that's what you're doing out with the riff-raff?'

'No, dear boy. Stop beating yourself up. It's, what did you call it, defying gravity. The problem with most people, Keith, is they are *so* damned ordinary.'

Defying Gravity

They clinked glasses and Henry continued.

'Changing the subject, did you spend a lot of time with Mark Osborne when you were Stateside?'

'All the time. I got bitten by a Black Widow at the Alamo. If it hadn't been for Mark rushing me to the hospital, I'd be dead now.'

'What were you doing interfering with a Black Widow?'

'I wasn't interfering with her; she took a fancy to me.'

'So, he's a good chap, then, Mark?'

'He likes a laugh. He came through selling on some JC Penney bonds I had. He's alright.'

'Well connected, I imagine.'

'Very. Call themselves good ole boys. You scratch my back. Yeah, he knows people. Why?'

'No reason. You just be careful with these Black Widows and Dusky Maidens. We don't want to see any more brushes with the law – or death. Not now.'

'Not now?'

'At any time. Perhaps we'll buy a bank. Just be cool.'

'Cool! Blimey, don't let your old house master hear you saying that.'

14. MURDER IN THE PARK

Six weeks had gone by since the robbery and the three Irishmen arrested at Heathrow with £77 million in bonds were still on remand at Wormwood Scrubs. The Operation Starling team under DCS Dickinson were still building a case to show that they were not, as they claimed, innocent horseracing fans bamboozled by persons unknown planting the stolen certificates in their luggage, but career criminals with terrorist connections on both sides of the Atlantic.

Keith still didn't know how they had got their hands on the bonds but it had become obvious that the United States was a more viable market than the UK. The coin had finally dropped for Ray Ketteridge. He did not have an inside track with major players in the US and called Keith to discuss the merits of employing Mark Osborne.

'What time is it?' Keith said.

'Just gone eight,' Ray replied.

'What are you doing up this time of day, watering your bloody garden?'

'You're a funny man, Keif. So, what about it?'

'I can't talk now, I'm in bed. Let's meet at Pellicci's. Do you know it?'

'Course I bloody know it. I used to have breakfast there with Reggie Kray back in the day.'

'And you lived to tell the tale. I'll be there in an hour.'

Keith had been putting off having a face to face with Ray since his fruitless trip to Amsterdam. There was never going to be a good time. He shaved, dressed and checked that the sheet of paper he'd been carrying around for weeks was still in his wallet. He glanced at his image in the mirror. 'Keep your chin up, son,' he said, then looked back into the bedroom where Kerry had rolled over and was sleeping like a fallen angel. He thought about writing her a note, but it wasn't something he'd done before and he didn't want to appear paranoid all of a sudden.

'Hasta la vista, baby,' he whispered.

Pellicci's in Bethnal Green Road was close to the flat. It was Keith's favourite place for a full English to start the day and, at night, he enjoyed a spaghetti vongole served in the art deco surroundings unchanged since the turn of the century. Gangsters like to eat in nice places.

'Two eggs for you, Keith,' Maria called as he walked through the door and found Ray waiting with his jacket on the back of the chair and an open-necked shirt with the sleeves rolled up as if ready for a fight. It was June, hot enough to have been the east coast of Sicily let alone the East End of London.

Ray stirred his tea and started in before Keith caught his breath.

'What do you think of this Osborne geezer, any good?'

'You met him at Trader Vic's. He's a businessman. He's shifted bonds for me in the past.'

'I don't recall …'

'Little guy, big smile. Everyone's best friend.'

Ray shrugged. 'What kind of numbers did he do?'

'Small denominations, £5,000, £10,000.'

'What about 10 mil?'

'Same concept. More zeroes.'

'Didn't you get bitten by a spider in Texas? That's what I heard.'

'A Black Widow, mate, nearly died. They sucked the poison out in hospital.'

Ray pulled a face and shook his head of good hair. 'Who'd want to live in a place with killer spiders?'

'Might be the place to make a killing with toxic bonds.'

Nevio set Keith's plate down on the table: eggs, bacon, black pudding, a pork sausage, button mushrooms, fried tomatoes and two slices of toast. He was wearing a white apron as clean as bedsheets on a washing line with a pleated toque on his head.

'Signor Keith. Happy I see you. Too long.'

'Been busy trying to earn a crust.'

'You eat crust.' He tapped the top of his head. 'It make-a your hair curl.'

He left for the counter, poured tea from a big silver pot and refilled Ray's cup.

'Bloody hell, you going to eat all that?' Ray said.

'Eat breakfast like a king and supper like a pauper.'

'That's how I'm going to end up at this rate.'

'Have a bacon sandwich, for Chrissake. On me.'

'Go on then.'

Keith caught Maria's eye and ordered.

'I know things haven't been easy, but it's early days still,' Keith said.

'My experience is when things go wrong, they get worse, they don't get better. If you're on a break in and you hear a night watchman, what do you do?'

'I wouldn't know, to be honest.'

'You down tools and you're out. You don't want to kill someone. It ain't worth it.'

Ray was hard to pigeonhole and Keith wasn't sure what he meant exactly by 'it ain't worth it'. That the police would be all over it, or 'it ain't worth' taking a life for mere larceny? The sandwich came. Ray looked at it for a moment, took a bite, then looked back at Keith.

'So, Osborne?'

'Very American. Funny guy. Gambles. Likes the ladies ...'

'Don't we all.'

'Throws money around like one of those buddhas with eight arms. He's got a good network. Texas good ole boys. They all know each other. All got each other's backs.' Keith laughed.

'You're not going to believe it, I got made a Deputy Sheriff. Got a badge, certificate, the lot.'

'Nothing would surprise me about you, Keif.' He scratched the side of his head as if to shake up his brain cells. 'You fix it up. Twenty-five per cent on what he can get. If he comes through there'll be more. You make your own deal with Osborne.'

Ray and his syndicate would make less on the deal than they would have done sending the bonds to TJ in Indonesia, not that Keith was going to mention it. When someone makes a mistake, they don't want to be reminded about it.

'Sounds good to me,' Keith said. 'How's the sandwich?'

'Not bad, as it happens.'

'How are you going to get the bonds to Osborne?'

Ray wiped his fingers on a napkin and lit a fag. 'I've got someone in place. Let me worry about that.'

Keith finished his tea. Breakfast had gone down well but now his stomach was in knots.

'Ray, I've got something I want to show you. Not here. Let's take a stroll through the park.'

'You kidding me?'

'Weavers Fields is just round the corner. You like bloody flowers, don't you?'

Ray glanced at the £3,000-Rolex in the nest of hair on his wrist. 'Alright, a walk in the park if that's what you want. At least it ain't fucking raining.'

Keith paid the bill with a tenner on top and they set off down Bethnal Green Road towards Weavers. Half-past nine and not a soul to be seen. They followed the path across a field dotted with daisies – two big blokes in smart clobber who would easily have been picked out from a police line-up as a couple of gangsters. Keith could see the new glass towers with bank logos rising over the City, warehouses for looted Saudi and Russian resources. It wasn't the dear old London Town of Henry Nunn's fantasy, it was what he'd heard someone call Londongrad, in the Thamesky Prospekt. Greed is good.

'So, what have you got to show me?'

'I'll come to that, Ray. First, if you don't mind my asking, how did Tommy Coyle and his mates get hold of £70-odd million in bonds?'

'Where are you going with this?'

'It's just too much of a coincidence they were caught with them red handed.'

'You're telling me.'

Ray had stopped and leaned his jacket over the back of a bench. He was not a happy man and Keith was about to add to his woes.

'Remember I went to Amsterdam with Martin Newman to see Ben Blessing? He'd agreed to take three bonds.'

'And you've got some money for me, right?'

'No, Ray, wrong. Let me tell you. As we were lining up to get on the Harwich Ferry, Customs was pulling out black BMWs. They searched the cars and took the passengers off to a hut for a body search. I had to strip down and drop my boxers.'

'So what did you do with the bonds?'

Keith took from his wallet a sheet of notepaper with the three thin strips torn from the bonds sellotaped to the surface.

'These are the serial numbers. I hid them up inside my tie. I ripped the bonds into pieces, stuck them in a coffee cup and dropped the cup in the bin.'

Ray's shoulders went back. 'Three-million fucking quid! Are you having a laugh? Three fucking million …'

He stared down at the sheet of notepaper as if he couldn't believe his own eyes. His big hands were shaking.

'They would have been confiscated. I would have been inside. It was a fuck up. We were in a black BMW and that's what Customs were searching.'

Ray looked up from the paper. His suntan had faded. 'I'll tell you som'ink, I feel like fucking killing someone.'

'We were fenced in by concrete barriers. We couldn't have done a runner even if we'd wanted to.' He held Ray's stare. 'The thing is, no one knew I'd be travelling in a black BMW. There has to be a grass. Customs must have been tipped off, same as Coyle's party at Heathrow …'

'Someone's taking the piss ...'

'Someone is taking the piss, Ray. I know it's not you and you know it's not me. Am I right?'

'You're always fucking right.'

It was the answer Keith expected but he had hit a chord. Ray Ketteridge had the face of someone who'd just been kicked when he was down, and he looked around the park as if for inspiration or guidance or a weapon. He was the boss behind the biggest robbery ever, anywhere. £427 million posing as £291.9 million. The numbers were like the stars in the sky. Astronomical. He had made history, and it was fading like a mirage before his eyes.

'If you can't trust me, Ray, you can't trust anyone,' Keith said.

Ray clenched and unclenched his fists as he visibly calmed himself. He reached for his cigarettes in his jacket and lit up.

'How long were you inside for, Keif?'

'Over three years. I don't want to go back.'

'You know something, I only like dealing with our sort of people. I don't like foreigners and I don't like people who talk like their mouths are full of fucking silverware.'

'My feelings exactly,' Keith replied. It was what Ray Ketteridge wanted to hear. 'I'll set things up with Mark Osborne, at least settle some of the debt, if that's alright. I've still got the other 2 mil, safe as houses.'

Ray took a long draw on his fag and blew the smoke out through his nose.

'If you're fucking with me, Keif ...'

'You've seen the serial numbers. They were circulated by the Bank of England the day they were stolen. You can't sell bonds with the numbers ripped off. Broke my bloody heart tearing them to pieces.'

'And mine.' He took a breath. 'Where do we go from here?'

'Cut our losses. Get the ten pieces to Mark Osborne and see if we have more luck across the water.'

Ray stared at Keith for a long time. Keith could almost hear the wheels and cogs clicking and churning as he put things together in his head. He knew there were problems in the organisation and knew Keith wasn't the problem. Keith wasn't in on the robbery itself and had only been brought in after the event.

'Three-fucking-million down the khazi. Get Osborne. You keep whatever you can get out of his piece.'

'Good on you. That's decent.' Keith lit a cigar. 'When we came through the gates I had this headline in my head: "Murder in the Park".'

'Don't think I didn't think about it.'

Ray looked down again at the three serial numbers stuck on the notepaper and screwed it up in a ball. He gave it to Keith.

'Burn it when you get home,' he said.

15. ABOVE THE LAW

Mark Osborne had the gambler's sixth sense that inviting Keith Cheeseman to Texas would pay off. He had been right. He knew about the Bank of England bonds robbery – it was headline news around the world – and he was not entirely surprised to hear Keith on the phone with an offer that would change his life in ways he couldn't begin to imagine.

'If you're up for it, someone is going to fly into Houston with ten £1-million bonds for you.'

'Not you, Keith?'

'A courier. This is the deal: we take 25 per cent on what you can get for them, split down the middle, 50–50. That suit you?'

'You're the man.'

'You're sure you can handle this, Mark?'

'If you were here, I would place my hand on the Holy Bible and swear an oath.'

'Another believer like Billy Bob?'

'That's the way it is in Texas.'

'Then believe this: these are serious people. They don't mess around.'

'You can trust me, Keith.'

'If you place the ten pieces there will be more. Maybe a lot more.'

'Bring 'em on. I'm ready for it.' He laughed and paused for thought. 'How will I know this person coming with the merchandise?'

'He'll contact you. Speak to the people you know. There's a player out there who can handle this. You've just got to find him.'

Keith was taking a chance. Mark had an excessive supply of self-confidence but tended to leap before he looked and often landed on his backside. The bank deal with Ryder could have paid off by bringing in the right people, but Mark showed his cards too early and the deal fell apart before the dotted line was signed.

Mark was probably not aware of Keith's doubts, that was his nature, but heeded his advice. The penthouse carried a mortgage and he had gambling debts across the state. This was his chance to clean up his act. He stayed home with Alice and went alphabetically through his Rolodex calling the good ole boys. Placing low-figure bonds in dollars was one thing, not even delinquent if you don't get caught. Sterling bonds guaranteed by the Bank of England with six zeroes was the big time.

Two days later, the bonds arrived and were exchanged over a drink in the lobby bar at the downtown Hilton, close to Osborne's apartment. The courier was young, good looking and spoke 'like the croupier in Mayfair' – Mark's idea of posh, Keith assumed. If he was young and good looking, it wasn't Henry Nunn, and if he sounded posh, it wasn't Ray Ketteridge or the Irish bulldog Houlihan. With the nervous disposition of a bent banker, John Bowman would not have been sent on such an assignment. He was keeping a low profile back in Geneva.

That meant there was a new player in the game.

Finding a buyer was not as easy as Mark Osborne had thought it would be. The mere mention of pounds sterling sounded too exotic and alien. He was beginning to run out of names in his Rolodex when a bond broker in Galveston, who Mark had worked with when he still had a licence, lowered his voice to tell him there was a big shot out there by the name of Dipino, who was 'above the law' and had, he'd been told, a liking for bonds. He gave Mark the telephone number of a guy who knew Dipino. It was a lucky break – *didn't he deserve it!* – that the contact happened to be lodged at a flophouse close to the main bus station in Houston.

Thank you, God.

Mark got a description and tracked him down: 'A tall guy, skinny as a string bean with a moustache like Pancho Villa, the Mexican bandit.' They drank beers in a bar with Astros baseball memorabilia on the walls.

'I'm told by a friend of mine you are acquainted with Dipino?' Mark began.

'Who wants to know?'

'Someone with some hot bonds.'

The thin guy wiped beer froth from his 'tache. 'You know what you're dealing with? Tony Dipino's connected.'

'Connected?'

The man grinned and drank his drink. 'Mafia,' he said.

'How do you know him?'

'That's for me to know, brother, and you to mind your personal questions. You want to find him or are you just out for a beer?'

'I do, sir. Very much. Do you have his number?'

'Do you have $500?'

'How do I know you've got his details?'

'What are you doing sitting here? You came to me.'

He called the bartender and waved two fingers. The glasses were refilled. The country music station played soft and there was nothing Mark could do but ride his luck and play the numbers. He discreetly slid the bills from his wallet and folded them into the man's palm. The skinny dude asked the barman for a pen and wrote a New York number down on a coaster.

'Good luck, bro,' he said, finished his beer and walked out.

Mark drove home in the Cadillac with the radio on full volume singing along with Dolly Parton's '9 to 5'. He waited until ten o'clock the following morning, a decent hour to call the Cosa Nostra. Dipino's number rang seven times, then a voice out of a movie answered.

'Speak.'

'Tony Dipino?'

'Who's asking?'

'My name is Mark Osborne. I got your number from a guy in Texas.'

'I don't know no one in Texas.'

'Thin guy. Big moustache.'

'You see him, tell him he's a dead man. What do you want?'

'I'm sitting on some hot bonds …'

'Then mind you don't burn your ass. Why are you calling me?'

'He gave me your number …'

'Not interested. I don't know who you are. I don't deal with stolen goods. I only do business with people face to face …'

'Wait, wait. Could we meet?'

'I told you, I'm not interested.'

'Give me five minutes.'

He heard Tony Dipino shout: 'Some asshole wants five minutes.'

He heard the reply: 'Maybe it's the Salvation Army? Give it to him.'

'I'll give it to him if he's wasting my time,' he said and aimed his voice back into the telephone receiver. 'What's today, Monday? Come tomorrow. I'll be at the bar on 42nd Street, Ray McFadden. You know it?'

'I'll find it.'

'Eleven in the morning.'

He hung up and Mark Osborne punched the air like the winner of a talent show. He'd had his doubts that the number on the coaster was for real and now he had a date with the Mafia. He got back on the phone to arrange a flight to New York that landed early morning. He then called Keith and told him that he'd found the man and was meeting him the next day.

'You done good, son,' Keith said. 'Don't go jumping at the first offer. If he's interested, he'll start low to test you.'

'I know that, Keith, I'm a pro.'

'Is your man a pro?'

'By heck he is.' He lowered his voice. 'Tony Dipino. He's Mafia.'

'Nice family man, then.'

They laughed. They hung up. Life was good. Mark took Alice out for enchiladas and tres leches cake in a Mexican place with a mariachi band and the best tequila cocktails in Texas. He was feeling happy, but it was more than that, he had a happy disposition. He felt relieved. He'd done everything Keith had told him to do and it had paid off. The lights were low, the music was loud and he had to shout.

'We're gonna be rich, baby,' he said.

'I thought you *were* rich, honey.'

'Yeah, but I mean rich-rich.'

He snapped his fingers like a flamenco dancer and two more cocktails appeared at the table as if from heaven.

He drank plenty of hot coffee and slept on the flight.

···◆·•————•◆···

It was Tuesday, 31 July 1990. Hot in Texas with a robin's-egg blue sky. Hotter in New York, grey with fumes hanging like shrouds between the tall buildings. Bent-over people scurried in a hurry through the hot haze while the rich out in Long Island were sitting by their pools with freshly pressed juices and the sound of the Atlantic pounding into shore. There's the good life and there's no life at all.

Ninety days had passed since Patrick Thomas had relieved John Goddard of hundreds of millions of pounds in bonds on 2 May, and he, Thomas, was the only person who had seen a return. According to the sums paid into various building society accounts later uncovered by the police, Thomas had scored between £100,000 and £150,000 to pull a blade on Goddard a few minutes after he left the Bank of England.

Mark Osborne didn't know that, and didn't know that later that morning Ray Ketteridge would be sitting in his garden in shorts reading the *Daily Mail* and hoping the biggest bank robbery of all time would begin to pay off.

Sometimes, Ray wished he'd never been in on the heist in the first place. Big scores bring big headaches and long stretches when they go sideways. Ray was more of a chiseller. While the man in the street was earning £12,000 a year and a house cost £50,000, he could make £10,000 shifting a Transit van full of nicked televisions from thief A to fence B with two telephone calls. Easy money. Bonds were like hand grenades and you never knew when the backdraft was going to blow your own head off.

Mark looked good in his off-white linen suit with a string tie and Cuban boots. Inside the lining of his four-button jacket, unpicked and resewn, were ten bond certificates in an envelope. He took a yellow cab to 42nd Street and stepped out in a sweat at 10.58am.

Ray McFadden's was empty except for the barman spit and polishing glasses at the window end of the wooden bar. A man sat on a stool at the far end studying the girls in a cheesy magazine. Tony Dipino was waiting at a bare table in the annexe, a dark, windowless room off to one side beyond the bar. He studied Mark in his white suit as he entered.

'You carrying?' he asked.

'I've got the bonds?'

Dipino grinned and glanced at the guy sitting at the bar. He was young, pumped up in a white T-shirt and blue jeans. Dipino turned his attention back on Osborne.

'I said, are you carrying?'

Osborne broke out in his concertina smile and shook his head. 'No, no.'

'You being from Texas, an' all.' He rolled his big shoulders. 'Let's see what you got?'

Mark removed his jacket. 'Do you have a knife?'

'You gonna cut me, Mr Osborne?'

'They're in the lining.'

'Frankie,' Dipino said and, as he spoke, a thin blade flashed like a silver fish from the knife in Frankie's hand.

He picked at the jacket lining. Mark removed the bonds from the envelope and fanned them out on the table like a magician doing a card trick.

'That's £10 million, like $13 million.'

'Are you a cop?'

'No, no, sir, not at all. No way. I'm a bond broker,' he said and did the big smile. 'I *was* a broker till the SEC took my licence away.'

'Why'd they do that?'

'Dealing hot bonds.'

'Drink?'

'Sure. That's very kind. I got a thirst on.'

'You came in from Houston?'

'I did.'

Frankie carried a bottle of Bushmills and two glasses to the table. He filled them and Mark threw his back in one gulp. There was sweat on his back. Tony Dipino refilled his glass and studied one of the bonds.

'Are these counterfeits?'

'They are the real deal, solid as gold, minted and guaranteed by the Bank of England. They were robbed back in May, big heist, biggest ever they're saying.'

'So we hear.' He paused. 'You got more bonds, or is this it?'

'I have access to as many as you can handle.'

Tony Dipino looked back at Frankie. 'You hear that, the big man can get hold of as many as we can handle?'

'Everything's big in Texas,' said Frankie.

'Not everything.' Dipino tapped his glass against Mark's and Mark took another sip of Bushmills. He was feeling more relaxed.

'If these are for real – if you're for real, I've got $2 million in seven bags not ten yards from where you're sitting.'

Mark knew his numbers. $2 million on £10 million was about 15 per cent of the face value. He remembered what Keith Cheeseman had told him. This was a game. He starts low, you start high.

'We were looking for something closer to $4 million. That's only 30 per cent,' he said.

'Who knows you're here?'

Mark shrugged. 'Nobody.'

'Then we can take you out and take the lot.'

Mark laughed. He wasn't sure if Tony Dipino was joking or not, but the laugh came out and he finished the whiskey in his glass.

'Then you'd have problems accessing the rest.'

Dipino laughed now. 'I like this dude in his fancy boots. He's okay.' He paused. 'We'll talk about numbers. First, you tell me how you got hold of these bonds?'

'A courier brought them from London. We met at the Hilton. He gave me the bonds.'

Dipino turned to his companion. 'You see. Everyone loves Mark Osborne. They fly in from all over the world to give him millions of dollars.' He looked back across the table and his tone changed. 'Who the fuck is this guy? Who are these people?'

'I don't know his name. It was set up by my friend Keith Cheeseman. He handles the distribution …'

'You lying to me? Keith Cheeseman? Who's he? What does he do? Sell fucking cheese?'

'No, no. He's a fence. The robbery was set up by a dude named Ketteridge, Ray Ketteridge.'

Frankie spoke. 'Osborne, Cheeseman and Ketteridge. Sound like lawyers to me,' he said.

'They are the reverse side of the coin, Mr Dipino,' Osborne assured him.

'Seeing as we're going to be partners, Mark, why don't you call me Tony?'

'Sure, Tony.'

'Sweet. Now, we're friends, are you going to accept my $2 million, or does Frankie have to drive you down to the canal?'

16. AN OFFER YOU CAN'T REFUSE

Keith had no idea that Mark Osborne had Ray Ketteridge's contact details and by the time he found out, the brakes had failed and the car was careening out of control heading for the cliff edge.

Mark called Ray and told him he was in a sit down with Tony Dipino with $2 million 'sitting here' on the table.

'Two-million dollars for £10 million sterling. You're having me on?'

'That's 15 per cent.'

'Fuck me. You must have asked for more?'

'I did, Ray, but he's – you know, he's not moving.'

'That's taking the piss.'

'The thing is, Ray, he won't hand the money over to me, only to you.'

'What's that supposed to mean?'

'He said, you're the boss and that's the way he does things.'

'Tell him I'll send my courier to pick it up. Same bloke who brought you the bonds.'

'I don't think he's going to go for that. Why don't I give you his number?'

'Right, you do that.'

The call took place the following day between the mafioso and the East-London gangster. There was a lot of ego, a lot of machismo, a lot of respect. They were men who know what men are capable of.

'Tony Dipino?' Ray said.

'Ray Ketteridge. Appreciate you calling. I got $2 million for you.'

'Fifteen per cent. That's not a lot.'

'That's what I am prepared to pay.'

There was a pause on the line. Inside Ray's head numbers were going round like lottery balls.

'I'll tell you this, Tony, I only like dealing with our kind of people. Fucking can't trust no one else.'

'We're living on the same side of the street. We should meet. Come to New York. I'll give you the cash in person. I'll take you out for the best meal you've ever had in this life. Place in Little Italy.'

'Sounds alright to me but I've got things to do. Give the money to Mark Osborne.'

'There's something not right about that guy.'

'I trust him, Tony. You've already got the fucking bonds. You don't need a receipt.

'I'll tell you what I'll do, you send your own bagman.'

'Jesus Christ. Two mil is peanuts, what the fuck you worried about?'

'It'll make me feel comfortable. London's booming. We can do a lot of business. Let me know what time he gets in, I'll send my boy to pick him up.'

Ray felt trapped. He was trapped. Three months had gone by and he had not earned a single penny from the biggest robbery in history. Dipino was holding the bonds *and* the money. Getting fifteen points was a joke, but at least it opened a door in the United States, and something is always better than nothing. How was Jeffrey going to get the money back to the UK? That was another worry he put aside for another day.

An Offer You Can't Refuse

The courier was Jeffrey Kershaw, also known as Jeffrey Kirschel, 'the *very* attractive young solicitor', as Henry Nunn had once said, who had brokered the deal between the IRA and the Protestant UDA to launder Sir Alfred Beit's £20-million collection of old masters.

Kershaw crossed the Atlantic, flying first class to New York next day on Ketteridge's tab. Frankie was waiting for him at the airport in a red Chevrolet Corvette that reminded Jeffrey of the old E-type Jag.

He sat down with Tony Dipino at McFadden's with the $2 million stacked up on the table and Mark Osborne nowhere to be seen. Unlike Osborne, who drank too much and was terrified in the company of the Mafia, Kershaw understood the rules of the game. This was just business and he was just the messenger. He reminded Tony Dipino that $2 million was a bargain basement price and that his client would be happy to negotiate for more bonds, though not necessarily at the same price.

Kershaw sipped his iced coke as Dipino stared at him across the airless gloom at the back of the bar. The New Yorker was a beefy guy with heavy jowls and a drinker's puffy lips. He could do – and in fact did – a good impression of Marlon Brando playing Don Vito Corleone, the Godfather in Francis Ford Coppola's movie.

'I'm going to make you an offer you can't refuse,' Dipino said, sending up the role. 'I will pay you for the ten bonds when you bring me 50 more pieces.'

'As you already have the bonds in your possession, it would show good will if you were to let me take the cash and allow my client to arrange delivery of further bonds.'

The Godfather guffawed. 'You hear that, Frankie, he wants me to show good will.'

'What's that?'

Tony Dipino stabbed a finger towards the piles of dollar bills. 'That stays where it is until I see the boss here in New York, in a place of his choosing.'

Jeffrey Kershaw was legally trained, charming, clever, a good talker who made a living on both sides of the law. He had dealt with Irish terrorists, Irish nationalists, Ray Ketteridge and killers serving life sentences in gaols across the United Kingdom. Except for the maniacs and sociopaths, they all knew that in a negotiation a moment comes to compromise so that the deal gets done without anyone losing face. It's all about face. Tony Dipino didn't have that safety valve. You did things his way or no way. Jeffrey was, to use the phrase favoured by the sports master around the older boys at his private school, royally fucked.

When Mark Osborne called Keith, he sounded like a boy who'd just scored his first goal for the A team.

'Keith, it's me. I'm back in Houston.'

'You got the money?'

'I did the whole ten, $2 million.'

'How much are we getting?'

'Twelve percent.'

'I know that, dear. How much is that? He's sending his man over, isn't he?'

'Yeah.'

'Have you got the money on you?'

'I have it in seven big bags.'

'Where the fuck are the seven big bags?'

'In my car.'

Typical, Keith thought, and couldn't help laughing. 'Well, get them the fuck out of there.'

'I've got somewhere to stash it. I just wanted to let you know. You're my friend, Keith, I want you to know that.'

The line went dead, and Keith sat there in his tower apartment that August day with the sun shining on the bookshelves and the telephone receiver still gripped in his fingers like a chicken drumstick he didn't fancy eating. He placed it back in the cradle and wandered over to the window. The NatWest was hidden in the haze. Something wasn't right. Mark had sounded his usual buoyant self, but he was trying too hard.

An Offer You Can't Refuse

You're my friend, Keith, I want you to know that.

Why would he say that? And would he really be so stupid as to leave $2 million in the back of a car and not stash it before making the call?

Keith tried to call Henry Nunn but he was out of reach, cruising the Greek islands with Roger.

When pretty women go to the police to report that their boyfriend is missing, the old sergeants at the desk don't take them too seriously. That was Alice Walker's experience when she stepped in the downtown police station on 16 August and told the duty officer she had not seen Mark Osborne for three days.

She explained that Mark had 'pissed off the wrong people', as she put it. Tears slipped down her cheeks and the sergeant took pity on her. He assigned an officer to conduct a risk assessment and decide on the correct response. Alice didn't tell the cops Mark laundered dirty bonds, she didn't know about that side of his life, and his being a good ole boy, one of them, meant the police began to take the case seriously.

After interviewing Alice about Mark's movements and mental state, it came as a surprise to the assessment officer to learn that her boyfriend also had a wife in the suburbs. They went out for a visit and Mrs Osborne lost her cool. She had not seen Mark for at least a week and going missing was something he did all the time. She didn't know where he was, where he had been, what he was doing or why in the good name of Jesus they were on her porch questioning her.

Whether the outrage was real or theatre, maybe the cops just didn't like hysterical women raising their voices on quiet summer mornings. Whichever way, they then proceeded to search the house, the stretch limos in the half-acre garage, the lawns rolling out to a white picket fence, the flower beds to see if the earth had recently been turned. They motored back to Houston, searched the penthouse and went through Osborne's Rolodex, the names and numbers telling a story if you had a mind to put the clues together and write it.

Mark Lee Osborne turned up five days later in the trunk of his Cadillac with two bullets fired execution-style in the back of his head. Mark was a funny guy. He would have enjoyed the irony of the car's numberplate – ADIOS.

Keith on a recruiting tour in Bedfordshire after passing out as best recruit 1961.

Left: Keith with Angus, Duke of Manchester.

Below: Mark and Alice dining with Keith at Galveston Country Club Texas.

Gerald Harper, Patrick Cargill, Fiona Richmond, Trevor Howard and Dawn.

At the Alamo.

Eric Morecombe, Dawn, Anthea and Bruce Forsyth.

Dorothy Squires and Keith.

Keith with Alice at Graceland, after meeting Lisa-Marie Presley.

Eric and Ernie with Dawn and Keith.

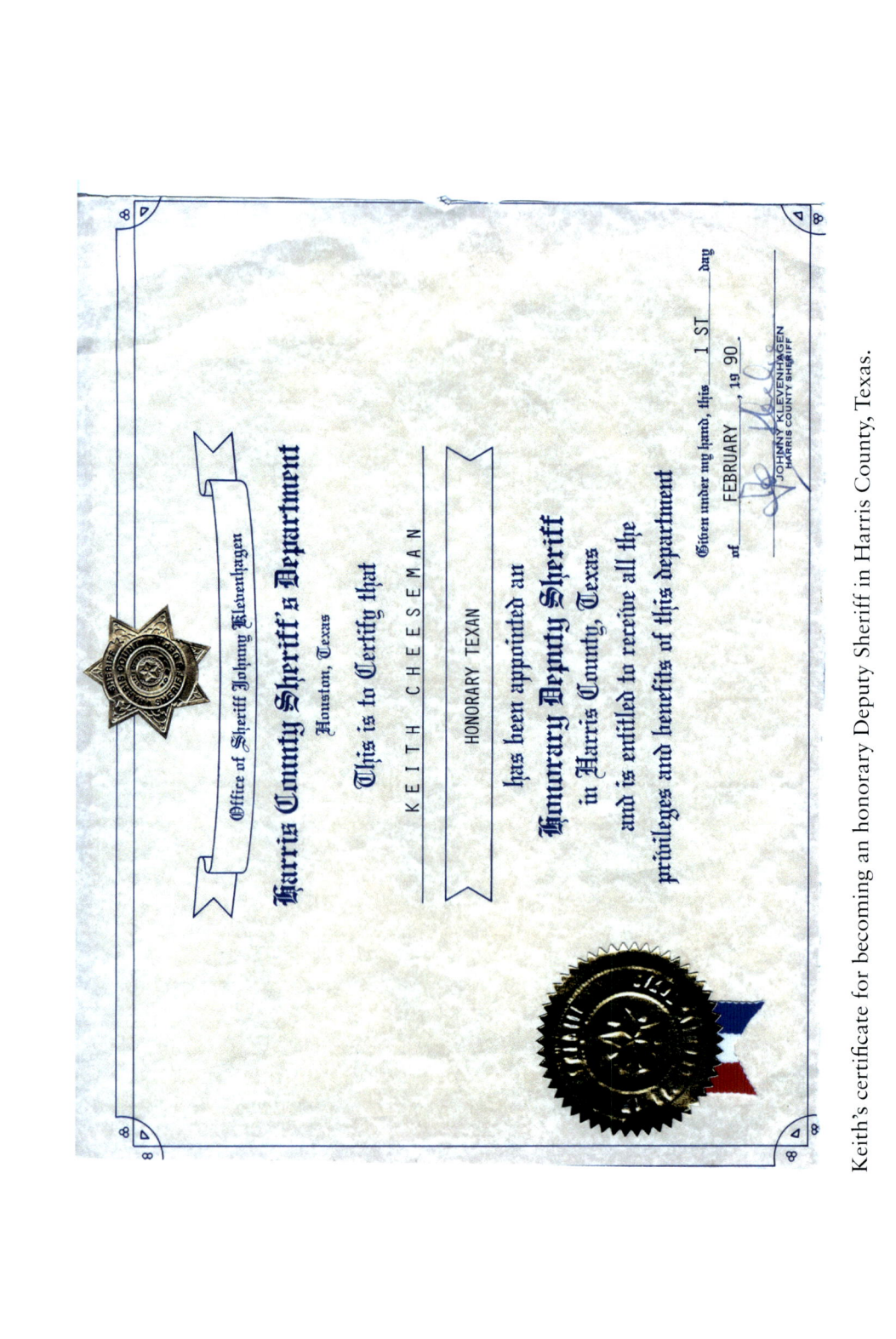

Keith's certificate for becoming an honorary Deputy Sheriff in Harris County, Texas.

Programme from 'An evening with Barry Fry' in Chelmsford.

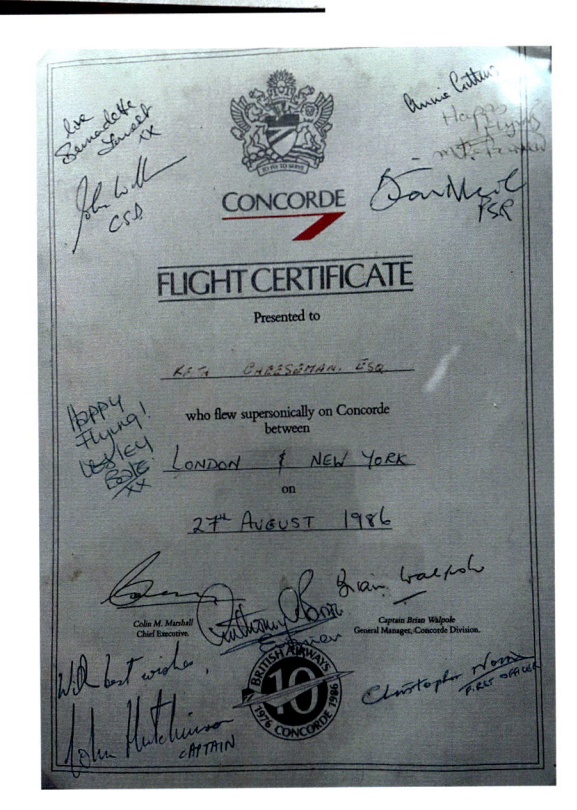

Keith's certificate for flying supersonically on the tenth anniversary of Concorde.

Keith married Sarah in Barbados, 2008.

17. THE STING

David Maniquis.
What a performer!
What a star!
What a bloody nuisance.
Who is David Maniquis?
In a Chinese locks puzzle, the interconnecting parts are held together by one key piece.

David Maniquis was that piece – the digit pulled from the dyke that let the flood waters rise up the floors of the Barbican to Keith Cheeseman's penthouse in the clouds. There Keith sat with a cigar between two fingers and a glass with the last sip of something amber in colour wondering if the dollar bills in those seven big bags had been safely stashed or spread in chips across the green baize of the roulette table.

I thought I could double our money, Keith.

He did consider calling Houston, but Mark was a big boy. He knew what had to be done. He didn't like people chasing him and didn't chase other people.

Keith stubbed out the Montecristo. The windows in the NatWest building shone like eyes in the sky. August in London. The rich away in their country houses. The poor at the seaside. He could hear Kerry in the kitchen. He loved Kerry but she had loose lips. Gossip was her hobby, her *divertissement*, Henry once said. With so much going on, it would have been better had she stayed in Bethnal Green, but there she was in his kitchen doing what, he couldn't imagine. He took his ashtray and empty glass with him.

'Blimey, we've got a new maid,' she said.
'Fancy Brighton for a couple of nights?'
'That'll make a change. I'll get me hair done.'
'It'll just get blown all over the shop.'
'Then I'll get it done again, won't I.'

Meanwhile, unknown to Keith, far away across the other side of the world, the local TV news station arrived at the parking lot shortly after the body of Mark Osborne had been discovered. They filmed gory close-ups of the splattered blood and brains coating the trunk of his car. The presenter had been given a tipoff by Houston police and the crew captured live coverage of Alice Walker rushing into the lot and falling heart-torn into the big arms of a uniformed officer.

Two frames of Mark's wife, dry-eyed and stoic, intercut with Alice Walker in a flood of tears was good television, as was the tobacco-darkened voice of the police spokesman with his confusing assessment.

'The death was done professionally and we believe there was a connection to the (Bank of England) bonds as a message sent to other individuals in as far as if you lose 'em you're gonna die.'

Fraudsters passing bonds had always been an international enterprise. What the execution of Mark Osborne did was bring the story into the newspaper columns around the world. While the three IRA-linked Irishmen, Thomas Coyle, Anthony Rooney and Edward Dunne, were still on remand, twenty more suspects were now behind bars awaiting trial dates in various countries after bonds in small and substantial amounts were recovered in

The Sting

Cyprus, Miami, Cologne, Singapore, Belfast and New York. How the smugglers got hold of the bonds, who distributed them and why they were picked out at baggage checks was a mystery Keith Cheeseman was anxious to solve.

An ex-Special Forces intelligence officer, codenamed Walter, a man with the style and panache of a John le Carré spook, had set himself up as a fraud investigator. He received a faxed copy of a £1-million bond from a contact in the Dutch underworld and went straight to Sheppards, the moneybrokers that lost the bonds in the first place. A senior manager met the 'bearer' at an Amsterdam hotel with a view to retrieving the certificate on a 'mutually acceptable basis'. How much the broker was prepared to pay to buy back their own bonds was not revealed. The deal fell through, but it showed the syndicate that Sheppards was in the market if the price was right.

When Osborne was found with two slugs fired at close range in his skull, it was clear to all parties on both sides of the Atlantic that buying, selling and laundering the Bank of England's missing millions was a hazardous occupation. In the coming months, more bonds would be found – as well as a naked body with the head cut off – and another key player in the heist would be shot dead on his doorstep.

Keith had always suspected that Operation Starling knew when the bonds were taking flight before the cuckoo rose from the nest. The entrapment and death of Osborne was the first firm evidence that the London mob had been penetrated or, more likely, that there had been an informer leaking intel from the beginning. Why, after the perfectly planned crime, the syndicate was eating its own tail was the £430-million question.

Peter Gwynn, the head of City of London CID, was asked by the documentary team at Carlton Television in 1994 if the police had 'inside help' when customs stopped the three Irishmen in what they claimed was a random search. Gwynn replied cryptically: 'I couldn't possibly comment, as the expression goes.' He then smiled and added: 'You can draw your own inferences from this. If it wasn't random, it came from sources.'

In fact, one of the officers involved in the find confirmed to David Strahan at Carlton that customs had received the whisper and knew exactly what they were looking for.

Before Keith had left Houston back in January, Mark had mentioned that he had 'upset a few people' – 'pissed off the wrong people', as Alice Walker had told the police. Keith didn't think much about this at the time. He had always given Mark the benefit of the doubt and had seen with his own eyes that he was well respected in the Lone Star State by sheriffs as well as outlaws.

As more details were revealed by Houston police, a sharper picture of Mark Lee Osborne emerged like a photograph in a developing tray. He had hefty gambling debts, which tends to upset people, and had been under investigation by federal officials after Anthony J. Lama, aged 36, a clerk from Staten Island who processed securities transactions at Salomon Brothers, stole $7 million in bonds in 1989. Like Osborne, Lama was a gambler and needed to pay off the two alleged bookmakers, Robert R. Rosenfeld and Ted R. Ballison, who had threatened to kill him. Rosenfeld was also charged with having attempted to sell $19-million worth of the stolen Bank of England securities to an undercover FBI agent posing as a narcotics dealer.

Through its network of snitches and undercover agents, the Global Research Unit set up by the FBI to work with Operation Starling had dropped the name Tony Dipino in the criminal ocean as someone interested in buying 'hot' bonds. They knew it was only a question of time before the stolen City bonds floated to the surface.

When Mark Osborne met the tall skinny guy in a downtown bar and drove home with a New York telephone number on a coaster, his fate had already been sealed. The call the next morning to whom he thought was Mafia boss Tony Dipino, was picked up by David Maniquis, a skilled thespian and high-ranking FBI operative running a sting that must have made Mr Dickinson and his team of 40 agents in London look on red-faced with embarrassment and green with envy.

The Sting

It was surprising to Keith that Mark wasn't a tad suspicious when he stepped out of a yellow cab at 42nd Street and looked up at the sign for Ray McFadden's. The Mafia are not known for operating Irish bars. They take their *caffè neros* in the Italian bars they own or control. Serving the Irish whiskey Bushmills was like kicking a man when he's down.

After performing his Marlon Brando act to entrap Osborne, Maniquis offered him a plea bargain that would allow Mark a period of bail so that he could 'sort out his affairs', and a lighter sentence when he came to court – a few years in a country club prison for good ole boys pinched in white collar crimes. Mark jumped at the chance. He made calls taped by the FBI to Keith Cheeseman and Ray Ketteridge, implicating them in fencing the stolen bonds and prompting the Feds to issue extradition orders to the British authorities that took months to process.

When Maniquis let his stool pigeon fly the coop, he had no way of knowing that waiting for Osborne in Houston was a revolver with six bullets and the safety catch off.

Who ordered the killing?

Texas private investigator Clyde Wilson told Houston Television that 'someone from England had hired a hitman for the Osborne job'.

A week later, homicide detectives announced that they wanted to interview a British subject by the name of Raymond Ketteridge.

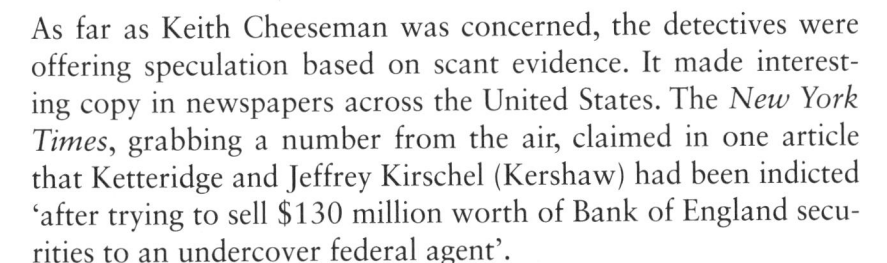

As far as Keith Cheeseman was concerned, the detectives were offering speculation based on scant evidence. It made interesting copy in newspapers across the United States. The *New York Times*, grabbing a number from the air, claimed in one article that Ketteridge and Jeffrey Kirschel (Kershaw) had been indicted 'after trying to sell $130 million worth of Bank of England securities to an undercover federal agent'.

Before Osborne was found dead, Ketteridge was still trying to get his $2 million. In a conversation taped by Maniquis in his Dipino skin, he told Ketteridge he would get the $2 million for the ten bonds when Ketteridge supplied him with 50 more. Ketteridge said he had 'the 50 pieces' and would have 'his man' deliver them after he had received the money he was still owed. There was no firm resolve but the mafioso and the gangster hung up on good terms.

Jeffrey Kershaw – Kirschel in the US – returned to McFadden's for a second attempt to collect the $2 million. If he was carrying 'the 50 pieces' Dipino-Maniquis had demanded, with the original ten, £60 million at the 1990 exchange rate of £1 to $1.6 would have brought the total to about $100 million – short of the $130 million, but close enough for the *New York Times*.

Maniquis must have decided that he was not going to persuade Ketteridge to fly into US jurisdiction and fessed up that he was not the Mafia but a federal agent who had taped the telephone conversations. He told Kershaw that Mark Osborne had been slotted in a contract killing and it was likely that he, Kershaw, was on the same hit list. He was going to serve time, but it would be to his advantage to come clean and the FBI would give him protection.

Jeffrey Kershaw did come clean and added a new twist to the tale. He told the Feds that he was not a bagman moving stolen securities, but a London solicitor and police informer working on retrieving the bonds. While he, Maniquis, was there to entrap him, Kershaw was there trying to entrap presumed Mafia boss Tony Dipino.

One can imagine the long pause as the two men studied each other across the table. Frankie must have been at the bar operating the tape deck beneath his girlie mag. Did he make eye contact with his boss? It must have been late afternoon, the summer heat stoking up the temperature at the back of McFadden's. Had Maniquis drunk too much coffee? Or not enough? Perhaps it was his wedding anniversary and he wanted to get home? Whatever the reason, just as he had allowed Osborne to fly back to Houston, he merely confiscated Kershaw's passport, told him

The Sting

he would be needed for further questioning and let him walk out of the Irish bar straight into a taxi.

Kershaw crossed into Canada on a second passport before nightfall and returned to Blighty where DCS Dickinson was waiting with his characteristic smile, big glasses that gave him the look of a wily owl and a warrant with the ink still fresh from Bow Street Magistrates Court. When Kershaw appeared, shoulders back in the polished oak dock, it was revealed that he was indeed a registered police informer and he left the court in the swift strides of a born soldier.

The fact that Operation Starling did not have details on Jeffrey Kershaw's status was not surprising. UK security is spread across numerous departments responsible for collecting, analysing and exploiting foreign and domestic intelligence. The four main agencies are the Secret Intelligence Service, SIS, better known as MI6, dealing with overseas security; the Security Service (MI5), home security; the Government Communications Headquarters (GCHQ) and Defence Intelligence (DI). The agencies are administered by three government departments, the Foreign Office, Home Office and the Ministry of Defence. Then there's the Metropolitan Police, Special Branch, the Fraud Squad, the Flying Squad and chief constables with knighthoods who know where the bodies are buried and only reluctantly share information.

Agencies across Whitehall are ivory towers with department heads zealously guarding their positions and reputations, informants and knowledge. They dine at the same clubs. They are polite to each but do not trust each other and only talk to rival colleagues about the weather, their dogs and Lucinda's love of horses. When there's a disaster and we hear the spokesman with misty eyes and a set jaw on the television say mistakes have been made and lessons have been learned it is not true. Lessons are not learned and mistakes are repeated again and again.

For shrewd birds like Jeffrey Kershaw, stashing second passports in safe boxes and finding a way through the smoke and mirrors is not difficult.

David Maniquis must have realised he had made a mistake letting his man go before Kershaw's plane hit the tarmac at Heathrow and issued an extradition order on Kershaw for the 'Alleged conspiracy to sell bills worth $53 million originating from the Treasury in London'.

$53 million?

It was just a number.

18. THE CROOKED SIXPENCE

Keith was not in a good mood. He was in a bad mood. A contemplative mood. It would have been so simple to have sent the bonds to TJ in Indonesia but criminals with their big egos and lack of humility always make life hard for themselves. They are showmen, comedians with scant management skills or the ability to admit when they've got things wrong.

The weekend away in Brighton with Kerry had not gone well – his fault, naturally – and when he got back, he went against his own policy of not chasing people and called Mark Osborne.

Alice picked up the phone and burst into tears the moment she heard his voice.

'They killed him, Keith. They went and killed him,' she cried.

'What?'

'Mark, they killed him. Shot him like a dog. Blood everywhere. They gone and put two bullets in the head.'

'Jesus Christ, Alice. You serious?'

'I am, Keith, I am serious. Those people put him in the trunk of his car and left him in a parking lot. Like a dog.'

'Who did it?'

'I don't know. A pro. That's what they're saying. They're looking for some British dude. Raymond … something …'

'Not Ray Ketteridge?'

'Yeah, that's the one.'

He let that sink in.

'I'm sorry, darling. I don't know what to say …'

'I'm going to lose the apartment. Everything. The money's gone. Mark's gone. They even took his car.'

What could he do?

'If I can get my hands on some spare cash, I'll get it to you. Can't do more than that.'

'You're a real gent, Keith. Mark always said that. I can't believe he's gone.'

She cried some more. He said goodbye and stood there with the receiver in his hand wondering why the hell Ray hadn't called to put him in the picture. And why had Henry Nunn sailed off across the Aegean with Roger when millions of pounds – hundreds of millions of pounds – were in play?

Mark dead. It was hard to take in. Ray was the wrong man in the wrong place in the wrong business. Keith had never found out how the Irish got hold of £70 million and lost it again. And there's Mark rubbed out over ten pieces. Fencing bonds is a clean crime. No one gets hurt. Like it or not, *the banks have to pay*. If they'd taken 10 per cent on the bonds' face value they'd all be sitting in villas in Marbella with the Guardia Civil on the payroll and piña colada on tap. If ever the word clusterfuck was appropriate, this was it.

Keith had promised Kerry that he'd go straight when he came out of Parkhurst and she'd never got tired of reminding him. She had overlooked the Dusky Maiden and NatWest scam – she couldn't stand James Burrows, the 'slimy' branch manager from Streatham. But the bonds robbery was all over the news and she knew with what she called her female intuition – or listening at the door – that Keith was up to his neck in it.

They had bickered all through the weekend in Brighton and bickered in the car driving back to London. When he pulled up with a screech of the brakes in Bethnal Green it was as good as saying their marriage needed its annual MOT.

Kerry turned in her seat.

'If you go down again it'll be ten years. I won't wait,' she said.

'Wouldn't expect you to.'

The Crooked Sixpence

'You said you'd go straight, Keith.'

'I am. I'm going straight. As straight as I can.'

'What's that supposed to mean?'

'It means what it means. You know that nursery rhyme? "There was a crooked man, he walked a crooked mile, he found a crooked sixpence upon a crooked stile"?'

'Yeah, what about it?'

'The crooked man nicked the sixpence. Couldn't help himself. That's me. I got the crooked gene. Some men like playing golf or, I don't know, chasing girls half their age. I don't do any of that stuff. Banks rob everybody. I rob banks.'

The passenger door clicked and swung back over the pavement. Kerry stepped out and leaned her bouffant of curly hair back in the car.

'You, Keith, need to get another hobby or get another wife.'

She slammed the door and as she strode off in her tight skirt, he thought *that's the problem with good looking women, they always expect a bit more than you've got to give them.* Truth is, Kerry enjoyed the gangster world but could never quite connect the dots between the good things larceny buys and the crime that carries the jail time.

He drove back to the Barbican with the windows open and his thinning hair slicked back by the wind.

Rodney Miller, the doorman, was sweeping fag ends into a dustpan when he parked the Jag in its usual spot. Rodney put Keith's own life into perspective. He did his job, collected his pay, went home to watch the telly with a plate of bangers and mash and got up and did the same the next day. He felt safe with his routines and didn't let his gaze stray up to the heavens.

'How's it going, governor?' he called.

'Well, Rodders, looking on the bright side, I ain't sweeping up dog ends.'

'You know what they do, empty the bloody ashtray under the car. Not right, is it?'

'Don't think of no one else, these people. Selfish times, that's what we live in.'

'Never a truer word. You see what those Iraqis have gone and done in Kuwait? Taken all the Brits off a plane and made them hostages.'

'Maggie'll sort it out, don't worry.'

'You said it. Want me to give the car a clean?'

'Why not, my son. I might go and have lunch with the QM.'

'What's that then, one of those intelligence things?'

'No, that's IQ. I'm talking about QEQM, the Queen Mother.'

'I'll give it a polish an' all in that case.'

'You've got a bit of a tan, you been away?'

'Yeah, the missus and me had ten days in Ramsgate overlooking the harbour. Lovely place. Best jellied eels in the world, I reckon.'

'Ever go abroad?'

'Don't like abroad, Mr C. All those foreigners. Everything they've got we've got only it's better.'

'You know something, you've hit the nail right on the bloody head.'

···◆•————•◆···

Keith was in a better mood after talking to Rodney. He took a shower to wash away the bickering and made three calls. First to Henry Nunn, back finally from his hols, then Ray Ketteridge, and finally to George the maître d' at Simpson's in the Strand to book a table for lunch the following day. The eatery had once been his local and he felt the need to be on home turf for a powwow with his partners in crime.

Like Keith, George was a Millwall supporter. They met occasionally at matches and, beyond a love of football, had in common an eye for detail and an offhand vaguely dismissive approach to the upper classes with whom, in different ways, they frequently mixed.

Keith was a bit of a psychologist on the quiet and was fascinated by the class system with its dos and don'ts, secrets and tells. What he'd noticed was that those who were snobbish

The Crooked Sixpence

and arrogant, as well as privileged, were often masking a lack of self-confidence and diminishing bank accounts. The loud, plummy voices came from a hard, knotty lump in the chest like a sealed box containing bloodlines and pageantry, the heroic past deeds of their glorious ancestors and their fear that if they ever opened the box, what they would find is nothing.

Those from the upper classes with no need for bluster and reverence were the most charming people you could meet. They looked upon good living as a duty and, having inherited or increased family estates acquired through some ambiguous past chicanery, they recognised their mirror image in the dark-suited villains who shared the same taste for fine dining, fancy motors, horse racing, five-star hotels, foreign travel and lunch at Simpson's. Titles and posh accents said to the common folk that these people were special. What it said to Keith was that they were almost certainly crooks. Angus Montagu was the perfect example.

One lunchtime at Simpson's, Keith was sitting with an Arab sheikh when Lord Snowdon entered wearing a polo neck jumper under his jacket.

'My apologies, sir, ties only,' the maître d' told him.

'But George, you know who I am,' His Lordship replied.

'I do, sir, and you know the rules.'

'Then you must make an exception.'

George shook his head. 'Make one exception and it leads to two exceptions. Then where would we be?'

Snowdon realised George wasn't going to back down. 'Then what can I do?'

'Come with me, sir.'

They left the restaurant area for the maître d's office beside the kitchen. Lord Snowdon returned with a tie over his polo neck and joined the miscellany of minor celebrities, debutantes, bankers with double-barrelled names and hangers on with bright smiles gazing up from the long table next to the entrance. The set up at Simpson's was that gentlemen dined on what was termed the 'floor', with booked groups on the slightly raised dais with booths around the sides. Ladies dined upstairs. When the restaurant was busy, gentlemen shared tables on the 'floor', allowing the right kind of people to meet the right kind of people. In this way, at different times Keith had become acquainted with the TV polyglot Robin Day and the Duke of Kent.

Keith's dining companions that day were the Arab and three Saudi businessmen who had a plan to build a medical training facility with a new road to connect the complex to Riyadh, the capital. They needed someone to oversee their investment portfolio and Keith had been recommended by Angus Montagu. Saudi money was pouring into London – much of it pouring out again to secret accounts in pure blue waters.

When Keith had arrived with his party, George the maître d' had led them upstairs to a circular table by the window, not in his usual place on the 'floor'. George leaned closer to whisper.

'Don't worry, guv. I know what I'm doing.'

He was a Millwall supporter. Keith trusted him implicitly.

They had settled down with their sparkling water and bread rolls when, at 1pm on the dot, the door opened and the Queen Mother entered with her ladies who lunch. She paused for a moment, as was her custom, everyone stood, and she turned with a smile towards the window table and gave Keith a little wave with her gloved hand.

Did George set this up? Did she recognise Keith from his regular presence at Simpson's? He didn't know, but the Saudis were suddenly as malleable as the soft butter in the silver butter dish.

19. EVERYBODY'S AT IT

Arabs don't talk business while they are eating. They like to chat about shopping at Harrods and how much they admire the royal family. After lunch, flaunting sharia with a glass of Château Margaux, they left Simpson's and piled into Keith's nicely polished 2.4-litre Jaguar to drive to Claridge's where a score folded into the hand of the doorman secured a parking spot beside the entrance.

In the sheikh's suite, over a pot of tea, Ali Ahmed took the floor. He was no more than 30 with a moustache as fine as spider thread, a degree from the London School of Economics and, as he'd mentioned in passing at lunch, his blue linen suit came from Camps de Luca in Paris. Shame about the brown shoes. The plan was to raise money to build the new medical facility from international investors and donors and move the commissions into an offshore trust Keith would set up and manage. Ali Ahmed explained that a 20 per cent management fee on transactions was normal practice.

The sheikh rattled his amber prayer beads.

'There is no hurry to build the facility and roads are long as well as short. Prices always escalate,' added Ali Ahmed.

'They most certainly do, my son.' Keith nodded thoughtfully. Preferential shares, privatisation, expense accounts, council contracts – he'd dipped his Hovis in that gravy boat himself when he was in the building game. Keith knew two sisters, one a baroness in the House of Lords, who sat on a dozen quangos – quasi-autonomous non-governmental organisations – eight hours' work a year at four meetings, picking up £20,000 here, £40,000 there, all above board, bank accounts bursting.

'We saw a pretty little cottage in the country and just bought it.'

'Then we saw an even prettier cottage ...'

'So, we bought that one as well.'

Someone had opened Pandora's box and made skimming from the public purse respectable. Everyone was at it and now everyone had found their dark side, being an honest crook had lost its cachet. The Thatcher years had been good if you knew how to play the game. It was a shame that after the ten years of free market free-for-all the Iron Lady was on her way out. Keith loved England: the history, its people, the humour, rainy Sundays, fish and chips, the horse races that were fixed and the NHS sold off by stealth to who knows who. From the ladies in straw hats playing bowls to the poor fiddling their gas meters with fake coins, the country was corrupt to its core and he wouldn't want to be anywhere else in the world.

He was still listening to Ali Ahmed in his blue linen suit.

'Are you acquainted with the Dutch Caribbean?' Ali asked.

'I am, as it happens,' Keith replied. 'Mostly Curaçao and Aruba.'

A broad smiled crossed his face. Ali glanced at the sheikh, then back at Keith. 'What exactly are the advantages of setting up a company on one of the islands?'

'Basically, you do whatever you like and pay bugger-all in capital gains tax. Share transfers are unrestricted with no transfer tax or stamp duty. There's no withholding tax, gift tax or estate taxes.' He paused, and in the silence, the only sound was the amber beads softly clicking through the sheikh's fingers. 'Share capital can be held in any currency. There's no legal obligation for companies to appoint external auditors and there's no limitation on foreigners owning shares. Safe as houses in other words.'

'This is what we are seeking, Mr Cheeseman.'

Everybody's At It

Keith was offered a £150,000 fee to set up the offshore company and a salary – to be negotiated – to oversee its management. Easy money. Job for life. He could call Paul Whitney in Aruba to open an account and watch the long sunsets over the sea.

···◆—•————•—◆···

Keith met Ray Ketteridge and Henry Nunn for their lunch at Simpson's the following day and told them the story of the Arab's offer before getting down to business.

'An offer to die for?' Henry Nunn said.

'I walked away from it.'

'You did what?' Ray said.

'You know how it is, you can't take Bethnal Green out of Kerry and we'd have had to move out to the Caribbean. Another thing, I didn't fancy getting involved in Middle East politics. I mean, look what's happening now. Bloody war going on in Iraq.'

'Where there's war there's brass, isn't that the saying?' Henry Nunn said.

'Maybe where you come from, Henry. Anyway,' Keith said. 'I'd have missed having lunch at Simpson's with you two old bastards.'

'You did the right thing.'

Henry watched the waiters moving between the tables pushing trolleys laden with tureens filled with massive joints of beef, venison, lamb and pork.

'What would you recommend?'

'They do a lovely pudding; steak and kidney with mushrooms and oysters. That'll do me.'

'Sounds,' Henry paused. 'Epic. I'll have the same.'

Ray Ketteridge was a traditionalist. He ordered roast beef, 'bloody and pink'.

There was an awkward silence as they broke bread, tried the wine and waited for their food. They all knew why they were there. It was a time for explanations, recriminations. Where do you start? The hiatus was broken by Robin Day on the way to his table.

'Keith, how are you, old man?'

'Not bad on a good day.'

'Come, come, you'll have to do better than that.'

Keith took a breath. 'It's one of those days,' he said, holding up his palm. 'So, there's a group of anglers casting their lines round the edge of a lake, the hooks filled with fat juicy worms. Delicious. Two fish under the water are looking for an easy catch. One says to the other: keep your mouth shut. That way you won't get caught.'

'Not bad for a Tuesday.'

'Hold on. One more, true story. One night in Holland I was in bed with a blind girl and she said, "Keith, you've got the biggest todger I've ever laid my hands on." I said, "You're pulling my leg."'

That got a laugh.

Keith introduced his companions: 'Robin Day. Ray Ketteridge and Henry Nunn.'

They shook hands.

'We've met before,' Henry said.

'Really?'

'At Kempton. Never forget a face.'

Robin Day adjusted his polka-dot bow tie. 'I shall look out for you. *Bon appétit.*'

He joined his table. The food came and Keith glanced at Ray as he spooned English mustard on to his bubblegum-pink beef.

'I spoke to Alice Walker the other day.'

Ray shrugged his shoulders, suggesting he didn't know who she was, or at least feigning that he didn't.

'Mark Osborne's girlfriend.'

'Yeah, we met.'

'He's dead.'

'So I heard.'

'No one told me.'

Everybody's At It

'No one told me until someone did.'

'Who told you?'

'What the fuck's this, Keif, third degree? We having fucking lunch, or what?'

'I just feel like I've been left out of the loop, Ray.'

'There is no loop.' He chewed and swallowed. 'Fucking hell. Always something with you.'

'This is exquisite,' Henry said, breaking the flow. 'I spent some time on Aegina, tiny island, a woman I know, so rich she makes life difficult travelling with ten cats, half-a-dozen dogs, a parrot in a cage, three maids and a Nubian chef who doesn't speak a word of any language she knows and so she's learning Nubian.'

'What's that got to do with anything?' Ray asked him.

'De Beers money. Diamonds. Always safe.'

'Same as bonds. Or they should be,' Keith said.

Ketteridge put his utensils down and took a long breath as if ready to dive off a high board.

'Fucking right. Press have been knocking on my door asking about Mark Osborne and some FBI fucker in New York pretending he's Mafia and buying up bonds. I told them, and I'm telling you, I don't know nothing about Osborne being wiped and I've never spoken to no one in America.'

'So what happened to the ten bonds your man delivered to Mark, what's his name?'

'Jeffrey Kershaw,' Henry Nunn responded. 'Playing a double game, apparently.'

Ketteridge turned to Henry with an expression like he wanted to stab him in the neck, then leaned forward, lowering his voice as he stared back at Keith. 'Fucked if I know. It all went tits up. Looks like the Feds have got their mitts on them. Every time we send the bonds some place there's some fucker waiting for us.'

Keith recalled the day in Weavers Fields when he told Ray he'd ripped £3 million in bonds to shreds and chucked the pieces in a bin. He'd warned him then there was a snake in the grass, but Ray had carried on making the same mistake expecting a different result, Einstein's definition of insanity. Ray was either a brilliant operator shedding the £292 million the police were chasing while concealing the unaccounted £135 million no one ever mentioned, or he was a blind man driving the bus while someone in the back seat gave directions.

He glanced at Henry, at his Greek island tan, the neat knot in his striped tie, the navy jacket with unembellished brass buttons, his half-closed grey eyes that gave away nothing. Was he, Keith wondered, the puppet master playing the game simply as an amusement? Henry shifted quantities of stolen art and artefacts. He didn't need the money. Bonds were not his cup of tea, all numbers and maths, no glitter or glam. And what about Jeffrey Kershaw? He had never met the man but his name kept popping up like a jack-in-the-box.

'We should have sent the bonds to Indonesia when we had the chance,' Keith said, the words slipping out because he couldn't hold them in.

'Yeah, well, we didn't, did we?'

Ray polished off the beef on his plate and left the vegetables. He downed his wine and a waiter refilled the glass.

'Another bottle, sir?'

'Yeah, why not?' Ray told him. He glanced around Simpson's as if inspecting the joint for a robbery. It was all very *la-di-da*, tinkling voices, faces from TV. 'How come you know Robin Day, Keif?'

'Keith knows everyone,' Henry said.

'Not asking you.' Ray looked back at Keith. 'In our business, you only need to know the right people.'

Keith wiped his lips on a napkin and sat back in his chair.

'Who are the right people? You don't know until they turn out to be wrong'uns,' he said. 'When I went down for the loans fraud, a mate of mine in the Sweeny, Tony, an inspector, he offered me the chance to walk away with no charges. He was going to put me on the payroll. All I had to do was name names and put my mates inside so I could stay on the outside.'

'That's not you, Keith,' Henry inserted, sipping his wine.

'So, what's your point?' Ray insisted.

'I'm not sure. What I do know is, if we're going to place the rest of the bonds you got left and come away with a few shillings in our pockets, you're going to have to close the circle, no more leaks.'

'That sounds like a toast,' Henry said.

The waiter replenished the glasses from the second bottle and as they touched the rims, Keith thought that he could trust Ray Ketteridge about as far as he could throw the Saudi sheikh with the amber prayer beads.

20. THE BIG FISH

A couple of days after lunch at Simpson's, Ray picked up Henry and drove out to his favourite boozer in Romford. The Plough was one of the oldest pubs in England and had stood on the same spot at Gallows Corner since about 1500 when farmers and field workers would come in for jugs of ale and a ploughman's lunch. No one drank the water, it was polluted by the waste that ran off the fields.

While Ray was at the bar, Henry found a window seat and let his eyes drift over the pinched East London faces. He was the first to tell you that he liked a bit of rough. His gaze wandered off to the trees and bushes outside the window. It was a perfect end of summer morning and a few words from Blake's *Jerusalem* came into his mind ... *And did those feet in ancient time, Walk upon England's mountains green.* He was not a believer, but he liked to think so.

Ray placed his pint and a glass of Cabernet Sauvignon on the table, sat and lit a Senior Service. They were the odd couple. Jekyll and Hyde. Beauty and the Beast. Everything had come easy to Ray. Blind to his limitations, comfortable in his own skin, the sort of man who gives regulars a chill up the spine when he walks into a pub. A gangster has to be bloody sure of himself to wear shorts. Henry with the rosebud in his buttonhole was a leftover from another time, overripe, overrefined, the queen bee with friends in the highest of high places and a *ginger*, as they say in prison (ginger beer – queer), the cut-glass accent that irritated Ray from others he tolerated from 'Enery.

They were like flies on flypaper glued together. Keith had no idea how or where they had met and had never got a straight answer when he asked. What he did know was that in 1989 – not long before the big one – Ray was stuck in a French prison cell for nine months for his alleged involvement in a multi-million-euro bank fraud, and Henry must have had a good reason, as well as the contacts, to pull strings across the Channel and persuade *le magistrat* that they had the wrong man.

Was Henry's motive to prepare Ketteridge as the front for the robbery? Before that morning on 2 May when John Goddard was relieved of the bonds, Henry had encouraged Keith to stay close to his Indonesian friend TJ, knowing that he was in the market for bent bonds. Henry had introduced banker John Bowman to the party the night of the robbery, but they were clearly well acquainted before then. This was Henry's package. Ray did the talking but Henry was the ventriloquist throwing his voice through sealed lips.

Bowman's plan was to place small tranches of bonds in Lichtenstein and Zurich before the Bank of England circulated the serial numbers, maximising their value. That didn't happen, but the bulk that remained still provided myriad underworld options. A £1-million bond might be held as security for a debt. A drug dealer holding a high-end certificate would be able to get product and pay off the supplier after the drugs have hit the street. A stickup merchant could borrow a gun for a one-off robbery.

TJ would have sailed bonds through the Indonesian Treasury and, as the bearer, at some future date demanded full payment, which he would have received from the Bank of England, no questions asked. That was how the system was set up. If you were to blow the dust from the account books and study the small print written in invisible ink, this exchange of goods or services was a blindfolded eye being turned to politicians and dictators across the planet in order that they could take advantage of our bent rules and we could rob them of their natural resources. They sent

The Big Fish

their children to private schools and we controlled their silicon, platinum, lithium and gold mines.

Juggling the bonds through criminal means remained viable, but the ability to slip them into the system John Bowman's way was immediately lost when Patrick Thomas stopped off in Charlie's Bar to show Jimmy Tippett the briefcase full of certificates. It gave the Bank of England twenty minutes to circulate the serial numbers and it occurred to Keith that the lost time had set up a pattern with Operation Starling always twenty minutes ahead of their every move.

When during lunch at Simpson's Keith had asked who had delivered the ten bonds to Osborne, Ray looked as if he was going to explode when Henry named Jeffrey Kershaw. All through his plate of roast beef, Ray had the air of being at a loss and was probably mourning the short-lived promise of juicy deals with the New York Mafia. Kershaw was clearly more than a bagman with a more prominent role in distributing the bonds than Keith had thought. It was Kershaw who had put the IRA and the Prods together to shift Alfred Beit's stolen paintings, and it was reasonable conjecture that Kershaw had a connection to the three IRA-linked bootleggers collared holding certificates worth an unimaginable £77 million.

Ray had got burned on every deal he'd set up and wasn't sure who to blame. He had taken Henry to The Plough to meet someone who knew someone who had spoken to someone, as you do, and Ray kept looking at his gold Rolex because that someone hadn't turned up. Why did he take Henry along with him? A toff accent has a ring about it when you're talking big numbers and Ray, for all the braggadocio, needed the back up. He stabbed out his fag and lit another one.

'Fucking sorry, 'Enery. Bastard's not coming.'

'Look on the bright side, we should have a bite. Let's have another drink. I'll get them.'

'Nah, nah, nah. You sit there. What d'ya fancy, ploughman's lunch?'

'That would do nicely.'

The bar had filled up and almost fifteen minutes had passed before Ray returned to the table. They ate their English Cheddar and pickled onions with crusty bread and after another pint Ray was back in his polished shoes feeling confident that the unlucky run was coming to an end.

'We've lost half the fucking bonds, you know that, 'Enery.'

'That means the glass is still half full,' he replied.

'Then let's drink to that, then, shall we.'

They touched beer glass to wine glass. Ray had some colour in his cheeks and ran his hand over his wave of bronze hair. He finished his pint, straightened his shoulders and the mob at the bar parted as, in his rolling gangster walk, he led Henry towards the exit. They crossed the car park to Ray's Land Rover and he could barely believe his eyes as he watched a dozen or more bobbies in uniform swarm towards them from every direction. They were waving truncheons and arrest warrants.

'Just carry on and act surprised,' Henry said.

The cops let them reach the vehicle, then two big young coppers grabbed Ray by his arms.

'What the fuck's going on?'

Another two grabbed Henry.

'Like you don't know?' said a cop in plain clothes. 'Open the vehicle.'

'You speak to my fucking lawyer.'

'Don't worry, I will. Now give me the keys.'

They opened the car and a sniffer dog slobbered over the upholstery inside.

'Got so'mink 'ere, guv,' the dog handler cried.

He peeled back the rubber matting and there, inside a plastic freezer bag, was a thin wedge of HM Treasury Bills, numbered and embossed, engraved in copperplate like bank notes and promising to pay the bearer the sum of £1 million – each. There were nine of them. An inspector fanned out the file – contaminating the evidence – and produced his badge.

'Raymond Ketteridge?'

The Big Fish

'What of it?'
'What are these?'
'No idea. Never seen them before in my life.'
'Who put them under your carpet?'
'No idea. Unless you put them there?'
'I'm asking the questions. Is this your car?'
'Course it bloody is, wouldn't have the keys otherwise.'
'Don't take that tone with me.'
'I'm not taking any bloody tone. Just had a quiet drink and look at all this.'

Ray glanced round at the circus of policemen, onlookers arriving for their jug of ale, blokes from the bar pouring out with pint glasses in their hands. The dog was on its hind legs barking, expecting a treat. Henry Nunn looked on as if part of the crowd, not a participant in the scene.

'Cuff him, Andy,' the inspector said.

The plump sergeant, who looked as if he hadn't chased a criminal for two decades, stepped forward.

'Hands, sir, behind your back, if you please.'

Ray held out his two wrists. 'I've got a bad back. Golf injury. I ain't going to be able to get in the car with 'em behind me.'

The sergeant took a long look at Ray and cuffed his wrists in front of him. Ray was royalty. He did the same with Henry Nunn.

'Thank you, sergeant, that's so kind.'

They were lowered, hands on heads, into the rear seats of different police cars and driven, via Eastern Avenue, the fifteen miles back to the City of London copshop in Bishopsgate where Detective Chief Superintendent Dickinson was waiting like a Muppet with a wide grin on his face. It had been four months since the City bonds robbery and he had the big fish in the tank.

Ray was remanded in custody on two principal charges: holding stolen Bank of England bonds and conspiring to launder stolen bonds.

The evidence was overwhelming. An open-and-shut case. A good reason for the Super to take his 40 hard-grafting agents down the pub for a pint. They deserved it.

Ketteridge had been caught with the bonds, not on his person, but among his personal possessions; hidden in his car. Thanks to the nimble footwork of David Maniquis and the FBI's Global Research Unit, Operation Starling had taped evidence of Ketteridge discussing the stolen bonds, his anger at not receiving the $2 million he was owed and his guarantee that he could supply '50 more pieces'. Speech recognition experts would show that the voice on the tape came from the mouth of Ray Ketteridge.

Keith got all the details the following day when Henry Nunn called him to say he had a white marble figurine of Pauline Borghese for a knockdown price of £10,000. It was a lovely piece and £10,000 for an early nineteenth century Capodimonte in mint condition was a steal. Keith, though, wasn't in the pink, and had an intuition that his spare cash was best left where it was, inside a hollow book on the bookshelf.

They had met at Henry's house of wonders and crossed the road to the Carpenter's Arms.

'You know the police have got Ray?'

'No. I'm always the last to know.'

'Poor me,' Henry said. 'Actually, after me you're the first to know.'

'How come you know?'

'I was there, dear boy. Frisked by a young officer and put in handcuffs, the first time that's happened since a night in Soho with Francis Bacon that would make your toes curl.'

'I don't think our toes have the same taste, Henry.'

He smiled, paused, drank his wine. 'We should organise another night at the opera. And Groucho's. It's been ... overwhelming.'

'So, come on then, what happened?'

Henry told Keith about the arrest at The Plough.

'It was all very polite and dignified,' he added. 'No flashing lights and sirens. Someone with their head screwed on the right way quietly went about the arrest and we were taken into Bishopsgate.'

The Big Fish

'And they let you go?'

'They did.'

'That don't happen, Henry.'

'I mentioned a name.'

'Of course you did. You don't want to share it, do you?'

He smiled and shrugged his thin shoulders. 'Some things are not for sharing. Even with you, Keith.'

'That's what's been worrying me.'

'You worry too much.'

Keith swallowed his brandy. 'What have the Old Bill got on Ray?'

'Well, apart from the £9 million he had foolishly stored in his car, by all accounts they have taped evidence from the FBI.'

'Doesn't look good, does it? When one skittle falls it knocks all the rest down.'

'Time will tell.'

'It's doing time I'm worried about,' Keith said. 'They'll be coming for me next, you know that.'

'Why?'

'That's the way it works.'

'Ray isn't a grass.'

'No, but they'll trace his contacts. I'm the link to Mark Osborne and the poor sod's dead. The FBI are like bloody bulldogs. Don't let anything go. I don't have a name to drop. Except yours, of course.'

21. THE OLD BAILEY

'Defend the Children of the Poor & Punish the Wrongdoer.'

This odd inscription above the entrance to the Old Bailey gives the impression that one is entering not merely a place of justice, but a venerable institution where one can expect respect and English fair play.

It is a false impression. The Old Bailey is terrifying. You enter 1,000 years of history and implacable legal process that has sent hundreds of men and women to the gallows and an uncountable number to hard labour on long prison terms.

On the bronze dome above the court stands F.W. Pomeroy's 1906 sculpture of Lady Justice with a sword in her right hand and what Keith calls the scowls of justice on her face – her expression is not benign. It is a grimace, a glower, a steely scowl. Abandon hope all ye who enter here.

Executions took place outside the Old Bailey until 1868 with huge baying crowds calling for blood and a wave of applause as the masked hangman stepped into the drama like a rock star coming on stage. The best way to watch was with a plate of oysters and a stein of ale from across the street at the Magpie & Stump, still a nice boozer today. In fact, that's where Keith sat with Henry on the morning of 4 July 1991, fifteen months after the bonds theft, waiting while Ray Ketteridge stood before the beak after months on remand. Henry had given an usher a £20 note to hurry across the road and let them know the moment the verdict came down.

'Six to ten, I reckon,' Keith said, and lit a cigar.

'You think so?'

'Open and shut. He hasn't got a chance.'

'Fancy a flutter? £500?'

'You're joking, a monkey?'

'Easy money, dear boy, if you're right.'

'Thing is, I don't really gamble.'

'Really? So what are you doing exactly when you're at the casinos?'

'I've got a system. Never win much, never lose much. It ain't gambling.'

'Is this some childhood trauma I don't know about? It's very popular now. I have a friend who's a psychologist. Apparently, our parents are to blame for *everything*.'

'Don't doubt it. Look at you …'

'A square peg always trying to get into a round hole.' He laughed at his own humour. 'So, no games of chance?'

'I'll tell you. I was at the Elephant one night talking about different riding styles with Lester Piggott and Stevie Cauthen, the American jockey. I mentioned that I'd ridden a few times and they showed me the best ways to ride using a bar stool. I must have had one too many because they persuaded me to climb up on the stool, stick my bum in the air and wave an imaginary whip. Naturally, I fell on my arse and Lester said if you fall off a horse you have to get straight back on again.'

'Well, he would, wouldn't he? And what has this got to do with gambling?'

'I'm getting to that. Stevie gave me a copy of his book, *English Odyssey*, with the signed dedication: "For Keith, from the winner of the King George VI and Queen Elizabeth Stakes 1987."'

'What's so strange about that?'

'The thing is it was Saturday. The race wasn't run till the following Wednesday,' Keith answered.

The Old Bailey

'Agh!'

'He won, as he knew he would. So, anyway, I told this story to two different people at different times. John Banks, he's a bookmaker in Glasgow, and Mickey Duff, the boxing promoter. They both raised their eyebrows and asked the same question: "Well?"'

'Yes, somewhat naïve on your part, dear boy. Everything is fixed.'

'No, Henry. Everything is broken.'

He laughed that high feminine laugh he had. 'The thing is, the trial can't be fixed ...'

'You having a laugh?'

'Don't be a spoilsport. £500 says he'll walk.'

'Go on then. Your round.'

Across the road, Ray Ketteridge stood in the dock at Court Number One, uniformed like a banker in a suit, white shirt, plain tie and polished shoes. His good hair was neatly trimmed and his strong features showed a Buddha-like insouciance. His legal team remained seated, files closed, a contented look – not quite smiling – about their pale London faces as they pondered what they were going to have for lunch.

Up in the gallery, journalists from the nationals sat with pens hovering over spiral notebooks. The court was called to order and the Crown Prosecutor came to his feet, robes swishing in a draught of air like the black sails of a Barbary coast galley. He removed his half-moon glasses, coughed into his palm and announced that it was not in the public interest to proceed with the trial. The charges against Ray Ketteridge were dropped and the judge hammered his gavel into the block like a carpenter with a stubborn nail.

Ray shook everyone's hand and walked through the corridors of the Old Bailey with his lawyers like bats with fluttering cloaks behind him. Camera bulbs popped as he stepped from the entrance and the paparazzi massed about him firing questions. Ray recognised the man from the *Mail*.

'How'd you get off on this one, Ray?' he called.

He'd been told by his lawyer not to speak to the press but Ray was not a man who liked being told what to do.

'They had no evidence against me, that's why,' he answered. 'The evidence they had was from paid informers. Who's going to believe a grass against the word of an honest businessman?'

'What do you know about the stolen bonds?'

'I'll tell you what I know about bonds and that's absolutely nothing. It's a case of mistaken identity.'

Someone else shouted: 'They say the FBI have got you on tape. Is it true?'

'No, load of cobblers.'

He would have said more, but the usher had earned his £20 bringing the news across the road the moment it was announced. Keith and Henry had left the Magpie at pace and a 1955 Bentley Continental with Henry at the wheel tooted as it pulled into the kerb. From the back seat, Keith swung the door open, and Ray waved as he edged through the crowd.

'Excuse me. Excuse me. Thank you very much.'

The door slammed shut, and Henry drove back to Mayfair where Roger was waiting with the Bollinger on ice and the figurine of Pauline Borghese watching from the mantel with the faintly amused expression naked women assume in the presence of those who are dressed.

Ray was happy to be out and angry that he had been picked up in the first place.

'Thing is, Ray,' Keith said, 'when someone nicks £427 million out of the Treasury, they're going to go after them.'

'That's another fing that gets me. I sent £135 million up the line and that's vanished into thin air.'

Keith glanced at Henry, then back at Ray. '£135 million?' he repeated.

'Cost of doing business,' Henry remarked.

'And every time we try and shift a few pieces there's some cunt with a badge waiting for us,' Ray added.

'There's an informer,' Keith said, that big fat 135 mil still running through his mind like an itch he needed to scratch.

The Old Bailey

'So you keep telling me. But who the fuck is it?'

'Jeffrey Kershaw?' Keith suggested.

'That bastard. I'm going to kill him if I get my hands on him.' He shook his head. 'I don't fink so. What do you fink, 'Enery?'

'I think it's Roger.'

Roger's mouth dropped open. 'No, it's not ...'

'I was joking,' Henry said, and turned to Ray. 'The important thing is you now have a Get Out of Jail Free card. The charges have been dropped here, so the FBI will have no legal case to extradite you to the States.'

'You're sure about that?'

'Please.'

This was news to Keith. He gazed around the room at the carefully placed pieces as if they were objects in a museum. It is difficult to say what is good taste and what is kitsch, what's pretentious and what shows no taste at all. It all came naturally to Henry and Keith appreciated having learned so much about art and culture from him. The hours are long if you go down. The broader the mind the shorter the time.

'Can I fill your glass, Keith?' Roger said.

'Yeah, why not, son, live for today.'

···—◆—●————●—◆—···

Ray was in the clear. Keith wasn't. When he heard the knock on his door at 9am he didn't know if it was Rodney Miller with his copy of *The Times* or the boys in blue wreathed in smiles because it's always a pleasure nicking people in posh places even if they aren't posh.

Kerry had moved a lot of her stuff back to Bethnal Green in what she had called a trial separation. It had given Keith a lightness of being, that sense that he could do whatever he wanted without having to take Kerry's needs into consideration. If he felt like sitting up till 2am reading, he sat up till 2am reading.

Laundering the City bonds had turned into slapstick. Keith's calling, as he saw it, was fooling banks, and he had to scan the financial press every day to keep up with the constant changes in banking laws and practices. Back in the sixties when he ran his first scam, banks had already begun to use mainframe computers to automate cheque processing and customer account management, the birth of digital banking. The Bank of America introduced the first automated teller machines (ATMs), which allowed customers to withdraw cash without entering the bank. Citibank created the first online banking system in the 1980s. The robbery that May morning was going to speed up digitalisation and the days of ex-military type couriers walking treasury bills and certificates across the City were coming to an end.

He heard Mrs Primrose let herself in, folded his paper and straightened his tie.

'Morning.'

'Morning.'

'You're looking very chipper, Mr C, if you don't mind my saying.'

'Now, why would I mind a compliment like that, Mrs Primrose?'

'You know, everyone's a bit touchy these days.'

'Must be the weather.'

'You're right there. Did you see the news? Hottest August on record, 95 degrees in some places. Makes you think.'

'That'll stop everyone buggering off to the Costa del Whatsit. It will be cheaper to stay at home.'

'And better. Anything special today, Mr C?'

'Nah, just the usual. You look after yourself.'

He rode down in the lift and strolled into Smithfield meat market with its stalls draped in curtains of gory carcasses like a scene from Dante's *Inferno*. The butchers in their bloody aprons sharpening knives on honing steels were powerful men with arm and shoulder muscles firm from chopping meat, men with red faces, bright eyes, voices out of Shakespeare's Globe. Sandy put his tools down.

'Morning, Keef, you old fucker. What are you up to?'

'Think I'm going to tell you? How's your daughter doing? She get that part in *Cats*?'

The Old Bailey

'She bloody did, mate.' Sandy's expression changed as he welled up in pride. 'I can get you a ticket?'

'I'd love that. Get two. Don't matter about the cost. I'll take a mate of mine. He looks like a bloody cat.'

'Cost? What're you talking about, Keef? Not to you.'

'Nice one, son.'

Keith walked on and ran into Mickey Balls. He leaned in close with bad breath and a secret.

''Ere, I'll tell you what, Kief. Got an E-Type, redder than a pillar box, belonged to a lady driver who got the Big C.'

'How much?'

'Two grand.'

'Is it nicked?'

'Course it ain't fucking nicked.'

'Not interested then.'

'You bastard. Keeping alright?'

'Ducking and diving.'

Mickey touched the side of his nose. 'It's a lovely motor, mint condition, if you hear anyone give me a shout.'

'I shall think about nothing else.'

Spare – as he was known – was sitting on a flattened-out cardboard box like an advert for Save the Children, sixteen going on 60, face like a blunt axe, eyes big as dinner plates.

'Got any spare change?'

'Spare change ain't spare, son, it's just change,' Keith replied. He dug into his pocket and pulled out about £2 in coins. 'You're not going to use it to buy drink and drugs, I hope?'

'No, Keith, I fancy a nice salad. I'm watching my cholesterol.'

'Me too.'

Keith took a seat in Jimmy Arnold's place with a copy of the *Sun* open on page three and the salt and pepper pots on the red-and-white checked tablecloths.

'Usual?'

In five minutes he was sitting in front of what Henry Nunn once called a heart attack on a plate: egg, bacon, blood sausage, mushrooms, fried bread and a pint of Guinness. Smithfield had extended hours for the butchers, hauliers, night workers, the brain surgeons and student doctors from Barts – St Bartholomew's – the teaching hospital just around the corner. If you want a drink at any hour, as most coppers, judges, lawyers and criminals do, the licensing laws had been fixed so there's always somewhere open pulling pints.

'Another, Keith?'

'You ain't in my will if you're trying to kill me, Jimmy.'

'You look a bit down in the mouth. On me, this one.'

'Go on, then.'

Keith let out a sigh and lit up a cigar. *So there we have it.* For the first time Ray had admitted that the 'missing' £135 million had 'gone up the line'. It was food for thought while he sipped his second.

22. THE IRISH CURSE

What do you give a man who has everything?
In the case of Pablo Escobar, you might send him the bearer bonds he needs to guarantee the exchange of hard cash stored in facilities in Venezuela and Panama for wild animals trapped and crated in secret from Africa and Asia.

At Hacienda Nápoles, Escobar's estate in Puerto Triunfo, 250 kilometres from the Colombian capital Bogotá, the head of the Medellín Cartel, el Padrino, the Coke King, the richest criminal who ever lived – worth at one time $30 billion – was stocking his private zoo with rhinos, hippos, elephants, zebras, giraffes, ostriches, every breed of ape and monkey, exotic birds and rare creatures only seen in David Attenborough's documentaries.

How did he get away with it?

Escobar always looked after the little people. He paid his staff well, securing their loyalty, and spent millions building roads, power lines, soccer fields and housing for the poor. He was shot dead by security officers backed by the FBI aged 44 and tens of thousands of people wept as they followed his cortège through the barrios of Medellín, his home city.

Back when Escobar was buying endangered species from smugglers and needed bonds as an insurance, he kept a post office box with a false name in Peru's capital Lima, where one of his lieutenants was expecting a delivery.

The package never arrived. It was seized by US Customs in what was described – once again – as a 'routine inspection' in late September 1991 at the Miami offices of Aeroperú. Inside, they found two Miami phonebooks with £71 million in Bank of England securities tucked between the pages.

According to customs officials, a man with an Irish accent had delivered the package with the name Anthony Gallagher and a return address in Miami hand-written on the top left-hand corner. The address was real but no one by the name Anthony Gallagher had ever lived there and no Anthony Gallagher was ever traced.

The books and bonds were paraded before the TV cameras that night by two customs officers.

The Irish connection had come as no surprise to Keith. He had suspected IRA involvement in the robbery and distribution that first night at Henry's house when they counted the bonds with Houlihan looking on in his donkey jacket like a union rep at a pay dispute. However exaggerated, the IRA had cachet as freedom fighters and Escobar would have trusted them to come up with 71 mil and paid them 30 or 40 per cent. They talk about the luck of the Irish. There was none of that. Keith believed the whole enterprise had been cursed from the start.

There was another sting involving Irish villains during the same period. Keith kept press cuttings about the robbery and David Strahan at Carlton Television had acquired videos from law enforcement interviews. What they described was a separate operation where undercover agents from Miami FBI posing as drug traffickers got their hands on photocopies of eight £1-million bonds brought to them – according to the *South Florida Sun Sentinel* – by 'two Irish Canadians Duncan Rapier and Stephen Orr'.

Rapier was asked by the agents if the bonds were stolen, to which he said a lot more than he needed to have done.

'I don't know if the bonds are stolen. The IRA gets stuff. They raid places. They claim this belongs to them or that belongs to them. We really don't know. Somebody ... in the middle of some action, somebody picks up a briefcase and all of a sudden they consider that to be theirs.'

'You can get hold of the originals?'

'That's why I'm here.'

The Irish Curse

The FBI established that the bonds were linked to what the *Sun Sentinel* called the 'largest bond heist in British bank history'.

Were the IRA involved in the City bonds theft? Or the distribution? Or both?

Rapier and Orr admitted to the FBI 'that was likely'.

The agents looked at each other and grins of relief appeared on their faces. They had everything they needed on camera.

'I have a surprise for you, gentlemen,' said one of the agents pulling his badge. He pointed up at the cold silvery eye in the corner of the room. 'You are on candid camera.'

They were remanded with co-conspirator Jean Paul Giudicelli, from Costa Rica. The FBI never recovered the eight original certificates.

When the bonds robbery occurred in 1990, the Northern Ireland conflict known as the 'Troubles' had dominated the UK security agenda for more than twenty years. The fact that Irish paramilitaries, with their capability to acquire heavy armaments and change governments, may have been involved in the heist was a major concern in Washington as well as Whitehall.

Since the robbery of old masters from Alfred Beit's County Wicklow property in 1986, the authorities had suspected that the Irish Republican Army and the Protestant UDA worked together when it suited them. This had never been confirmed and proving it one way or the other was an obsession for security agents and journalists trying to break great stories.

David Strahan interviewed Keith Cheeseman for his documentary. Strahan begins:

'Were the IRA involved in the robbery?'
'So they say.'
'Were they [the IRA] involved with Protestant paramilitaries?'
'So they say.'
'Were they involved together?'

'It would not be unusual.'
'It would not be unusual for the two politically opposed groups to work together?'
'No.'
'They jointly finance their operations?'
'Yes.'
'Can you tell us more about that?'
'Not really. It's business. Business is business. It is not unknown for them to be cooperating with each other.'
'You understand that this was the case this time?'
'Yes.'

Strahan interviewed DCS Dickinson on the same subject. The Super answered in his cautious way that 'the same sort of individuals involved in the Beit case linked to paramilitaries we ended up dealing with in Operation Starling'.

Strahan asked Dickinson about the Ketteridge trial. 'If I were reading between the lines, by withdrawing the prosecution, were you protecting the identity of an informer?'

'No,' he replied. 'You are reading too far between the lines. I would describe that there is a number of reasons when we would seek to withdraw cases, and that is only one of them. It is not identified in court as to the reason why we withdraw. It would not be appropriate for any particular case to identify why we did so.'

Dickinson and the Operation Starling team seemed to be content that the majority of the £291.9-million worth of stolen bonds had been traced, but appeared to have no clue that there were far more missing bonds than they knew about. They still didn't know who robbed John Goddard at knifepoint and no one had yet been imprisoned for the crime.

While the reporters and the Old Bill were intrigued by the Irish connection, no one was taking much interest in who organised the robbery and where a big chunk of the money had gone.

Was the Irish obsession just a cover?

Keith took a puff on his cigar and watched the windows on the NatWest building turn orange as the sun went down.

23. THEY'RE ALWAYS WATCHING

In response to the bonds heist in May 1990, just five months later, in October that year, the Bank of England opened the Central Moneymarkets Office and introduced a computerised system designed to superannuate couriers striding across the City with huge sums in briefcases. The mugging of John Goddard at knifepoint was the last of its kind.

'What they want to do is make cash transfers more secure,' Henry Nunn said in the serious voice he saved for serious matters. 'I do believe it will have the opposite effect.'

Keith kept up to date reading *The Economist* and the *Financial Times* – the pink one – and was still getting his head around the changes computers would bring to banks and how to rob them.

'That's good news then?' he said.

It was chilly. They gathered pace as if walking to the beat of kettle drums, two men in suits and good leather shoes, Henry with the collar turned up on his camel-hair overcoat. He continued his train of thought.

'Computers convert data into binary numbers, ones and zeros, then change the numbers into words or actions. The numbers are just codes.'

'Then breaking them will be like breaking into a safe?'

'No, I think it will be much easier. With a computer, you'll be able to dip into the NatWest from your living room, or the Bahamas.'

'So, no long lunches with dirty bank managers?'

'Thing of the past, dear boy. It's going to be all takeaways and sports clothes. We have reached our sell-by date.'

They had watched a German orchestra perform Mahler's 'Ninth' at the Barbican and walked back to Willoughby House where Mrs Primrose had laid out plates of mozzarella with avocado, tomatoes, Iberica ham and a bottle of Ribera del Duero.

'Did you enjoy the concert?' Henry asked.

'Hated it.'

He laughed. 'That's Mahler for you. Worked like a maniac. Died at 50. My age.'

'Yeah, but you don't work, Henry. Unless you call thieving work.'

'My good fellow, I don't steal.' They entered the building. 'I think of myself more as a distributor. I move objects of interest from one place to another.'

'Creaming off a percentage.'

'There's always a delivery charge.'

'You'd have made a good living as a lawyer if you hadn't got struck off.'

'The trouble with lawyers is they're never trustworthy. They all want to be actors or writers. Those outside the law are far more honest.'

'Blimey, have you been speaking to that psychologist again?'

'Every day,' he said, and laughed his high-pitched laugh. 'He's from *Up North*, a bit rough around the edges, but cute.'

They rode up in the lift. Henry looked about the apartment, judging the décor, the bookshelves, *the objets d'art*, pieces of which had gone through his own hands. His eyes fell on the glass-covered chessboard with onyx pieces represented by figures from the Battle of Waterloo.

'You play?'

'I learned a few gambits from John Stonehouse.'

They sat at the table by the window with the London lights like silent fireworks across the horizon. Something Kerry had said before she moved out rang true, he had in recent months spent more time with Henry than he had with her. It happens when you're on a job. It is all consuming. When things are going well you ride your luck; when they go badly, you need to find out why and fix it. Five months had gone by since the big one and all he had to show for it were two unsold bonds folded between the pages of *Smiley's People* and a handful of scrap paper he'd chucked in a bin.

Keith had opened the wine earlier to allow it to breathe. He poured two glasses; it was ruby red and glowed in the soft lighting. Henry tried a sip and his eyebrows went up.

'Mmm. Rather good.'

'Goes with the ham. People bang on about Rioja, and it's good, but the Ribera del Duero is more subtle. The vineyards are further south. The grapes get more sun.'

'You are a man who knows how to enjoy life.'

'That's the thing, Henry, I'm not in it for the money, but what it buys.'

'Freedom, you mean?'

Keith tapped the side of his head. 'Freedom's all up here. A lot of blokes doing time feel freer behind bars than the people outside running for trains, afraid of the boss, yelled at by their old lady when they get home. Always short of money. Bills. Hire purchase. That's not freedom.'

Henry clinked the rim of Keith's glass. 'You have perfectly described my idea of hell.'

'So, when you go inside, and you will, be positive, read, learn a language. You're a lawyer, give the old lags free advice and they'll look after you.' He tapped his head again. 'Freedom's up here, not on Wandsworth Common after midnight.'

'Now you're being cruel.'

'You have to be cruel to be kind,' rang the old cliché. Keith put his cutlery down. 'So, Henry, what next with the bonds?'

'How do you mean?'

'How many are left, for a start?'

'That's Ray's department.'

'Ray was never up to this, was he? He's a front man. A face. You're pulling the strings.'

'Not at all.' His voice rose. 'It's Ray's gig. I have made a few introductions.'

'What was he doing with nine certificates in his car?'

'I thought you knew. He'd arranged to meet someone at The Plough. They never turned up.'

'The police turned up, though, didn't they? How come they followed you out to Romford? They must have known he was carrying bonds. That's why they searched the motor.'

'It's a mystery to me, Keith.'

'He was bloody lucky to walk out of the Old Bailey and not downstairs to the dungeons. Did you arrange it?'

He laughed. 'Lovely piece of ham,' he said.

'Black pigs fed on acorns. So, did you?'

'Fixing judges at the Old Bailey is even out of my league.'

'Is it, though?'

Henry drank his wine. Keith refilled the glasses. He glanced out at the skyline and had the sudden feeling of being – not alone, exactly, but on his own. Kerry had gone. Mark Osborne was out of the game. Executed. He remembered his last words to him on the telephone.

You're my friend, Keith, I want you to know that.

You say that sort thing after you've betrayed someone, or you're about to. Mark must have grassed because he was afraid. He had 'pissed off' the wrong people and those people had sent a pro to do the business. The private investigator Clyde Wilson had looked pleased with himself telling the TV cameras that the hit was ordered in London and that local law enforcement had put out that they wanted to interview Ray Ketteridge.

But that was a smokescreen. Ray couldn't pass a nicked bond in the criminal underworld. He certainly couldn't have organised a hit in Houston, Texas.

Keith glanced back across the table. He liked Henry. He thought of Henry as a friend. But Henry didn't have friends. He didn't have enemies. Henry had interests, as the statesman Lord Palmerston described England's relationship with the rest of the world.

After his trial at the Old Bailey, Ray had said that he'd sent £130-odd million up the line 'and that's vanished into thin air'. What that told Keith was that the 135 ghost bonds were never recorded or registered. They had been placed in John Goddard's case by someone inside the Bank of England who knew in advance they would be robbed before he delivered them. The unrecorded bonds would, in however long it took, be cashed through foreign banks – much as TJ had proposed – or deposited in bank vaults to secure loans until the borrower defaulted and would likely not come to light for years.

The scheme was perfect. While coppers around the world chased after the £292 million in bonds they'd been told was the amount lifted from Goddard, those behind the robbery were quietly sitting on the rest. With the exception of the individual or individuals inside the bank, only the six people who had been present that night when the bonds were counted knew the true figure was £427 million – Henry Nunn, Ray Ketteridge, John Bowman, Houlihan the Watcher, Roger the Dodger and Keith Cheeseman.

Nearly half a billion quid and not a penny to show for it.

It wasn't late and he wasn't tired.

'You want a lift home, Henry?'

'That would be lovely, darling.'

He drove Henry to Mayfair and drove back with a Dean Martin cassette on the stereo. He'd once shared a house in America with Dean Martin, but that was a story for another time.

⋯⋯◆⋯●⋯⋯⋯⋯●⋯◆⋯⋯

The following morning Keith woke just before 8am to the sound of a long double knock on the door.

Fuck it. They've come.

He slid his feet into leather slippers, pushed back his thinning hair with his palm and a long sigh rose from his chest as he tramped heavy footed down the corridor in his pyjamas. He fixed a smile on his lips. No point in looking angry or crestfallen.

Be friendly. Crack a joke. Deny everything.
Bloody Rodney.
'Morning ...'
'Fuck me, Rodders, it's a bit early.'
He gave Keith his copy of *The Times*. 'I know it is, guv, something I want to show you in the garage. It's important.'
'Can't it wait?'
He stiffened his jaw and shook his head. 'No, guv.'
'Give me ten minutes.'

Keith cupped his palms under the tap and washed the sleep from his face. He dressed, combed his hair and found Rodney Miller in his little office in the basement.
'What's all this then, son?'
Rodney held his finger to his lips and pointed. 'See that car over there, the black one?'
'The Vauxhall?'
'Yes, guv, the Vauxhall. It faces the entrance, right? In the headlights there's a camera recording all the vehicles as they come and go.'
'I always thought you worked for MI6.'
'Thing is, guv, your apartment's also being watched.'
'You sure?'
'Saw it with my own eyes. Two geezers who looked pretty bloody dodgy came with a long ladder and put a camera up at Lazard Brothers. It's right opposite your apartment and they turned the camera up at your windows.'

An old Vauxhall with an eye in the headlights sounded like City of London Police. A camera at Lazard's was a different department. Was he being watched? Was the surveillance coordinated? Who could say?

He thought about giving him a couple of twenties but didn't. Rodney Miller had gone out of his way to help him as a friend. A gratuity would have been gratuitous and undermined the act.
'Rodney, I appreciate this. You're a real mate.'
'Any time, Kief. You watch your back.'

Keith walked around the building. He found a spot where he could study the façade of Lazard Brothers without the camera studying him. What were they waiting for? What were they hoping to see? What had they seen?

Henry bloody Nunn in the picture window drinking wine in his pinstriped suit and yellow waistcoat, little black eyes curious as a cat, the black-and-gold cufflinks on his double cuffs matching the black band and gold casing of his Omega dress watch. Perhaps he was right, 1990 was drawing to a close and with it their sell-by date. That day, 22 November, Maggie Thatcher had resigned as prime minister after ten years in Downing Street.

He strolled down to Jimmy's place in Smithfield and sat at a table next to two men in bloodied white aprons and wasn't sure if they were butchers or surgeons.

'The usual, Keefy?'

'Yeah, you only die once.'

24. THE DARKEST HOUR

The penthouse was five floors up – this was the Barbican, not New York – with wide balconies and big windows. Lord and Lady Donaldson lived next door on the same floor. They were nice people. Very obliging. Once when Kerry had fried pork sausages, Keith couldn't find any mustard and couldn't imagine eating sausages without it.

He went next door and explained his dilemma. Lady Donaldson scurried off to the kitchen, calling in her high, tinkling voice:

'I'm sure we have some here somewhere. Oh, yes, here it is.' She came back with two jars. 'English or Dijon?'
'English pork, English mustard,' he said.
'You are a man after my own heart.'
'There'll always be an England, Lady D.'
'There will, indeed, Mr Cheeseman.'
'Although, I dunno, now Mrs T's gone.'
'A sad day for us all.'

···◆·•———•◆···

Tuesday, 27 November 1990.
06.00. Keith woke suddenly and glanced at the green numbers on the digital clock. He wondered for a moment if he was dreaming about codes and binary numbers, but the sound of his

front door being smashed down sounded real, and reality was confirmed as the numbers rolled over to 06.01.

He was fully awake now. It was just before dawn. He heard fast-moving steps approaching along the corridor. His bedroom door swung open and two men burst in with grins as wide as the Thames. More happy faces appeared like winners when the betting shop opens, shouldering their way in one after the other, a dozen or more with loud voices.

'FBI,' they cried.

'Put your hands where we can see them.'

'FBI.'

It was like an episode of *Starsky & Hutch*. They shouted at him, they shouted at each other. Everyone seemed inordinately pleased with themselves. The Americans waved guns like they were in Texas. They were gun people; they felt safer with a firearm. Like going out without your trousers on, they couldn't imagine being without their guns.

During the next ten minutes, Keith worked out that the first two into his bedroom were plain-clothes detectives from City of London Police at Bishopsgate. They must have acquired a lift key from the concierge and broken down his door.

The rest, men in black with moustaches and twitchy eyes, were from Operation Starling and the FBI's Global Research Unit. They had crossed the balcony from the obliging Lord and Lady Donaldson's place and entered his apartment through the unlocked balcony doors. Why they needed guns, and how they got permission to carry them in London, Keith had no idea. In fact, the twitchiest of the group, an older bloke with oiled black hair, pushed the barrel of his .40 Smith & Wesson into Keith's cheek.

'You armed?'

'I beg your pardon?'

'You heard me, motherfucker. Where's your piece?'

'Except when I was serving my country as a soldier, I have never had or carried a gun in my life.'

One of the Bishopsgate cops intervened. 'It's OK, Mervyn, he's clean.'

The Darkest Hour

'Clean, my ass!'

The two detectives from Bishopsgate looked embarrassed as far as Keith could tell. Up till now, his brushes with the law had only been with the nicely manicured accountants and auditors in the Fraud Squad – hence the telegram when he married Kerry. They were numbers men, same as Keith, polite and civilised. Their relationship was more like that of chess players who appreciated each other's skills. The agents from Starling and their counterparts with drawn guns were acting like the Sweeney taking on a violent armed gang, rather than a solitary plump chap in his pyjamas.

After one of the detectives read him the warrant, Keith knew damn well that anything he said could and would be used in court as evidence.

'Anything you say …'

'I'd like to get dressed, if that's alright?'

Mervyn nodded. 'Watch him,' he said to a colleague.

Mervyn slid his revolver into a worn shoulder holster, and it occurred to Keith that the difference between the Brits and the Americans was that the Feds assumed he was guilty and feared that he would come at them with guns blazing. The English police clung to the *habeas corpus* notion that you were innocent until proven guilty – although in the case of Ray Ketteridge, he was guilty and walked out of court as if innocent. Keith, though not a gambler, thought it was 50–50 that the same would happen to him.

He was in the shower before anyone could stop him and dressed in a suit with terylene in the blend so it didn't crease. The dawn light was cracking through the windows and a touch of pale pink lit the glass on the NatWest building. It was going to be a nice day.

Mervyn had gone through the drawers in the bedroom and tossed all the underwear and socks Mrs Primrose had folded away into a messy pile on the floor. He moved on to the pockets in his suits and pulled out a roll of twenties about the size of a cigar tube that Keith had forgotten about.

'What's this?'
'Looks like a few quid in twenties.'
'Drug dealers roll their cash.'
'Oh, really,' Keith answered. 'What the hell were you doing coming over my balcony? You must think I'm bloody Batman and I was going to leap off ...'
'What?'
'If you'd have knocked on my door, I'd have opened it for you.'
'Fuck you.'
'Put the money back in the pocket. I haven't been found guilty of anything.'
'You've got some lip on you, boy.'
'Just put it back and be nice.'

Mervyn shook his head as if he had no idea what he was talking about.

'Fuckin' Brits,' he said.

Keith took a deep breath, held it for a count of five, and had a sudden attack of pride in who he was, where he came from. We are decent people, polite people, he thought; basically kind, basically generous. He hoped that didn't change in the fuck-you age of yuppies, takeaways, mixed toilets, traders in red braces, greed is not only good it's the only way to be.

The Feds continued to search the apartment, under carpets and beds, behind picture frames, in the cutlery drawer, the crockery cupboard, the fridge, the pasta pot, the broom closet; down the back of the sofa; on the underside of the coffee table, the dining table, the dining chairs. One of them studied the polished wood floor to see if any planks had been pulled up and pushed back into place.

On the three tiers of bookshelves among the books were various keepsakes: an antique miniature globe, some sculptures and Capodimonte, a bell from a Tibetan temple, family snaps in silver frames, a picture of Keith in his army uniform and one of him with a big grin on his face from the day he signed George Best to play for Dunstable. They studied his curios and bibelots. They dropped books on the floor where they opened like shot birds, and for some reason they neglected the just-out-of-reach row of volumes on the third shelf where £1,000 was buried in the hollow of one book and a pair of certificates nestled among the words of John le Carré.

He glanced at the clock. More than an hour had passed. The two City police detectives started bustling around him, and then escorted him down to their car in the basement. He noticed the black Vauxhall had gone. Rodney Miller gave him a wave and he waved back as he was driven off without handcuffs to Bishopsgate.

The DCS was waiting in his big glasses with a thin smile and a suit that had seen better days.

'I have been expecting you, Mr Cheeseman,' he said.

'I'm not sure why, Mr Dickinson, I haven't done anything. May I ask you a question?'

'Of course you may.'

'Are you going to pay for my front door? Your blokes went and broke it down. They could have tried knocking first.'

'Protocol,' he replied. 'You are entitled to make a claim.'

He was led to a cell. A bobby too young to shave with a back as straight as a poker stood at the door, but it was never locked. It would have been too much bother with all the coming and going. Members of the Starling team and the FBI in turn played good cop, bad cop asking the same questions. Who organised the robbery? Who did the mugging? They asked him about Ray Ketteridge and Jeffrey Kershaw. How long had he had links with the IRA? What was his relationship with Pablo Escobar? The only name that never came up belonged to Henry Nunn. Keith denied everything.

'We have you on tape talking to Mark Lee Osborne,' said Senior Special Agent Mervyn Parr. He opened a black notebook and read the neat block capitals written in black ink. 'The first thing you said when Osborne called is: "You got the money?"'

'Don't recall that at all.'

'He told you he'd got the whole $2 million, and you asked him how much you personally were getting.' Keith made no response.

Mervyn continued: 'You asked him where the money was, and when he told you it was in his car in seven big bags, you told him to stash it somewhere. It's all on tape.'

Keith shook his head and sucked air through his teeth. 'I've had a lot of worries lately. My wife's moved out. She's talking about divorce. It's been a confusing time for me. Do you think I could have a glass of water?'

Mervyn said he was going to pistol-whip the truth out of him, and Mr Dickinson brought him a plastic glass and a bottle of Perrier. He seemed a decent type, old-fashioned. Finally, they had a moment alone.

'We're not charging you with anything, Keith,' he said, but there was venom in the tail. 'You are being arrested pending extradition proceedings by the Americans. You'll be held on remand until your bail hearing. The FBI are petitioning for you not to be given bail.'

25. ON REMAND

End of November, a bleak grey sky made bleaker divided by the geometric lines of prison bars and the familiar smell of sweat, fear and damp. Empty-eyed men shuffling along with bent backs and no future, imagination knocked out of them by poverty and bad luck. Hard men and wannabe hard men with prison tats illustrating their dreams: a Harley, a death mask, a crucifix, the name of the woman they had abused or raped or killed, knuckles suggesting their desire for love or death. They turn their toothbrushes into blades and plan breakouts that never happen.

Keith was back in Wormwood Scrubs. He had previously spent more than three years in different jails but those months he spent on remand in late 1990, early 1991 felt not unfair, exactly, but irksome. He didn't nick the bonds. He hadn't sold any bonds. He hadn't made any money out of the bonds. He didn't deliver the bonds to Mark Osborne and their banter about 2 mil in seven big bags was more of a *Two Ronnies* comedy sketch than a conspiracy to fence stolen property.

He had not been present during the bail hearing – as is the custom – and it was Kerry who came to the Scrubs to tell him that the FBI had objected to bail because, they said, there was a risk of Keith doing a runner.

What, me?

The judge did grant bail but set it at a staggering £500,000 – a sum more appropriate for a Nazi war criminal.

At least he had a sharp legal troika with his old friend Ralph Haeems – Mr Fixit from back in the Dusky Maiden days, his assistant, Michael Brooks, a solicitor, and Kerry, with her own contacts and the sort of personality with which people were reluctant to use the word 'no', and usually changed their mind if they did. They were estranged, but she fought like a panther to get him released.

Kerry made sure his newspapers were delivered first thing every morning: *The Times* and the *Sun* during the week, the *Sunday Times*, the *News of the World*, *The Economist* and the *Financial Times* at the weekend. At the café opposite the Scrubs, in her polite, convincing way, she arranged to have his lunch and dinner delivered by a waiter who twice daily defied death dodging between the cars on the Du Cane Road to make sure his food was hot when it reached the prison gates. She lobbied MPs, contacted Home Secretary Douglas Hurd and also dealt with David Strahan from Carlton Television to make sure Keith got a fair hearing now he was interviewing more people for his documentary about the robbery.

When Keith came out of the Scrubs in the 80s, he was invited to the staff Christmas party. He always showed respect and had a good rapport with the wardens. They were only doing their job. He knew that and they knew he knew that. During the bonds robbery investigations, being featured regularly in the tabloids gave the impression that he personally had scarpered with £292 million. This made him something of a celebrity and, for some reason, having money – real or imaginary – endows people with a charisma that draws others to them. A couple of the screws got into the habit of giving him a mock salute.

'Morning, Mr Cheeseman.'

'I see you're in the *Mirror* today, page seven.'

'With your money you should have your own set of keys.'

'Thing is, Charlie boy, I like it here.'

'Wish I did.'

On Remand

Remand prisoners were housed in a different area from those serving their sentences and were allowed a lot of leeway if they didn't take liberties. Keith had visitors almost every afternoon, lawyers, reporters, mates. The screws would leave him unguarded and get on with other chores. One time, a young lad from a family he knew had been arrested. He had never been in prison before and that evening Keith was taken to his cell so he could smooth the way for him.

One regular visitor was Martin Newman, ten years older, making a living doing PR for rock bands and guilty of a one-man population explosion, having fathered numerous children with his numerous dolly birds. He brought in packets of tobacco and a box of ten cigars which Keith opened immediately just to savour the sweet smell of the Caribbean.

'What's this, one each for all your kids? You must have a season ticket to the maternity wing.'

'Every year there's another one. Like clockwork.'

'I'm going to have a whip-round and get you a vasectomy.'

'Is that where they cut the end bit off?'

'No, son, that's circumcision.'

'Blimey, I think I told a mate of mine it was the other way round.'

One of his women was struggling with addiction. Their two boys would have been taken into care, but Martin had gone to court to get custody and was looking after them with his mum.

'Thing is, I've always been loose. Peace and Love.'

'There's your answer, too much love and now you haven't got any peace.'

'I've got all these bloody kids running riot and you have to show some discipline or, you know, they'll go off the rails. Sometimes I feel like I'm a bloody dictator.' He glanced at his watch. 'Got to go, mate, Jason and Aaron are shepherds in the nativity play.'

'We used to talk about robbing trains,' Keith said. 'Now it's all school runs and childcare.'

'The times they are a-changin'.'

'Is that Bob Dylan?'
'Yeah, best of the lot, mate.'
'Prefer Dean Martin, myself.'

Christmas and New Year came and went. It was 1991 and the cells were filled with new calendars from the *Sun* and *Playboy*. When you go down for a few years, you get into a routine and make the best of it, as Keith had advised Henry Nunn. On remand waiting for a bail hearing, there is a sense of life being suspended, that you're neither here nor there, one leg inside and the other outside. There are no days to count off. No remission. Just the minute hand on your watch on a slow march to bedtime.

Keith rose early, when the prison was quiet, after restless nights when some chap in the main block with mental health issues wailed through the dark hours for his mum and kept the whole prison on edge. Half the people in jail should never have been locked up. They didn't need punishment. They needed Henry Nunn's cute psychologist.

He'd shave and dress in a starched shirt and cashmere sweater – nicely cared for in the prison laundry – and wait for the papers to arrive. Still in 1991 – and for a decade after that – the morning ritual in prison was slopping out. That is emptying the piss buckets, overseen by what they called the potwalloper. That was the purpose of the packs of tobacco Martin Newman brought in, currency to pay for these small inconveniences.

After slopping out, the cells were open for the rest of the day. Keith usually had breakfast in the canteen where there was a good supply of salt and pepper for his over-easy fried egg, but also because the prisoners enjoyed his presence, his humour, that sense that he was a rascal who had made himself rich and usually got away with it, something to aspire to and admire. He had come to this conclusion without arrogance. It was just the way it was, and he used the time to give advice when it was asked for and to help semi-illiterate blokes write letters to their mums and girlfriends.

While half the men inside shouldn't have been there because they had mental health issues, most of the other half wouldn't have been there if they'd had a decent education.

The hierarchy in prison was the same as it was out of prison. The Governor was the king, the guards his inner court, lackeys with low wages but power. Then you had the Lords of the Jailhouse, the psychopaths and murderers. They were deferred to and respected even by the Governor. He knew only too well that they had nothing to lose if they burned his prison down, so he gave them concessions and home leaves to make sure they didn't. As an entertainer, conversationalist and bon vivant, Keith Cheeseman was the wise fool, the court jester, trusted by prisoners and screws alike, the same person inside as he was outside.

Keith had just settled down at Wormwood Scrubs when he was told to collect his cashmere sweaters and get ready for the drive from Hammersmith to Brixton, a journey that would take him through Chelsea, where Georgie Best was still propping up the bar at the Phene Arms, and on through the avenues of trees on Clapham Common. HM Prison Brixton was a dedicated remand facility where the regime was even more liberal with all day visits and Kerry again arranging to have fresh food and the newspapers delivered.

He had no idea why he had been moved until he heard on the crimevine that Thomas Coyle, Anthony Rooney and Edward Dunne were being transferred to Wormwood Scrubs. There were cogent – if complicated – reasons why it would not have been a good idea to have Keith and the three IRA-connected bond smugglers in the same jail at the same time.

The media was all over the robbery story, especially since the murder of Mark Osborne. It was rumoured that the success of the police tracking down the bonds was due to an inside informer and that Keith Cheeseman was a likely candidate. This was untrue, but the rumours persisted and were put into print after the event by the *Observer* one Sunday. The Irishmen would have known they had been betrayed and keeping them away from Keith would have been for his protection.

But there was another more likely reason. Keith was not on the outside grassing to the cops; he was inside waiting for a bail hearing. Had he sat down with Coyle, Rooney and Dunne, they would have discussed mutual acquaintances and quite possibly fingered the snitch. Keith's guess was that he had not been moved to protect him, but to protect the inside man, the actual informer.

Weeks passed into months, spring into summer. A year had passed. Suddenly it was November 1991, and Martin Newman came to visit with a stash of tobacco and a picture of a squashed little bundle of new life named Lily.

'Not another one.'

'Well, you know how it is …'

'Not in here, mate, I've forgotten.'

26. DYMCHURCH

It was getting on for Christmas again when Keith dressed in his crease-free suit and was delivered in a windowless van to the appeal court where he stood, back straight like a soldier, before Mr Justice Turner.

'You are *the* William Keith Cheeseman?'

'I am, sir. Good morning.'

'It is indeed.'

The judge shuffled his papers, picked up a pen, made a mark, and sat back with his fingers knitted together. Under the Senior Courts Act 1981, the bail set at £500,000 was decreased to a slightly less absurd £310,000. Kerry had worked her magic on her ex-husband John Dedman. He stood up for £140,000, and an assortment of friends guaranteed the rest.

The guarantors also appeared in court. They did not have to deposit the cash. Their word was their bond.

'You do understand,' Mr Justice Turner intoned with a plum in his mouth and a twinkle in the eye, 'that should Mr Cheeseman abscond, you will have to produce and forfeit the money. If you do not, he will not be standing before the courts, you will.'

In turn they nodded. Keith felt his heart beating faster in his chest as the judge brought down his wooden hammer with a bang, *they love doing that*, and the court rose.

He was out.

He had dinner with his briefs, Kerry, John Dedman and his guarantors – he picked up the bill, naturally – and one of his pals gave him the number of a mini-cab driver that turned out to be one of those turning points in life, a moment when the road seems to be leading in one destination and you wind up somewhere completely different and unexpected.

The driver curved confidently through the back-doubles to the Barbican chatting amiably in a strong East London accent about how John Major was going to have his work cut out filling Mrs Thatcher's shoes.

'What man can fill her shoes?' Keith said.

'We're entering the unknown.'

'Sometimes that's better than the known, if you ask me.'

The meter read £8.50. Keith stuck a twenty through the partition and the driver gave him his card.

'John Miller,' he said. 'Call me any time.'

'Keith Cheeseman.'

'Cor blimey, I've been reading about you in the papers. Is that you? You almost brought down the Bank of England.'

'Strong foundations, Johnny boy, it's still standing.'

'Happy to make your acquaintance. I mean what I said, Mr Cheeseman, any time.'

'Nice one.'

The smashed front door had not been replaced but poorly repaired. Still, he was back in his castle; the night views of London like a photograph, fresh milk in the fridge left by Mrs Primrose with a note on the table saying, 'Welcome Home Mr C'.

It was handy that Bishopsgate nick was just around the corner from the Barbican. It was the condition of Keith's bail that he had to report to the station every day during the first week, then once a week, when he signed a form that was then co-signed by the desk sergeant. He usually saw Sam Smithers, an old copper near retirement who enjoyed a bit of repartee.

Dymchurch

One night they met by chance at Dirty Dick's in Bishopsgate and had a drink together, Sergeant Smithers in a tweed jacket with leather elbows and a pipe in his top pocket.

In its own literature, Dirty Dick's boasted of being described in 1866 as: 'A small public house without floorboards, a low ceiling with festoons of cobwebs dangling from the black rafters, a bar battered and dirty floating with beer, numberless gas pipes tied anyhow along the struts and posts to conduct the spirits from the barrels to the taps, sample phials and bottles of wine and spirits on shelves, everything covered with virgin dust and cobwebs.'

It hadn't changed that much.

'Didn't think this was your sort of place, Keith?'

'I haven't always been upper-class, you know. I used to be one of the workers.'

'One of the shirkers if you ask me.'

Keith smiled and took out his cigars. 'Your glass is empty.' He caught the barman's eye and waggled a finger. 'Two more, my son, and have one on me.'

'Blimey, it must be true, you did nick £292 million.'

'And the rest.'

Sam laughed, not that he got the joke.

They lit cigars and stood there with their pints like two old mates. Sam insisted on buying another round. They tipped them back and parted at the telephone box opposite Liverpool Street Station where Keith called Martin Newman.

'How are your kids?'

'That's like saying how long's a piece of string.'

'Fancy a drink?'

'What would a thirsty man in the Sahara say?'

'Meet me at Tramp in half an hour.'

Keith took a stroll along Liverpool Street and then did something he hadn't done for years: he hopped on a number 19 bus and watched London grow richer from the top deck. He stepped off at Old Bond Street and could smell, not dust and diesel, but the polish on the windows and perfume on the night air.

They say money doesn't buy you happiness. This is a delusion the poor cling to and the rich find comical. Money does buy happiness. Money equals freedom, the highest form of happiness. Money equals pleasure. The more you have the more pleasurable life is. People with money can never know what it is like to be without money. Money is a magnet and Maggie, whether she knew it or not, was telling porkies. It doesn't trickle down. It is sucked up.

In Tramp, Keith was a celebrity, the tabloid antihero, the last of the gentlemen villains with fantasy millions in his back pocket. In truth, his cash reserves were being sucked up by legal fees. He had never been much of an investor. Money was for spending and he needed to pass that £2 million in bonds or find a new source of income if he was going to continue to enjoy the quotidian demands of the good life.

Did Martin have any ideas? Not at all. He had his own money worries and a football team of kids to look after. They watched the beautiful people dancing and ate sea bass ceviche. They left early. Martin had to drive to Doncaster to arrange a concert date for The Kinks, and Keith called his regular driver to take him home.

Keith had grown fond of John Miller. He was a scallywag with more ambition than nous, but he was always there on the dot and talked a lot of lively nonsense like men on long stretches. He drove an old black Rover with the paintwork scorched and bubbled on the bonnet.

'What's all this?' Keith said before he got in the car. 'You can't drive me about in this.'

'It's got a good motor, Kief.'

'People don't see the motor, do they? Go and get yourself a respectable set of wheels. I'll lend you the money.'

'You mean that?'

'Course I bloody do. Come on.'

Keith climbed in the car and when they got to the Barbican, he invited John up for a drink.

'Better make it a small one, don't want to get nicked on the way home.'

'This time of night they'll be drinking their tea and eating chips.'

After taking the lift up to the fifth floor, John looked around the apartment. 'Did you really nick all that money, Kief?'

'If you believe what the papers say I did.' Keith gave him £500. 'That's free rides till you pay it off.'

'That's a deal.' He paused. 'I've been meaning to tell you, there's a bird I know, pick her up regular from Hendersons, you know, the private bank?'

'I do, as it happens. It's just around the corner, next to the Fraud Squad.'

'Works long hours. Pick her up at 2am sometimes and drive her out to Chelmer. She's well pissed off with it.'

'Chelmer?'

'A village near Chelmsford. She's got a cottage. Takes more than an hour, even at night.' He took a swig of his whisky and water. 'So, one time she says to me "they're all bastards" and she'll rob them if she gets half the chance.'

He spoke as if he was joking and Keith joked back: 'You should introduce her to an expert.'

'That's a bloody good idea.'

A few days later, John brought Elaine Borg to the Barbican. Keith got the firm impression that, while John was in fact married, they were an item, and robbing Hendersons may very well have been John's idea. Elaine Borg was vivacious and clearly astute, while John was none of those things.

She opened up after two glasses of wine. She described herself as the chief computer programmer with sole control of several high-value investment accounts including James Bond himself in the actor Sean Connery, Lady Beaverbrook, the Church of England and Russell Grant.

'You don't mean the astrologer?'

'That's the one.'

'We don't want to dip into his account. He'll know what we're doing before we do it.'

She laughed. The suggestion was out there.

'Money goes in and out of these accounts all the time,' she said. 'Huge amounts sometimes.'

'You do know, Elaine, that any money that vanishes from accounts is repaid by the bank? They are bound by law to do so.'

'I know, I wouldn't do it otherwise. And Hendersons can afford it.'

Keith had looked up Hendersons before their next meeting. The company had been established in 1934 to administer the estates of Alexander Henderson, 1st Baron Faringdon. In 1975 the company started managing pension funds and floated on the London Stock Exchange in 1983. With more than $1 billion invested, they wouldn't miss a couple of million.

Elaine stretched out her legs as if unwinding herself. She was a beautiful woman and Keith felt a mutual attraction that made no sense if she was having a fling with John Miller. That, on second thoughts, seemed unlikely. He was sitting across the room beneath the glow of one of the table lamps with a glass in his hand and a silly look on his thin face. Elaine had worked out how the fraud would work. As she had access to the unique codes on her client accounts, she could transfer funds to parallel accounts at Hendersons, then out to accounts at other banks that Keith would set up.

'That works for me.'

Keith went down to the garage in the lift with them. Elaine kissed his cheeks before climbing into a new-looking silver Mercedes John had bought to replace the old Rover.

'I did what you said, Keif,' he said.

'Good lad.'

···◆—•————•—◆···

A few weeks later, when John Dedman rescinded his bail agreement, Keith continued to appear at the police station until a further hearing took place before Mr Justice Morland.

Keith called on two good friends to act as guarantors, the financial advisor Tony Adams, who guaranteed £165,000, and the actor Gary Webster from the TV shows *EastEnders* and *Minder*, who topped up the remaining £145,000. Tony Adams had been declared bankrupt four months earlier, but he didn't mention it in court.

With the daily paper tucked under his arm and a new spring in his step, Keith went out for breakfast most mornings. John then picked him up and drove out to banks in the suburbs where Keith used small amounts to open accounts in false names taken from the telephone book.

On his next trip to the police station, Sam had an open file in front of him.

'Got something extra for you to sign today, Keith,' he said. 'This is the inventory of the stuff the FBI took out of your place. They're going to send it back and want you to sign that there's nothing missing and there's been no damage.'

'What, before I've even seen it?'

'Can't argue with the FBI.'

'No, they've got bloody guns.'

'The day that happens here is the day I take my pension.'

Keith read through the list.

'I see you've got a home movie of Dean Martin ...'

'What did the Feds want with that?'

'No idea. I love that guy. What a voice.'

'He's just how he seems, a really good bloke. I know him quite well.'

'You know Dean Martin?'

'It's a long story.'

'You in a hurry? Fancy a cuppa?'

'Go on then, Sam, two sugars.'

···◆·•————•◆···

Back in 1974 when his construction business was doing well, Keith travelled to Australia to bid on a construction job. One night he took Lynn Healy, his business partner, and her fifteen-year-old daughter to dinner at the Windsor Hotel in Sydney. Frank Sinatra was staying there with his entourage at the time, and he'd had a bad day. The entertainment industry was on strike and he'd been condemned in the press for crossing the picket line. He came storming into the dining room effing and blinding.

This was Frank Sinatra, so no one said a dicky bird. 'Effing journalists. Effing strikers. Effing Australians. If I had my effing way I'd ...' this, that and the other. It was too much and Keith decided to have a word. Frank's minders formed a wall as he approached. The cutlery stilled. The waiters stopped in their tracks. You could have heard the dust shift.

'Can you calm your language a bit, Mr Sinatra. I'm saying please. I've got a teenaged girl over there who doesn't need to be hearing this.'

The silence stretched. Keith shrugged and went back to his table. Frank Sinatra drank his Jack Daniel's. His companions nattered and he sat there drumming his fingers wondering who the fuck had the balls to tell Frank Sinatra to quieten down. As Keith stood to leave, Sinatra crossed the room towards him. He offered his small hand, which Keith took in his big paw.

'Bad day. Bad scene. My apology.'

'Good of you to say so. You're a gent.'

'And you're from London?'

'For my sins.'

'We've all got those. Are you in entertainment?'

'I rob banks, to be honest, that's entertaining enough for me.'

He roared with laughter.

'You kidding me?'

'Best job in the world. When you get away with it.'

He laughed again and his whole face changed, became Old Blue Eyes. 'I'm going to be in London in September. I can send you a couple of tickets.'

'That sounds like an offer I can't refuse.'

He was as good as his word. It was 1980. Keith took Dawn, then still his wife, to the Royal Festival Hall. They had a drink in Frank's dressing room and at dinner after the show the minders couldn't have been nicer.

Dymchurch

Another pair of tickets arrived for Sammy Davis Jr. at the London Palladium with another invite to go backstage. Keith mentioned that he was heading to Las Vegas on business – he had some JC Penney bonds – and was invited to Sammy's Halloween party at the Flamingo Hotel built by Bugsy Siegel and Meyer Lansky, the mobsters who developed the Las Vegas Strip. He danced with Debbie Reynolds and Ann-Margret.

'You're light on your feet for a big man,' Ann-Margret said.

'Have to be in my line of work.'

'And mine.'

Light on his feet and light in his wallet as well after losing $2,000 playing five-card stud with Sammy Davis, Dean Martin, Telly Savalas, Rory Calhoun, William Conrad and Ed Asner.

Keith had booked into the Barbary Coast because his old army buddy, Jerry Coccas, headed up the hotel security. There had been an armed robbery there the previous night and Jerry advised him to move to a different hotel. Dean Martin joined them as they were speaking.

'Come and stay with me, Keith,' Dean said. 'We don't have any of that. I have my own security.'

'Are you sure?'

'I wouldn't say it if I didn't mean it.'

···◆•――――•◆···

Sergeant Smithers had sweat on his brow and was panting for breath.

'You *stayed* with Dean Martin?'

'For three months.'

'Jesus.' He crossed himself. 'Are you in the home movie, then?'

Now Keith had more explaining. Dean Martin had made a movie called *The Caddy* with Jerry Lewis when he sang the song 'That's Amore' for the first time.

'Love that song.'

'And there's another one you'll remember, "Sam's Song",' Keith said, and began singing it to the sergeant.

Sam nodded in recognition.

'Dean and Jerry thought *The Caddy* was a load of rubbish, so they filmed themselves singing a skit of "Sam's Song", changing the words and taking the piss. They were both drunk and it was funny. Dean showed it to me and gave me the cassette as a keepsake.'

'I'd love to see it.'

'There's the problem, sarge, they have a different system in the States. The cassettes don't play over here.'

'What a pity.'

Someone came into the police station. Sergeant Smithers went to attend to them and gave Keith a wave.

'See you next time,' he said.

Sam had forgotten about the FBI inventory and the papers for the extension of bail. It wasn't a deliberate diversion on Keith's part, but that's how it worked out. As Keith had shown up at the police station but left without signing, he had fulfilled his obligations and by law, the guarantors were not constrained to pay *if* he absconded.

Time to go to Dymchurch.

27. ON THE RUN

Life tip: when you go on the run, don't run.
Keith left the police station and ambled unhurriedly along the road with the icy breath of the wind behind him and the busy morning traffic humming by. He turned left and passed the omnipresent eye at Lazard Brothers. It didn't matter that the camera was still watching. There are cameras everywhere, always watching. The Barbican rose up like a memorial to the past and he felt a dampness about the eyes. He passed Clive James in the lobby.

'Don't you have a coat, Keith? It's brass monkeys out there.'

'Warm heart, mate.' He turned back from the lifts as Clive was about to leave the building. 'Always nice to see you, Clive.'

'And you, mate.'

He stepped in the lift and stepped out again at the penthouse. Everything shone like young eyes and smelled of polish.

What do you take?

Nothing.

Soon as someone sees you with a bag over your shoulder, they know you're going somewhere.

He listened to the sound of his own footsteps on the hardwood floor as he made his way down the long corridor to the living room. He went up on his toes to reach two books on the third shelf. He took £1,000 in used tens and twenties from the hollow space in one and from the pages of John le Carré's *Smiley's People* he removed two bonds promising to pay the bearer £2 million. Keith's gaze ran along the shelves at the Capodimonte figures, the photos, the books. He noticed the new William Boyd novel *Brazzaville Beach* and decided to take it with him. A man carrying a book looks as if he's on the right side of the law.

He grabbed his car papers from the desk and changed his watch for the Patek Philippe with the square face. It looks like what it is: expensive; useful to trade or gift. He slipped the bonds into a Ziplock bag and scribbled a note to Mrs Primrose to explain that he was going to be away for a while, and that she should take the things from the fridge home with her. He thanked her for her kindness and left £100 in cash. He took a last glance out at the NatWest and a smile cracked his lips.

I said I was going to have you. And I did.

He rode the lift down to the garage where Rodney Miller was fiddling about with the keys hanging on a board. He took another ton from his wallet and stuck it in the top pocket of Rodney's blue overalls.

'Don't want any arguments from you, Rodders. I've got a question.'

'Bloody hell. Hundred nicker. Must be a bloody hard question.'

'I'll start easy. What's the name of that place where you stayed in Ramsgate?'

'The Sea View, right opposite the harbour. Lovely view.'

'Well, it would be, wouldn't it. I'm going away for a bit. You look after yourself.'

'And you, guv.' He tapped his overall pocket. 'You know something, you're the most generous bloke I've ever met.'

'What goes round comes round.'

Keith waved over his shoulder as he strode towards his racing-green, 2.4-litre Jaguar with the wood rim steering wheel, walnut dash and dark-green upholstery. The police wouldn't need to visit the DVLA to get his details. They knew the car. He knew the score.

She fired and drummed on the tick over, a low boom resonating over the walls as he lunged up the ramp, paused at the exit and left the Barbican not knowing if he would ever return.

···◆·•————•◆···

On the Run

If you are going to Ramsgate or Dymchurch, you take the same road south-east out of London. Where the road forks, Keith took a right and, just fifteen miles from one of the biggest cities on the planet, he was already in rural countryside on the way to Dymchurch.

He stayed on the backroads, easy on the pedal, through villages separated by stretches of winter trees, neat cottages with twigs of smoke motionless on the still air and empty fields with hedgerows iced in frost. He slowed to watch two girls on horseback at full gallop and remembered that night learning riding styles on a bar stool with Lester Piggott and Stevie Cauthen. Keith hadn't seen that much of the world. He'd been to America, Australia, a few countries in Europe, but nowhere could hold a candle to England with its big skies and making-do people still imagining they're fighting World War Two with humour and a stiff upper lip.

He stopped at the railway station in Tunbridge Wells where he found a photo booth and got his picture snapped, four black-and-whites with an expression he didn't quite recognise. *Come on, son, chin up. That's the discipline. Don't let your possessions possess you. Things are just things. When it's time to go, you up sticks and go.*

From the station, Keith crossed the road to the Post Office and collected the form for a British Visitor's Passport valid for one year for 'West European countries except surface travel to West Berlin'. At the end of 1989, they'd started to take down the Berlin Wall. Thatcher had gone. The wall had gone. The world was changing but the Passport Office still hadn't got round to printing new forms.

He drove on to Ticehurst, a tucked-away village where he had a pint of bitter with a steak and kidney pie for lunch at the Bell Inn. He borrowed a pen from behind the bar and filled in the passport form with the name Rodney Miller and an address in Bermondsey. On the title page of *Brazzaville Beach* he wrote the dedication:

For Rodney Miller,
Editor extraordinaire, bless you.
William Boyd, 1990

He returned the pen and asked for directions to the Post Office. He walked in the opposite direction until he was out of breath, turned and walked quickly back to the general store where the Post Office was located. Before he entered, he mussed up his hair, loosened his tie and took on an expression that was both amiable and anxious.

He waited his turn and passed the form and fee across the counter to a smiling middle-aged woman with a perm and red-framed glasses; he was relieved it wasn't a male jobsworth with a lifetime of disappointments and her at home telling him he was a waste of space. She checked the application, smiling, all good.

'Can I see your birth certificate?'

'Birth certificate?'

'It's necessary for identification.'

'Oh, God, I'm so sorry, I was in a rush to get out of the house,' he replied and took a breath. 'My wife's been in a road accident in Geneva. She's with the Red Cross. I completely forgot.'

'Do you have anything else?'

'No, no. I've made a stupid mistake. My old passport has expired.' He closed his eyes. He put his hand to his heart. 'It's all my own fault. I'm so stupid sometimes.' He sighed. 'All I have is this.'

He opened *Brazzaville Beach*.

'I'm a book editor.'

'For William Boyd?'

'Yes, he's a lovely man. The book is brilliant.'

He shrugged hopelessly as he looked back at the woman with the perm and brown eyes staring over the top of her glasses. And that's what he liked about the English. They keep to the rules but know that sometimes the right thing to do is break them. She inked the rubber stamp on her desk and brought it down like a judge with his gavel on a new one-year British Visitor's Passport, a sheet of thin cardboard folded to the size of a regular passport.

'Bon voyage,' she said. 'I do hope your wife is going to be alright.'

'Thank you. That's so very kind.'

On the Run

The caravan was just how he'd left it. He let himself in and sat with the door open for a few minutes smoking a cigar and planning his next moves.

Sergeant Smithers would have immediately alerted his boss that by some fluke – not *his* fault – Keith Cheeseman had complied with his bail conditions and reported in but left the station without signing the necessary form, relieving the bail guarantors of their obligations. DCS Dickinson and his agents would have broken down his broken door at the Barbican within the hour, searched the place, seen the note to Mrs Primrose and would be looking for a green Jag. If they had spoken to Rodney Miller, with any luck, the police would be belting down the M2 to Ramsgate.

As the one fingered by the FBI for extradition, the team from Operation Starling would spare no cost or effort to find him. Keith pushed back his cuff and glanced at the Patek Philippe. Nice watch. No time.

From beneath the insulated floor, he found the £2,000 he had stashed, two boxes of Montecristo No. 4s and a silver Cartier watch he'd bought for some girlfriend and forgotten to give to her. He changed into the tweed suit hanging in a laundry bag in the closet, and topped it off with a deerstalker that sat on his head like a flowerpot on a football. Keith surprised even himself when he turned to the mirror and found the booted and suited gangster transformed into a country gent. In a leather hunting bag that went with the outfit he had a change of underwear, a toilet bag with a hairbrush, toothbrush, toothpaste and an electric shaver.

Did the police know he had a caravan in a false name in a park in Dymchurch? It was hard to say, but he locked up and drove to Charlie Gray's place without looking back. Charlie was in the bar.

'Fuck me, it's Sherlock Holmes.'

'Cards on the table, Charlie. The Old Bill have got me on the bonds robbery.'

'Don't surprise me one bit.'

'I skipped bail two hours ago and I need to skip the country before the day's out. If you want me to bugger off, I understand completely.'

'Fuck off. That's not what mates do, is it? What do you need?'

'They'll be looking for my Jag. I need to borrow your Roller and drive down to Dover.'

'Bit showy for a getaway car?'

'That's the point. They won't give it a second look. Thing is, Charlie. They'll come here asking you questions, collusion, collaboration, all that stuff.'

'Fuck 'em. I ain't done nothing. Serving fish and chips every bloody night's a life, but it ain't *the* life, is it?'

'Let's have a quick one. A whisky,' Keith said. 'My car's outside. All legit. Papers are in the glove compartment. Keep it. Sell it. Tell the police I abandoned it. Whatever suits.'

Charlie poured two doubles. 'So, where you gonna go?'

Keith took a sip from his glass. 'Any suggestions?'

'You know I've got a place in Tenerife? It's empty. Just sitting there.'

'That's conspiracy to aide, support and assist someone suspected of committing a crime.'

'You a fucking lawyer? Do you want the fucking key or don't you?'

'I do. It's a life saver. I won't forget it.'

They crashed glasses together and swallowed their drinks.

'Bloody lovely outfit. I'll get the car key. There's a garage out back. Door's open. Stick the motor in there.'

Charlie Gray shouted to one of his staff to say he was going out for a couple of hours. Keith garaged the Jag and Charlie was in the driving seat of the yellow Roller, ready to go.

'What you doing?' Keith asked.

'I'm driving. You can have the apartment. You can kip with my bloody wife for all I care. But you ain't driving my fucking car.'

Keith climbed in with the hunter bag, deerstalker on his knees. Charlie backed up, turned around and set off along the coast to

On the Run

Dover. The wind whipped up white horses on the grey sea. It was mid-afternoon, nothing much on the road except two big blokes in a Rock an' Roller.

They had only done about five miles when Keith heard the whoop-whoop of a helicopter overhead. He bent to look out. It was a cop chopper, low over the road, swinging in the wind like a rocked cradle. In the distance, blue lights flashed and the sirens had the sound of the orchestra tuning up for Mahler's 'Ninth'. Rain splattered the windscreen and a convoy of police vehicles shot by on the other side of the road on their way to Dymchurch.

'Bloody hell, they were quick,' Charlie remarked.

'Secret service. Or the FBI. No one knew I had a caravan out here except Kerry, and she wouldn't have blabbed.'

Charlie turned away from the wheel for a moment, then looked back at the road. 'FBI?' he said.

'They're over here showing our cops which side is up. They want to take me back Stateside with them.'

'Don't do things by halves, do you, mate?' He dropped a gear and sped past a bread van. 'How are you going to get out of the country? They'll have your name at immigration.'

'Got one of those Visitor's Passports in a false name.'

'Don't you need a birth certificate for one of those?'

'Told the woman my wife was dying abroad.'

He laughed. 'And she gave it to you?' He pointed at a sign. 'Dover. Ten miles. Give me a call if you need anything. I'll be watching the news.'

28. FUNNY BONE

Keith had followed Robert Maxwell's financial dealings in the press without imagining he would be drawn into the tail end of the robber baron's mysterious demise.

The flamboyant owner of the *Daily Mirror*, the *New York Daily News* and the publishing house Macmillan, Maxwell's story had it all: vast sums of money, tricky deals on the Stock Market and his workers looted of their pensions. He fled on his 180-foot yacht *Lady Ghislaine* and vanished from the stern off the coast of Spain's Gran Canaria at 4.25am on 5 November 1991. His body was found by helicopters six hours later.

At the same time as pathologists were examining Maxwell in the mortuary, investment analysts on both sides of the Atlantic were studying the assets of the Czechoslovak orphan of the Holocaust who had arrived penniless in Britain as Ján Ludvík Hoch and built a business empire. Maxwell had kept his financial house of cards from falling by selling stock that was already pledged as collateral on loans and robbing the pensions paid in by his employees from the companies he owned. During a hectic six-month period, the value of Maxwell's publicly traded companies, Mirror Group Newspapers and Maxwell Communication Corp., went into freefall. He was in default on $1.6 billion in loans and bankers that had accepted the stock as collateral were asking for more security.

The day he left Britain for his last cruise around the Canaries, Goldman Sachs sold $2.2 million in Maxwell Communication Corp. shares, a move that depressed the price of the company's stock in such a way that bankruptcy was inevitable.

———◆———

The three-hour journey from Calais to Paris's Gare du Nord went by with the clackety-clack of the wheels beneath the carriage and William Boyd's prose as Keith turned the pages of *Brazzaville Beach*. Charlie had dropped him off at the passenger terminal in Dover where the immigration officer barely glanced at his Visitor's Passport and waved him through. The ferry rolled about in the choppy waters of the Channel but army life had prepared Keith for turbulence and he stood on the afterdeck watching the White Cliffs growing smaller with a twin sense of freedom and loss.

The Champs-Élysées was deserted as the taxi slid through the silvery streets and it was almost 10pm before he signed the register at the George V. The art-deco hotel was built in the twenties and had views of the Eiffel Tower. The concierge had wise eyes and a white moustache. With 100 francs folded in his palm, he moved heaven and earth to make Keith's brief stay commodious. His first task, nimbly executed, was to persuade the chef to stay on to cook Keith the Michelin-starred *Escargots de Bourgogne*, served in his suite with a bottle of red Burgundy.

He called Charlie while he was waiting for his food.

'It's all over the news. Car chases in Kent and Sussex. ITV had a picture of you that must have been taken ten years ago.'

'When I married Kerry. They like that one.'

'Is she alright?' Charlie asked.

'Oh, yeah, tough as old boots. We've gone our separate ways, but we're still fond of each other.'

'That's nice,' he said. 'Don't know what else to tell you, mate. Tenerife's a good bolt hole if you can get there.'

'That's the plan.' There was a knock on the door. 'Dinner's arrived. I'll be in touch.'

'Fucking enjoyed today, don't mind telling you.'

'You stay straight, mate. You've got a nice little thing going.'

Keith ate his snails and had to smile when he thought about Tom Dickinson in his big glasses surrounded by his team. He imagined Mervyn Parr itching to get his gun out and pop a couple of caps. The FBI had entrapped Mark Osborne, tracked down the bonds sent to Escobar and climbed over his terrace at dawn. They were on the ball. The British police were always congratulating each other and giving out certificates and commendations, but really they were extraordinarily amateur. He topped up his glass and drank a toast to that.

After breakfast Keith shed his tweed suit for Pierre Cardin slacks and a blazer in the hotel's menswear shop.

He snatched a bit of schoolboy French from his memory.

'*A quoi je ressemble?*'

'*Très bien. Un ajustement parfait.*'

Keith turned to his image in the three-way mirror and what he saw was a man back in his own skin. Louis, the concierge, had arranged his air ticket to Tenerife and a young Moroccan driving like Ayrton Senna taxied him out to Charles de Gaulle Airport with a change of clothes and toiletries in a new leather holdall. He had felt a bit down fleeing Blighty but one night in the City of Light and he was his old self again.

It was 6 November, the day after Robert Maxwell's dramatic fall, and the waiting lounge was crammed with journalists, writers with acid pens and photographers with lenses like riflemen on a firing squad. His flight to Tenerife went on to Gran Canaria and almost every seat was filled by reporters from all over the world, some of whom he recognised. He hid his face in his book and only looked up when the drinks trolley came down the aisle. The woman beside him kept turning in his direction.

'Do I know you?' she finally asked, and he tried on his Henry Nunn voice.

'I'd certainly like to think so.' He held out his hand for her to shake. 'Rodney Miller.'

'Shirley Hausman, *Daily Express*. Your face is familiar.'

'I edit books. I didn't know I was famous.' He showed her *Brazzaville Beach*. 'This is one of mine.'

She looked away. She had lost interest and they sat in silence drinking their gin and tonics until the plane touched down at Reina Sofía Airport. Keith grabbed his bag from the overhead locker and eased his way between the rows of hacks flying in like vampires to pick over the remains of Ján Ludvík Hoch.

He stepped out into a pleasant shirtsleeves afternoon and the taxi took just over an hour following the coast road to Puerto de la Cruz. The narrow lift took him up to the penthouse apartment with its hazy views of a solitary snow-capped mountain in the distance and the Atlantic stretching to infinity. Like the alpha-male chimps in Boyd's *Brazzaville Beach,* we are programmed to survive.

New day. New life. New name. A croissant with butter and jam. *Café con leche.* They went down a treat.

'*Otro, por favor.*'

'*Si señor, un momento.*'

The girl swivelled her hips and smiled. He liked Spanish people. They enjoyed the small things. They took time to chat and were happy staring up into the sky contemplating the great mysteries of the universe, which they knew damn well they were never going to solve. They did a few jobs in the morning, ate a big lunch and took a siesta. They went for a *paseo*, a little stroll, at sunset, and went to bed late after a bottle of Rioja and a few plates of tapas.

The first person he called was Kerry.

'Where the hell are you? You're in all the papers again.'

'Better you don't know. Call Charlie Gray for me. Tell him I've arrived ...'

'Charlie bloody Gray. You're in Tenerife. He's got a place out there.'

'I'm trying to keep a low profile.'

'You? Keep a low profile. That's a bloody joke. Why the hell have you buggered off? You do a runner if you've been sent down and you've got a chance of getting away. You don't do a runner when you may have got off.'

'And I may not have.'

'You're like a bloody big kid, you know that?'

'I did it because I could. Because that's what I do. There's one rule for them and one for us. I don't think that's right ...'

'It ain't right. But they can get away with it, you can't, Keith. You'll end up inside again.'

'That's the game. When I knew I could get away without the guarantors being liable I didn't think twice.'

'Jesus Christ. Look after yourself, you big idiot. I'll come and visit when they catch you.'

'I know you will. You're a darling.'

···◆—•————•—◆···

Kerry was right. Kerry was always right. But while ice rain gripped the streets of Bishopsgate, where he was due to sign his bail terms, he was in his underpants in a penthouse in Tenerife with the sun warming the windows and the shower spitting out water for two seconds then stopping again. There was a list of names of work people taped inside one of the cabinet doors in the kitchen. That's where he found PLUMBER – Del Boy.

He called.

'That Del Boy?' he asked.

'Yeah, who's calling?'

'Bloody funny name for a Spaniard?'

'That's because I'm from Wapping.'

'Best news I've heard all day,' Keith paused to take a breath. 'Rodney Miller, mate, got a problem with the waterworks ...'

'They've got bloody good doctors on the island.'

Keith had set that up for him and duly laughed. 'Shower don't work, mate, and all the pipes are clunking.'

'I should be able to sort that out.'

Keith gave him the address and the job was done within the hour.

'Best twenty quid I've spent since God was a boy.'

'Any time, Rodney, it's a pleasure.'

'You in a hurry?'

'Not particularly.'

'Let me take a shower and I'll take you out to lunch. I could kill a paella.'

They ambled down to the harbour and shared a bottle of Ribera del Duero, Keith's favourite red. The big square parasol with Ricard along the four sides shimmied in the breeze and the salty sea air carried the scent of saffron. Keith refilled their glasses.

'I thought you were supposed to drink white wine with fish?' Del Boy said.

'Nah, load of old rubbish. It's got no soul, no depth. The French made it up to get rid of all their white wine.'

'Typical.' Del sipped the wine. 'You going to be here long, Rodney?'

'How long's long? For a while. Might go into business. Always fancied being a plumber.'

Del had set himself up in Tenerife after his second marriage and had a young family. In the coming weeks, when he had jobs in Playa de las Américas, Los Cristianos and Los Gigantes, Keith travelled with him so he could see the south of the island. He'd give Del advice on how to do things he knew nothing about and Del held his chin as if considering his options and ignored him.

'You know something, Rodney, I think you're right, you'd make a bloody good plumber,' Del said. 'You just need to do the seven-year apprenticeship.'

'Blimey, sounds like a prison sentence. I'd rather rob banks.'

'I can just see you running out of a bank with a bag full of dosh.'

'No, mate, the secret is to walk out with two bags. Not that I know anything about that sort of thing. Like plumbing.'

Funny Bone

They'd drive back through the mountains and stop at tapas bars for a beer. Weekends, Keith often went with Del and his children, Alicia and Daniel, to watch Daniel compete in go-kart races. They never missed Tenerife home games and watched the team that season climb up *La Liga*, the Spanish football league.

Plumbers, doormen, Dean Martin, the Duke of Manchester, John Stonehouse: everyone, even Frankie Fraser, the gangland enforcer he'd shared the occasional cigar with in Parkhurst, was a complex mixture of good and bad qualities with the same potential for meanness and kindness. He'd once played chess with Frankie.

'Are you going to kill me if I win?'

'Damn right I will.'

'Thank Christ for that, I can't stand the bloody food in here.'

Frankie laughed. Keith won and survived to tell the tale. Everyone has a funny bone. Keith Cheeseman finds it and pulls at it like a harp string. He likes people and people can't help enjoying his company and liking him back.

One night in a bar he got talking to a rather gorgeous dark-eyed, dark-haired Swedish woman by the name of Pia Linstedt, the daughter of Sweden's great actor Carl-Gustaf Lindstedt. She insisted on taking him to her favourite Swedish restaurant and he endured the salty fish dishes for the sake of the good company.

Two nights later, he took Pia to an Italian restaurant. Then it was back to salt fish, the nights alternating through an international list of Tenerife's best restaurants and bars and finally Pia's apartment for salad and quiche.

'I'm leaving tomorrow, back to Stockholm,' she said. 'I'm going to miss the sunshine.' She paused and laid her palm on the back of his hand. 'And you, Rodney?'

'I'll still be here when you get back.'

'You're not going home for Christmas?'

'Seeing as you won't be here, I just might.'

'We must spend Chinese New Year together. I know a wonderful restaurant in Los Cristianos.'

'Swedish?'

'No, silly boy, Chinese.'

They walked down to La Orotava, the old port, to have breakfast in a café beside the customs house where the fishing boats unloaded and he borrowed Del Boy's car to drive her to the airport. From his pocket he took a small parcel wrapped in Christmas paper.

'This is for you.'

Inside the parcel was the silver Cartier he had brought with him from the caravan in Dymchurch.

'Rodney, it's beautiful. Thank you.'

'Happy Christmas.'

'I didn't get you anything.'

'I didn't expect anything.'

They hugged and he watched her stride off pulling her case on wheels. She paused as the glass doors opened and looked back to wave.

He drove back to Puerto de la Cruz and read the papers.

The Spanish autopsy on Robert Maxwell gave the probable cause of death as a combination of coronary artery disease and a plunge into the bitter cold seas of the Atlantic. The judge in charge of the investigation ruled out foul play but reached no conclusion as to whether Maxwell's death at age 68 was an accident or suicide. The *Daily Mirror* reported that Maxwell's business empire had gone into receivership with debts in excess of £1 billion.

Even the bonds couldn't have saved him.

Stella Rimington had taken the helm at MI5, the first woman to hold the post. Unemployment was up at 2.5 million and thousands of shops were defying trading laws and opening on Sundays.

He called Elaine Borg. Everything was tickety-boo. She was moving modest sums into the numerous accounts he had set up and those modest sums combined were becoming slowly more extravagant.

He lit a No. 4, sat for a moment staring out at the view, and wondered whether it was worth the risk taking a trip back for a couple of weeks.

29. '£290M CLUE TO HEADLESS CORPSE'

The 26 October 1991 was a clear bright day with a faint breeze and the leaves dropping in a palette of autumn colours. Colin Oliver would normally have taken the bus home but decided to take a leisurely walk from Cuckfield along Broxmead Lane to Burgess Hill. He did not imagine for one second that the events of the day would come back to haunt him long into the future.

On the way he needed a pee. He unlatched and closed the gate at the entrance to a field and made his way into Bolney Wood. He was miles from anywhere. There were no houses visible in any direction, no sign that anyone had stepped into those trees for years, except that in the undergrowth there was a rolled-up carpet. He was going to ignore it but on impulse, he pushed deeper into the thicket to take a closer look.

What he saw when he unrolled the carpet was a dead man with his head and hands cut off.

Colin froze. His heart pounded. He closed his eyes to block out the terrible sight. He took deep breaths to pull himself together, then set off on his shaky 62-year-old legs back across the field and down Broxmead Lane to Burgess Hill police station. He gave his statement to the desk sergeant, who gathered up every available constable in the Sussex Weald to search the woods. The body parts were never found. An ambulance took the decapitated corpse to the mortuary and Colin Oliver went home to listless nights and vivid nightmares.

The forensic report revealed that the partially dressed body wearing a shirt with a 'distinctive' logo and grey trousers had a distended belly and a star-shaped mole on the right thigh. Police authorities announced that they had identified the remains of Keith Cheeseman 'who was on the run from the FBI' and whose partner had been murdered in a gangland killing the year before.

Patrick Thomas was in the canteen at Belmarsh Prison when he saw a copy of the *Today* newspaper with the front-page headline: '£290m Clue to Headless Corpse'. He read the lurid account of Keith Cheeseman's mutilated body being discovered in the woods and what went through his mind was *they'll be coming for me next*. Was he safe behind bars? Not at all. There were nutters inside who would knife you for two packs of tobacco.

Thomas had been well paid to rob John Goddard of his bag of bonds back in May 1990, but however much crime pays, it is never enough, because crime, more than cash, is the addiction. He had never been charged or been a suspect of the bond's robbery and, that sultry autumn of 1991, he was on remand in Belmarsh after being found in possession of two kilos of cocaine worth – at the time – £30,000. Six months before, in March, Pat Thomas and David Summerville had been cutting up coke in the Greenwich flat they shared when the Drug Squad burst in and caught them with the white stuff on the table. One of the cops heroically licked his finger, dabbed it in the stash and rubbed it over his gums to be sure it was Inca's finest.

The duo were due in court two weeks later and, in that time, Thomas grew jittery and paranoid. He talked to prisoners he trusted at Belmarsh, a Category A prison in London's Thamesmead holding suspects involved in national security cases. When he got out, if he got out, should he go on the run? Head

'£290m Clue to Headless Corpse'

for a beach in Jamaica? Find the fairy with a plum in his mouth who had set him up to do the mugging? There was no shortage of advice. Criminals on the crimevine all know a thing or two. They know someone who knows someone who knows the score. Gossip is currency. They love to talk. Except for books, chess and violence there's not much else to do in prison.

Thomas and Summerville came before the judge in November. They faced the same charge. They had been caught 'white' handed with the marching powder ready to be spooned into gram-sized self-sealing bags. Open and shut? A dead cert? Not at all. The law is labyrinthine. The law is an ass – obstinate and stupid, as Mr Bumble says in Charles Dickens's *Oliver Twist*. Summerville was sentenced to seven years and, in a twist of fate that defies logic – 'like finding the Holy Grail on the Northern line' – Thomas was acquitted and went straight out to buy a gun.

He tried to withdraw cash from one of his several building society accounts, but the cashier asked for further proof of identity. Her reaction justified his feeling that he was being followed, as he told his stepsister, Rosemary. People were staring. There were cameras on the ceiling. He lost his nerve and fled back to the house he had moved into with Rosemary in Brockley's Turnham Road estate, a run-down part of South London. He kept thinking about the way Keith Cheeseman had been hacked up and dumped in the woods. If they could get to him, what chance did he have?

Thomas's ex-girlfriend and their daughter came to visit. He had expected them to stay overnight and was distressed when they left early. He drank a bottle of Jack Daniel's to calm his nerves. After Christmas, he did manage to withdraw some funds from another account and bought a gun from a contact in a pub.

On 28 December, Thomas met up with his old friend Jimmy Tippett Jnr. With the exception of Thomas, Tippett was the only person who had seen the bonds in neat colour-coded files before they were handed over to the actual organisers of the robbery.

Tippett, Thomas and some other friends began their night out at Sands in Blackheath. They went on to the Greycoat Boy in Greenwich and then to some night clubs in the West End. At each place, Thomas took a line of coke with a shot of Jack Daniel's. Tippet saw the pistol Thomas had tucked into the back of his trousers.

'What are you carrying that for?' he asked.

'Protection,' Thomas answered.

'Who's after you?'

'They all are.'

They moved on to the Ministry of Sound, the new club set up in a disused bus garage at the Elephant and Castle. When the bouncer went to frisk him, Thomas backed away and sprinted into the cold December night. Jimmy Tippett never saw him again.

What happened next is unclear, and we will never know for a fact. Thomas probably went straight home. No one ever came forward to say they had seen him. No camera recorded his image. His journey from the Elephant is a blank.

What we do know is that Rosemary woke with a start shortly before sunrise. She heard a scuffle in the hallway, then two gunshots. She rushed downstairs from her bedroom and found her brother lying across the threshold bleeding from a head wound. The front door was open and the eerie light of dawn was rising in the black silence. She called an ambulance. Thomas was dead before it arrived.

Detective Inspector Dave Bowen led the investigation. He learned that Thomas had £150,000 spread over various building society accounts, the bulk of the money paid in immediately after John Goddard was mugged. Detectives spoke to Jimmy Tippett and the other friends who had been with Thomas that night, but they knew nothing about the killing and had alibis for the hours after he fled from the Ministry of Sound. Tippett was arrested and questioned in connection with the bonds heist. The charges were dropped and the incident was recorded in his autobiography, *Born Gangster*.

'£290m Clue to Headless Corpse'

Police never found the gun Jimmy Tippett had seen on Thomas and never found the gun used by the assassin. Ballistic experts did confirm that the second bullet found lodged in the front door of Rosemary's council house came from the same weapon that killed her brother. The evidence pointed to a gangland hit, but Inspector Bowen swore on the Bible at the inquest that it was both his, and the opinion of his fellow officers, that Patrick Thomas had committed suicide.

The coroner returned an open verdict, and police had to quell friends and family members who rejected the decision and were ready to riot.

The urbane Peter Gwynn, head of City of London CID, told David Strahan from Carlton Television that it was 'good conjecture' that Patrick Thomas had committed the bonds heist based primarily on the discovery that he had a large sum of money spread over various building society accounts paid in on the days immediately after the robbery. Gwynn made no comment on Thomas's murder.

After eighteen months of investigations, Mr Dickinson had finally got his hands on a suspect involved in robbing the Bank of England, and he was dead.

Shortly after the shooting the police announced that they had mis-identified the Bolney Wood corpse and that it was not the well-known fraudster Keith Cheeseman. The investigation to find the murderer and the identity of the victim, codenamed Operation A23, employed 60 police officers and cost £150,000. Detectives led by DCI Peter Kennett searched the files of more than 100 missing men without finding a match.

In December, while Pat Thomas was running around London like a time bomb, police had a break when they found a copy of *Penthouse* magazine in an abandoned house two miles from Bolney Wood. It contained an article about dismembering bodies with numbers scribbled on the pages. They tracked down Gunter

Josef Knieper, from Dresden, Germany, who had rented the property. He was arrested in Spain in 1992, but there was no evidence to connect him with the murder.

On 2 August 1994, the remains of the headless corpse were buried at Western Road Cemetery, Haywards Heath, in a coffin marked 'Unknown Male'. The funeral was paid for by Mid Sussex District Council and was attended by representatives of the police, council and coroner's office. The case remains unsolved.

30. THE BENGAL LANCERS

Tenerife's problems were all in their own half. They'd had a run of luck that took them up the league, but the defence remained weak and the goalie was suddenly spending half his time picking the ball out of the back of the net.

'I thought they were going to top the league this year,' Del Boy said.

'You having a laugh? They're going to drop off the bottom at this rate.'

'Don't be such a pessimist.'

'You know what Mark Twain said?'

'No.'

'A pessimist is a well-informed optimist.'

'What's that mean?'

'No idea, mate.' Keith threw up his arms. 'Look at that, bloody gave it away.'

Tenerife were struggling against the mighty Real Madrid at their 22,000-capacity home ground, El Estadio Heliodoro Rodríguez López. It was almost a full house, the crowd alternatively cheering and booing. Flags filled the air. Someone was playing a drum. Keith loved the noise, the atmosphere, the passion and madness that makes soccer one of life's great pleasures.

Life didn't have to be complicated: a cigar, a glass of wine, a few good mates. He'd grown fond of Puerto de la Cruz with its cheerful barmen and the east wind that brought warm air and sprinkles of red sand from the Sahara. It was a Sunday afternoon, 19 January 1992 and Tenerife's eleven sloped back into the changing rooms with dropped heads and a 3–1 deficit.

'Told you,' Keith said. 'Fancy a drink?'

'No, got an early start tomorrow. I'll drop you home.'

It's a funny thing when your team loses, there's not much to say. They pushed along with the crowd to the car park. It took ten minutes to reach the gate and the road was blocked by fans with silent drums and folded flags. The cars honked. The fans shouted *puta madre*. We are programmed to win and losing strikes us as a personal insult. Even Georgie Best, after years at the top of his game, looked stricken coming off the pitch when his team got hammered.

Keith was going to tell Del Boy about the time when he owned Dunstable Town FC but held back. He enjoyed the anonymity of walking in Rodney Miller's shoes and, a lifetime later, when Del Boy and his wife Jo knew exactly who he was, they still called him Rodney. He stepped out at his apartment.

'Nice one, my son.'

'I'll pick you up Tuesday, Jo's doing her fish pie.'

'Hang on to that one. You got a winner there.'

Keith took the lift up to the penthouse and prepared a pre-prandial gin with a splash of tonic. He set it down on the table in the living room and sat gazing out at the view, the sun lowering without haste, the clouds gathering on the horizon. He fancied a nice baked *dorada*, sea bream, and would wander down later to the fish restaurants in the port.

He opened *The Economist*, and as he read the analysis of investing in sub-Saharan Africa, he had an idea. He could buy up the sand cheap, before it took flight to the Canaries, and turn Brighton's pebble beach into a soft red carpet. They could plant palm trees and fill them with green parrots. He'd read somewhere the world was getting hotter.

Who did he know in Brighton who'd have a flutter?

The intercom buzzed. He finished his drink, crossed the floor and pressed the answering device.

The Bengal Lancers

'Yes.'

'Hello. Is that Keith Cheeseman?'

Fuck it!

He tried his posh voice. 'Sorry, you must have the wrong address. Rodney Miller here. How can I help you?'

'This is Scotland Yard. Do yourself a favour, Keith, look over the balcony, then come back and open the main door for us.'

The L-shaped balcony covered two sides of the building. Keith peered down one side, then the other. The Guardia Civil, Spain's military police in olive-green uniforms and cheeky black hats, were down there with machine guns and snipers. There must have been twenty vehicles. He poured himself another gin and tonic and went back to the buzzer.

'Why don't you come up and have a chat.'

'That's good of you ... *Rodney.*'

English sense of humour. He loved it.

He pressed the button to open the main door to the building. He opened his own front door, stood back and listened as the lift slowly rose through the building. It had a maximum capacity of six, but ten men burst into the room all sweaty and dishevelled. He took a sip from his drink.

'I'll take a look, but I don't think I've got enough glasses for all of you.'

The first in was a dapper chap in an Armani suit and brown crocodile shoes. He introduced himself as Alain Barboteu, the head of Interpol. Next out were two grim reapers from Scotland Yard with expressions like kids who never got any Christmas presents. Behind them were two men in black with cocked guns, then a Guardia Civil officer as fat as a barrel in a red-and-yellow sash and masses of medal ribbons. He was joined by four more Spanish cops in different uniforms, moustaches and sub-machine guns. Keith shook his head.

'I don't see the Canadian Mounties? And where's the Bengal Lancers?'

He had a habit of taking serious things lightly and trivial things seriously. Scuffed shoes or a stain on a silk tie constantly stole his attention. The law coming with automatic weapons for a fraudster seemed absurd, even comical. He glanced around, glass in hand. Everyone was grinning and civilised. The men in black put their guns in their shoulder holsters and Keith remembered how the FBI had smashed into the Barbican like head bangers and still missed the 2 mil stuck in a book.

'I suppose this is a bit of a coup for you chaps. You'll be going out for dinner later to celebrate.'

'Trouble is, the banks are all closed,' Scotland Yard said.

'What are you doing going around arresting people on a Sunday?'

'So, you're not Rodney Miller, then?'

'What do you think?'

'We don't have any Mounties, but we've got our man,' he said, and took a long breath of Tenerife's warm sea air. 'Mr William Keith Cheeseman, you are being arrested and will be held pending an extradition request by the United States of America.'

'Held where?'

'Above my pay grade, I'm afraid.'

Alain Barboteu, reeking of *Gauloises*, accompanied the Guardia Civil to take Keith down in the lift. The others followed. Once they were all outside, Keith gave the Scotland Yard inspector 2,000 pesetas.

'Have a drink on me.'

And he took it.

Barboteu drew him to one side and put his arm around his shoulder. 'Keith, why didn't you tell us you were here? We could have sorted something out.'

'Is it too late?'

The Frenchman shrugged the way Frenchmen do and glanced at his watch. 'Three o'clock is always too late or too early for anything you want to do,' he said philosophically.

'Camus?'

'Jean-Paul Sartre.' He shrugged again. 'Hell is other people.'

Keith took his seat in the back of a car beside the Guardia Civil officer, two big men in the confined space wriggling their

The Bengal Lancers

bums to get comfortable. He turned with a nod, as you would on a train, and noticed that his companion had a similarity to the dictator Franco, who featured heavily in the portraits that hung on the walls of the bars in the mountains where he'd eaten tapas and drunk San Miguel with Del Boy. The journey took him to the north of the island and up through winding switchbacks to the prison called Esperanza – hope in Spanish.

He was kept in solitary for 24 hours. When he came out into the ground floor courtyard the following day, the first-floor walkway was packed with prisoners who burst into applause. They screamed '¡Olé! ¡Olé!' like he was a matador entering the bullring. A crossdresser in a red dress took the rose from between his teeth and threw it to him.

'Hola, guapo,' he called and Keith took a bow.

The £292 million bond haul converted was 35 billion pesetas – the largest robbery *ever*. The number was astronomical, phantasmagorical, the dream of every outlaw, racketeer, bootlegger and bandit who ever walked the planet. Keith had already made the local paper and the number was printed as a headline on the double-page spread.

The two Scotland Yard detectives appeared later that morning. They sat in a stuffy room with bottles of water on the metal desk, a tape recorder and open notebooks.

'Who organised the heist, Keith?' It was Detective Chief Inspector Mike Jones, the senior of the two in an old suit that needing cleaning, glasses pushed up on his brow and glazed green eyes like the fish that landed down at the port.

'You're asking me?'

'There's no one else here.'

'Do you talk to MI6?'

'What's that got to do with anything?'

'It's got everything to do with everything.'

'Don't be a mug, the more you help me, the more I'll help you down the line.'

'Can I get that in writing?'

'You're a cheeky bugger, you know that.'

'How'd you find me, anyway?'

Jones sat back and clasped his hands at the back of his head. 'Technology,' he replied.

'Machines always let you down in the end.' Keith smiled. 'I remember telling Clive James that one day when the lift wasn't working.'

Jones turned to his partner. 'You hear that, Jason? He knows Clive James.'

'We live in the same building. So, technology, was it?'

'Your old girlfriend wasn't as clever as she thought she was.'

'So it's not only machines that let you down.'

Elaine Borg had been arrested in what the *Sun* described as 'a plot to steal £5 million by hacking into the computer system of a top finance house in the capital'.

'Hendersons knew what she was up to right from the start,' Jones added. 'They traced her phone calls and here we are.'

'And here we are.'

'You're not doing yourself any favours clamming up. Everyone else is singing like a canary.'

'And I'm in the Canary Islands singing like Pavarotti.' He folded his hands on the table in front of him. 'Did you know, when he stays in a hotel they always move in a new bed and he has three security blokes who jump up and down on it to make it soft enough.'

'I suppose you know Pavarotti as well?'

'Nah, not really. We stayed one time in the same hotel in Manchester and had a drink at the bar.'

Jones looked at his empty notebook and shuffled his papers. 'What's this name, Cheeseman? Is that your real name?'

'Old English, mate. Cheesemans made cheese. While you Joneses were picking onions and shitting in the fields, we were in business, the middle-class, paying our taxes.'

'You talk a lot and say nothing.'

'Better that than you keep asking me questions and me saying no comment. No comment. No comment. You'd hate that.'

DCI Jones looked at his companion and switched off the tape recorder.

'I've got a wife and two kids. My boy's doing his A levels. He wants to be a human rights lawyer – that's the truth.'

'I don't doubt it.'

'If I go back with nothing, I'll get a sideways promotion from Scotland Yard out to some dump like Luton.'

'Do you mind. I was born in Luton, as it happens.'

'You know what I mean. Give me something.'

'That's not fair, Mike, pulling at my heart strings like that. You know I'm an old softie.' He took a swig of water. 'I'll tell you what I'll do. I'll find something that's better for you to take home than a stick of rock with Tenerife down the middle.'

'Stick of rock,' he said, shaking his head of thin, greying hair. He turned to Jason. 'What do you reckon?'

'Fucking hot in here. Let's go and have a swim. Start again tomorrow.'

There was snow on the ground in London and a heated pool in Tenerife. Scotland Yard was in no hurry.

···◆·•————•◆···

Keith returned to his cell where he found a red rose in a glass of water left by the crossdresser. Not a sign of affection, but respect for nicking 3.5 billion pesetas. The rumour had spread. He was in all the papers, a legend in his own jailtime.

Over the next two days, in their interviews the London cops switched their attention to Patrick Thomas.

'Where did you first meet him?' DCI Jones asked.

'Never met him.'

'That seems unlikely. You know who he is?'

'Course I do. It was in all the papers. Shot in the head on his doorstep. Professional hit.'

'Suicide, according to the coroner.'

Keith laughed. He had followed the story of Thomas's demise and reached his own conclusions, not that he had any intention of sharing them with DCI Jones and Jason Garvey, his sergeant.

Thomas had been groomed to carry out the robbery because he was Jamaican and fitted a mugging profile. He walked away from the drugs rap because out on the street there was a chance that he led them to those passing the bonds. When he was no longer of use, he was eliminated. It wasn't a gangland killing. It had all the hallmarks of an MI6 operation to protect the string pullers, the people out of reach, the people who own the country – the top dogs inside the Bank of England who planted the bonds and had set up the heist in the first place. Keith thought it odd that Scotland Yard hadn't considered the possibility.

'Ask yourself this,' he said, and Jones lowered his glasses as he leaned forward. 'Why would Pat Thomas kill himself?'

'Why does anyone kill themselves? Fed up with life. I mean, we all feel like it sometimes.'

'Well, you would, being a copper,' Keith said. 'He'd just been let out of jail. He had some money in the bank. He'd have been looking to hook up with something new.'

'He was paranoid.'

'Course he was. He was being watched – I know how it feels. But it still doesn't make any sense. Go back and read the papers. Your lot said at the inquiry Thomas fired two shots, the first to test the gun. That's tommyrot. If you are going to off yourself, you don't take a practice shot into your sister's front door, you just do it. You rev yourself up. When you're ready, you pull the trigger – once. And one more thing: they never found the gun.'

'What's your point?'

'The point is, Inspector, the villains you're looking for are Establishment people, people you salute and look up to,' he replied. 'Think about it. Why were Pat Thomas and the other bloke stuck in Belmarsh? That's where you put people who are a danger to the state. They were druggies. They were only a danger to themselves.'

'I suppose you know the answer to that as well?'

'When Thomas was inside, he would have talked. They *always* talk. And there are always snitches bartering gossip for a better cell or two packs of king-sized. If you'd have hauled the kid in, he would have given you everything he knew about his contact, the one who set up the robbery. They had to protect their man and to do that, they had to get rid of Thomas.'

Jason Garvey had been taking notes. The two coppers sat back. Jones pushed his glasses back up over his brow.

'Bloody hard to know with you, Keith, if it's all bullshit, or you really believe this stuff.'

'Thing is, Mr Jones, you know as well as me that your lot don't talk to the spooks because the spooks are too high and mighty to talk to you. Patrick Thomas fell into that empty space.'

···◆·•————•·◆···

Jones and Garvey went off for their swim and, that same afternoon, Keith was taken to the visitor's room where Kerry in a pink-and-white-striped summer dress stood hands on hips, waiting for him.

'You're a sight for sore eyes,' he said.

Her bottle blonde locks were up in a bouffant and she wore an expression that was somewhere between I told you so and poor old Keith stuck inside again. She put a copy of the *Sun* on the table.

'I want you to pay special attention to the picture on page three, darling,' she said. 'You know I was searched before they let me in.'

'Body searched?'

'Don't be so damned cheeky.'

Keith opened the paper.

'Not now, Keith. I didn't come all this bloody way to sit here while you read the paper.' She fluted her brows. 'Page three.'

He knew Kerry and he knew she knew he wasn't a bloke who gawped at teenage tits.

'I'll take a gander in my spare time.'

'I'm surprised you've got any. I've seen more bloody coppers in Tenerife than you can wave a stick at. As for bloody journalists, they're as thick as thieves.'

'I think you'll find that's a mixed metaphor.'

''Ark at him, Mr Know-it-all. You're the one who's in the clanker.'

She paused and lit a fag. He pointed at the sign.

'No smoking in here.'

'What they going to do, put me in prison?' She blew out a stream of smoke and pulled out a box of Montecristo No. 4s from her bag. 'Almost forgot. These are for you. You know they cost half as much here as they do at home.'

'You should move here.'

'Nah, can't take an old bird like me out of London. You should never have done a runner, Keith. I told you that. You never bloody listen. Now the Americans want you over there and you ain't on home soil to defend yourself. They treating you alright?'

'Oh, yeah, nice people.'

'Charlie Gray sends his regards. They went to the hotel to ask him how come you were staying in his apartment and he told them to fuck off.' She puffed on her fag, flicked the ash on the floor. 'They said he could make a complaint about you breaking and entering if he wanted to. You can imagine what he told them.'

'One of the best, Charlie.' He took a drag from her cigarette and coughed. 'You remember that night we had fish and chips in his restaurant?'

'Course I do. Good times, Keith. If you'd stayed straight we'd still be together.'

'You reckon?'

'No, probably not.'

They laughed. They were friends. You look back and that's what matters, the people you cared for and who cared for you.

The Bengal Lancers

They nattered on until a guard came in. He waved away the smoke. Kerry held her finger to her lips and gave him twenty Rothmans.

'Enjoy page three, darling,' she said.

Back in his cell with the rose on the ledge, he sat on his bunk and looked closely at Georgina on page three. She had just turned eighteen and was studying for her A levels at the grammar school in Tunbridge Wells. If Georgina wanted to be a human rights lawyer, it was all the rage, she had all the accoutrements she needed.

He looked closer and realised the photograph was slightly thicker than the rest of the page. He picked around the edge and peeled it back. Concealed inside were three $100-dollar bills.

31. FAKE NEWS

Andy Warhol said everyone gets fifteen minutes of fame. Keith reckons he got a full half-hour with journalists waiting in line to interview him outside the gates of Esperanza. He told them sweet FA, just funny stories and anecdotes. The man from the *Daily Express* had the good grace to slide a bribe in a distinctive yellow box across the table.

'Have you always smoked Montecristos?' he asked.

'You've done your research, then?'

'I read it in the *Sun*, to be honest.'

'Unusual quality for a journalist,' Keith responded. 'And to answer your question, I started out smoking Embassy Gold, which we pinched from the off-licence when I was a boy. Then I was out having lunch at Simpson's one day, this was years later, with Nigel Broackes and Vic Matthews, Lord Matthews to you, son, back when he owned your paper.'

'Before my time.'

'Everything's before your time. Anyway, I told Vic I was having problems raising funds for my building business and he said: "Smoke bigger cigars."'

'"And buy yourself a new Roller," Nigel suggested.'

'"You're not listening," I told him. "I don't have any money." "Get the car on HP and stick a big cigar in your gob. Money attracts money," Vic said, and opened a box of No. 4s.'

'You took his advice?'

'And his cigar. Vic Matthews wasn't one of those posh gits with a silver spoon up his jacksy. Served as an able seaman in the war and started out as an office boy. He was self-made. Those are the people to listen to.'

The lad scribbled in his notebook and Keith tapped his finger on the table as he leaned forward.

'Now you're on the *Express*, you don't want to try and be the editor, you want to be the proprietor. That's where the power is.'

'I never thought of that.'

'Power's contagious. Reporters are around it all the time. They all catch it in the end.'

'And what about you, Keith?'

'I'm happy being what I am.'

The clock on the wall showed 10.30am. Time was up. The man from the *Express* left through the visitor's door, still writing in his notebook. Keith exited out the back way where two guards were waiting. The protocol was to give him a search but Keith was never in prison long before the guards dropped all that. A smile, a bit of courtesy and they just waved you through. He opened the box.

'*Toman dos, son grandes.*'

It's an old joke: Take two, they're big. Each of the guards tucked a couple of cigars in their top pockets.

'*Gracias, Señor Dinero.*'

'*No pasa nada. ¡Viva la libertad!*'

He had picked up a bit of Spanish, which was going to serve him well when he was transported to the mainland.

David Strahan from Carlton Television appeared with his camera crew. He had already interviewed Kerry – she was loving it – but Keith kept mum. He had been linked to Elaine Borg's arrest and was unsure how that was going to play out.

····◆·•————•◆····

Back in October, when Elaine paid a visit to Keith at the Barbican with John Miller, she was confident that no one at Henderson Financial Investment monitored her activity.

'None of the senior people even know how computers work.'
'You're sure about that?'
'I promise, Keith. When I'm at my desk, no one even looks at me.'

What they planned was to transfer sums between £50 and £100 from high-net-worth accounts into the twenty dummy accounts Keith had opened. The sums were so modest they assumed they would go unnoticed, but would quietly rake in about £1,000 a day.

Safe as houses? Watertight? You can't plan for every eventuality, every misstep and Act of God. There is a tendency to overestimate yourself and your partners and underestimate Johnny Law and happenstance. That's the risk, the caffeine charge that makes crime addictive. Keith had always had doubts about this one but he closed his eyes and jumped.

The scam ran smoothly to begin, but Elaine was not aware that Hendersons regularly set up internal checks without the employees' knowledge, and her illicit activity was spotted. The Fraud Squad was called in and the smart boys in anoraks installed a hidden camera that recorded every stroke Elaine made on her keyboard. They also tapped her phone to trace her friends and contacts. They were in no hurry to gather evidence and used the investigation as a training exercise over the next three months.

Hacking was a relatively new way to rob banks. Mark Tantam of Touche Ross, the management consultants, told the *Financial Times* in 1993 that 'against other types of fraud, computer fraud is very small'. Most embezzlers were insiders with legitimate access to the system. 'In my experience, hackers are technology enthusiasts who want the intellectual challenge of working through the system,' said Mr Tantam. They are a nuisance but, he predicted, 'are unlikely to start moving money around the banking system'.

In the same article, fraud expert DCI Ken Farrow said the typical pattern is one of a disgruntled employee with knowledge of how to get into the system. 'He or she will work with one or more outsiders who may be organised criminals,' he said. 'We have known it to happen that people are approached in pubs after they boasted that they could take their employer for a fortune.'

The Fraud Squad listened in on Elaine's chats with Keith in Tenerife and, in a rare moment of international coordination, as the Guardia Civil, armed with assault weapons, surrounded Keith's apartment on Sunday, 19 January 1992, the Old Bill knocked on the door at Elaine Borg's cottage in Chelmer Village. It was one degree above freezing, the path slippery with melting ice, the sky grey like an old worn blanket. The cold breath of the two policemen condensed in vapor cones.

'Elaine Borg?'

'Yes ...'

'We're from the City of London police. May we come in?'

'Why? Yes. No.' Her voice lifts. 'What's all this about?'

It is the immediate reaction when criminals are caught. They can't believe it. The survival mechanism kicks in and they deny it. They deny everything. They wonder if they can slam the door and escape through the back window. The blood drains from their face. Their shoulders sag. Like a dropped vase, their dreams are shattered into a million pieces.

'I think it would be better to speak inside.'

Elaine opened the door fully and let them in.

She was arrested with what the newspapers described as 'an unnamed man'. She collected her handbag, put on a winter coat and was driven to London's City Magistrates' Court. She was charged under the Computer Misuse Act, which covers unauthorised access to computer systems with the aim of assisting a more serious crime, such as fraud or blackmail.

Keith suspected the unnamed man was John Miller, who would have provided information about him, Keith, to avoid being charged as an accessory. Miller then eagerly earned a few bob telling the press that Keith had 'forced him to sign a hire purchase agreement on a Mercedes, and then went on the run without paying his wages as a driver'.

None of this was true, but when the reporters sat across the table at the visiting room in Esperanza and asked for Keith's side of the story, he confirmed and denied nothing. The more you say, the more the words can be reshaped like plasticine to turn an elephant into a monkey and make two plus two equal five. The problem with John Miller was that he wasn't a villain with a villain's astuteness and subtlety. Miller was a bottom-feeder, a chancer, the man in the pub who talks as if he knows what's what and no one listens – except the tabloid journalists.

After eight weeks on remand, on 17 March 1992, Elaine Borg stood before Judge Richard Gee at Snaresbrook Crown Court and pleaded guilty to 'conspiracy to steal, and unauthorised access to, computer material with intent to commit a further offence'. The prosecution described her as a computer systems programmer who 'had devised a plan to hack into the accounts of company clients together with a male partner who was a known criminal based in Spain'.

The word 'hacker' to describe cybercrime was new and the moment the name Keith Cheeseman was mentioned in connection with the fraud, the tabloids reached for their biggest fonts for their headlines.

The *Sun* loved the story and ran with it daily with black-and-white shots of Keith with the Dusky Maiden and his arm around the shoulders of George Best. With his large head, ready smile, smart suits, distinctive ties and a twinkle, you wouldn't miss Keith in a crowd. He was on nodding acquaintance with the Queen Mother. When he asked Frank Sinatra to modify his language, Ol' Blue Eyes sent him tickets for his next show. He was a presence, a one off; a complex blend of cunning and compassion; wisdom and nonchalance; of acumen swindling banks and stupidity getting caught. That was the game. The way Keith poured a glass of wine or lit a cigar had a certain style, one that made you think that this was a man who knew how to enjoy himself, knew that this short, brutal life should be lived as if a bomb is about to explode and never mind the fallout.

···◆·●————●·◆···

Newspaper reports from the period make a fascinating case study of journalism in the 1990s and show how tabloid coverage of the period sowed the seeds of fake news and alternative truths a generation later. The fact that Keith had set up the fraud in such a way that only small sums went into the dummy accounts didn't make for catchy headlines. The press in response grabbed any number from the air.

On 21 March 1992, the *Sun* wrote that 'Keith Cheeseman was to be quizzed about a plot to steal up to £5 million by hacking into the computer system of a top finance house in the capital'.

Tony Thompson, author of *Gangland Britain*, upped the ante in an article in the *Independent* on 31 March 1992 under the heading 'King of the Sting'. 'Once they [the accounts] were opened she [Elaine Borg] would program the computer to credit the false accounts with £15 million. Then, after the money had cleared, it would be spirited away into offshore bank accounts.'

Nice big numbers, but what the coverage lacked was sex.

Not a problem.

The papers characterised Keith and Elaine as Heathcliff and Cathy from Emily Brontë's *Wuthering Heights*. He was the dark mysterious interloper and she the 'starry-eyed perfect stooge with a cunning plan to become rich beyond her wildest dreams'.

After 'he'd seduced her' they went to posh wine bars for intimate dinners. 'The divorcee from Chelmsford, Essex, soon became obsessed with the con man who already had a long list of scams under his belt. Although he was 59 [in fact he was 49], tubby and balding, he was pure charisma. As one of his ex-wives put it "He could charm crocodiles from the mud."'

Elaine's infatuation 'knew no bounds'. She 'never suspected he had no intention of sharing the booty. Once the money was stashed, Cheeseman planned to disappear with the lot.'

What's interesting about the last quote from the *Independent* is that the writer could not possibly have known if this were true or not unless Keith had made a public confession. It was pure invention. Fake news.

The police spokesman said in court that 'Elaine Borg was unlikely to have set up the scheme on her own'. She was an unfortunate dupe, and Judge Richard Gee took pity on her. 'You fell under the spell of an international con man,' he said and, 'after careful consideration', gave her an eighteen-month sentence suspended for two years.

'So now Elaine sits at home, jobless and living with the consequences of losing her heart and her mind to a charismatic, though ruthless crook.'

····◆·●────●·◆····

Judge Richard Gee had his own brush with the law in November 1995 when he was accused of a £1-million mortgage scam allegedly committed while he was a solicitor. The case was heard at the Old Bailey four years later, when he pleaded not guilty to charges of conspiracy to defraud banks and building societies by falsified mortgage deals and obtaining services by deception.

Prosecutors claimed that between 1980 and 1989, Judge Gee played a vital role in a string of 'utterly bogus transactions'. They alleged that he was involved in a plot to obtain mortgages on properties at residential interest rates, then let the properties to businesses at a profit.

From November 1995, when he was arrested, he had been suspended on full pay amounting to £300,000 paid by the taxpayer. His defence cost £806,000, 'of which he is thought to have paid about £100,000, with the rest coming from legal aid', according to legal correspondent Clare Dyer in her piece in the *Guardian*, 18 December 1999, under the heading 'Judge quits amid new allegations'.

After a 76-day trial, the jury failed to reach a verdict and Gee escaped a second trial by producing medical evidence from psychiatrists that he was a suicide risk. After the trial, a Metropolitan Police spokesman said that Fraud Squad officers were carrying out an investigation into 'the falsifying of claims to get legal aid'.

In October 1998, after the jury failed to agree on a verdict, 'the Attorney General, John Morris, caused an outcry when he placed a permanent stay on any further prosecution'.

32. SEÑOR DINERO

In jail Keith was popular with the staff and prisoners, but the language barrier meant he couldn't help men write letters or keep everyone amused in the *cantina*. Just as it was in the UK, most convicts had psychological, educational and addictive problems. What those men needed were all the things poverty denies and the system was designed in such a way that those things would never be forthcoming.

Being linked to the biggest bank robbery in history made him a folk hero, but he was a lonely hero in Esperanza with that uneasy sense of waiting, of the sand in the hourglass slipping by and nothing happening. The FBI was determined to whisk him off to the United States, but to the annoyance of the Spanish judge, when Keith appeared in court the American lawyers failed to present the correct documentation. There was also some resistance to make extradition easy because a Spanish doctor, in what turned out to be a case of mistaken identity, had recently been shot dead in Mexico by the FBI.

After the fruitless interviews with DCI Mike Jones and his partner Jason, Keith believed the palpable silence from the UK meant that those who had planned and were profiting from the bonds theft did not want him to appear at the Old Bailey, where everything he revealed would enter the public domain. He had counted 427 bonds that night at Henry Nunn's house, not 292. The tabloids had painted him as the criminal mastermind behind the robbery, which he wasn't, and those who were wanted to make sure Keith Cheeseman did not rise for the judge in an English court.

Someone had got to Mark Lee Osborne. Someone had got to Patrick Thomas. Two shots each time. These people didn't mess about.

He strolled down the corridor to his cell. He was reading *Animal Farm* in Spanish. He knew the story. It was easy to follow, but his eyes were tired. He closed the book and stretched out on his bunk. Winter had turned to spring. The afternoons were hot and humid. The water stains on the wall had dried in green contours like a map of the world. The ventilation shafts carried competing smells from the kitchen and latrines, fish, poo, vomit. Sometimes the electricity failed and the darkness was tactile and black. Prison sounds are universal and seem louder in darkness. The rattle of keys and chains, electric doors closing with a cushioned thump, the rumble of water pipes, dominoes slapping tabletops echoed in the beat of passing boots, guards yelling and the occasional scream from some lost soul who has been stabbed or just can't take it anymore.

'*¡Déjame salir! ¡Déjame salir!*' they cried. 'Let me out! Let me out!'

In the next cell, the Italian drug smuggler with the tattoo of a question mark on his neck played opera at full blast on a cassette and Keith remembered that night at *La Bohème* with Henry Nunn. They had gone to Groucho's for dinner and discussed Puccini's themes, the role of the artist, the narcissism of poets, the meaning of love. Henry was as tricky as a box of frogs with a mind like the ball that bounces over a roulette wheel. The bonds theft had blasted through the banking world like a raging storm and Henry was the calm eye at its centre. Kerry had tried to phone him but the number was out of service. Keith had managed to speak to her on a dodgy line from London and hearing her voice always cheered him up.

He picked up his book again as a guard with a grand moustache tapped on the open door. He entered and made a scribbling motion in the air.

'*Lo siento.* I sorry. You go.'

The guard had a form that had to be signed. Forests across the planet were vanishing and Keith had a hunch it was due to prisons with the endless documents forever being signed, stored in steel cabinets and never read. It was prison routine: forms, fights and transfers. He had been driven to Esperanza from Puerto de la Cruz and a van was waiting outside to take him back through the hills with their carpet of tiny yellow flowers and along the coast to Penitentiary II in Santa de la Cruz de Tenerife, the capital, in the south of the island.

Prisoners like to think of themselves as rebels, outlaws, men of the edge. In truth most were conformists, comfortable with the daily rites and rituals that brought order to their lives. They grew nervous being moved and rarely understood why, although the reasons weren't complicated. Often, it was to ease overcrowding, but mainly it was to prevent gangs organising their activity inside the prison. Vulnerable and high-profile offenders were moved to keep them safe. More than once, Keith had been transferred as a punishment when he stood up for other prisoners' rights. It was good for morale when he was the jester, and it irritated the authorities no end when he got serious.

The men came out on the walkway and rattled their tin mugs against the metal landing. They cheered and clapped. The cross-dresser did a repeat performance throwing a rose.

'*Adios, guapo.*'

One of the guards brought him his laundry, freshly washed and pressed, and he stepped out into a warm spring morning with a hint of jasmine in the salt sea air. The road curled like a corkscrew down to the coast and it was a pleasure seeing the fishing and pleasure boats bobbing in the harbour.

The gates opened and his new Governor was waiting in person on the steps outside the admission block.

'*Bienvenido, Mister Keets.*'
'*Estoy contento estar aquí.*'
'*Hablas español.*'
'*Estoy aprendiendo.*'

'*Excelente.*'

The Governor threw out his arm with pride. The prison, built three years before, in 1989, was open-plan, with red-tiled roofs on white-stucco buildings like the holiday villas English plumbers and train drivers were buying on time shares. Penitentiary II was close to the soccer stadium where he'd watched Tenerife crushed beneath the boots of Real Madrid. A short walk from the main gate was one of his favourite restaurants, La Aceituna (The Olive), where he had spent starry nights in candlelight with Pia Linstedt. While he was in prison, she arranged to have Keith's favourite dishes brought in from La Aceituna.

He filled in some more forms and it was time for tea in the canteen where the prisoners stood and clapped when he entered. A good-looking bloke approached and shook his hand.

'We heard you were coming, bloody good to have someone English here to talk to.'

'This looks like the beginning of a beautiful friendship. Keith Cheeseman.'

'Wayne Lineker.'

They sat and chatted. It soon came out that Wayne was the brother of Gary Lineker, England's football captain, Tottenham Hotspurs star, the striker who never got a red card.

'You must have got one to be in here,' Keith said.

'Rubbish ref, in my opinion,' Wayne replied. 'I shouldn't even be here.'

'They all say that, son,' Keith said, and he laughed.

'I should have stuck to football, I suppose.'

'Me, too,' said Keith, and Wayne laughed again. 'I wasn't always out of shape, you know. I played for the Gunners and scored a hat-trick in the cup final in 1963.'

'Hang on a minute, you played for the Gunners?'

'Not Arsenal, the Royal Artillery Gunners in the army cup final,' Keith explained, and Wayne's sceptical expression went back to normal. 'Funnily enough, we did play Arsenal once at Highbury, Gunners against the Gunners, just like a bloody war. I scored two goals and after the match, Billy Wright, the Arsenal manager, asked me about my plans. I told him I had trials coming up for Birmingham, Everton and Borussia Dortmund. He told me not to sign for anyone else yet as he was interested in signing me for Arsenal.'

'Why didn't you stick with it?'

'No money in it. The wages were nothing back then.'

'The money's big now, but they have to work for it.'

Wayne could have gone pro, the same as his brother.

'Barry, my dad, reckoned I was a better player, but Gary was dedicated. He's got real persistence.'

'Secret of life, mate.'

'You're right there. I couldn't put up with the early morning training sessions and it was always bloody raining where we grew up in Leicester.'

Wayne went into business instead. He opened what he called the World Famous Lineker's Bar in Tenerife in 1988, and launched a string of sports-themed bars and pubs that appealed to the millions of thirsty Brits abandoning Clacton and Blackpool for sangria holidays in Spain.

Business was booming and he had been charged on tax issues. He managed to walk away with a clean sheet and didn't serve jail time proper until 24 April 2006, when he was sentenced to two-and-a-half years at Southwark Crown Court. Wayne had pleaded guilty to smuggling pesetas and escudos worth £220,000 into Britain between 1999 and 2001, avoiding taxes of about £90,000 – which Judge Stephen Robins ordered him to pay.

Wayne was a businessman and businessmen have a complicated relationship with tax. They pay wages, rent, energy bills, the builders and painters who keeps their gaffes looking smart. They look for loopholes to lessen their taxes and sometimes loopholes turn into black holes that swallow every penny. They don't see tax as an obligation, a public service, but a game of Texas hold 'em. Keith had rich mates who would pay lawyers £20,000 to avoid paying £18,000 in tax. And even richer mates who kept their funds offshore and still complained that the roads were broken when they didn't pay any tax at all.

Only poor people pay their tax, always on time, normally out of their wage packets, without complaint and for reasons that are complex and deeply ingrained. Worrying about what 'people are going to say' and 'what the neighbours might think' is always in the minds of working people. They aren't afraid of failure. They are afraid of success and how they would have to make excuses to their friends if it ever came their way.

33. THE UNTOUCHABLES

When Keith was transferred to Penitentiary II, he was accompanied by two guards, and they stopped on the way for a round of *carajillos* – black coffee with brandy. Keith's treat.

Unlike Esperanza, HMP Wandsworth and the unknown jails calling his name from the future, the country club prison in Santa Cruz did have teachers, doctors and psychologists working on education and re-entry programmes for men who had not chosen crime as a lifestyle – like Keith – but had drifted into it through a lack of guidance and choices. They weren't detained for bank fraud but social security fraud, shoplifting, nicking cars.

Being a legend with a fabled £292 million stash, Keith was trusted to run the prison commissary where inmates bought their hygiene items, stamps and snacks. The guards corrected his Spanish and he was allowed to wander around the gardens as if it were his own country estate. He could have called Martin Newman to set him up with a getaway car on the perimeter and walked out of the gate at any time. He would have paid a fisherman to take him from the Canaries to Morocco … then where? Maybe Brazil to join Great Train Robber Ronnie Biggs. That would have been an earner with the tabloids.

Why didn't he? The people behind the bonds robbery weren't villains, they were more dangerous than that. He wanted to put the caper behind him, keep shtum, do the time – but there was another, more convoluted reason. The unsolved murder of Mark Osborne weighed on his conscience and he didn't want to leave Spain, where he had been consistently treated with respect and courtesy, while there was the slightest risk of violence hanging in the air.

····◆·•————•◆····

One warm afternoon, after a good lunch from La Acietuna, he was taken by car with two guards to the magistrates' office where he was told that the US government was still processing his extradition and he was being moved to the mainland to appear at a hearing in Madrid.

He collected his cashmere from the laundry and before sunrise shook hands with the morning shift guards Pepe, José, Santiago, Carlos and Rafa, who had a tear in his eye as he took Keith in *un abrazo fuerte.*

'Adios, Señor Dinero.'

The Guardia Civil were waiting. They came heavily armed in a dark-blue van with bars on the windows. Prisoners in the first-floor cells raised clenched fists and he felt like George Orwell going into battle during the Spanish Civil War. He was leaving good friends and good memories behind in Penitentiary II and came away with the feeling that prisons dedicated to rehabilitation are far more cost effective than those designed for punishment.

The gate slid open. The van accelerated away as the sun rose and lit the empty streets. They turned the corner towards the sea front and he watched the waiters spreading linen cloths on the café tables ready for another warm day in Santa Cruz. He was marched across the tarmac at Tenerife airport and strapped into a military Hercules plane like Hannibal Lecter in *The Silence of the Lambs* – an image which took him back to a convivial lunch with Anthony Hopkins at Langan's Brasserie some twenty years earlier. When he made fun of this foolishness they tightened his chains. They landed in Seville, not Madrid, as he had expected, and he was sure the FBI must have arranged the transfer.

Two vehicles, one filled with commandos armed for war, left the airport with spinning blue lights and Keith saw nothing of

The Untouchables

the ancient city except the spires and towers of churches and castles. The convoy drove from Seville to Granada before entering a national park and came to a halt at a remote, high-walled compound in Albolote. The building with polished stone walls had once been the stables of a royal palace.

His reputation had preceded him. There was no clapping or red roses being tossed, but within 24 hours he had found his way to the top table with Roberto Escobar – Pablo Escobar's brother – and Jesús Gil, the former mayor who had turned Marbella into a private fiefdom and was in jail charged with real estate corruption and a cash-for-votes scandal that saw €670 million paid in bribes from municipal funds.

Apart from being in jail for fraud like Keith, Jesús Gil was also the former owner of a football club – Atlético de Madrid. Roberto was a keen player and former world-ranked racing cyclist known as Osito – Little Bear. They both spoke some English, Keith spoke some Spanish and they became known as *Los Intocables,* The Untouchables.

Roberto had escaped from prison in Colombia where he was accused of illegal possession of arms, illicit enrichment and drug smuggling as the accountant and head of logistics in Pablo's Medellín Cartel. He had given himself up in Spain and was waiting in Granada to learn if he was going to be extradited back to Colombia or, worse, every drug smuggler's fear, to the barbarous steel-walled prisons of the United States of America.

Keith missed his sizzling steaks coming in hot from the grill, the Albolote stables were miles from anywhere, but Jesús had a man running the kitchen and they dined on gourmet dinners with wine transferred covertly into green water bottles. Buckets of oranges appeared every couple of days and the kitchens were stocked with fresh fruit and vegetables shipped in from nearby farms thanks to the folded peseta notes that passed from Gil and Escobar into the hands of the prison staff.

The prisoners and guards had more in common than just eating well in Albolote. The summer months were a furnace, hot and humid. Even the walls ran wet. Books turned sticky and disintegrated. You came out of a cold shower and were sweating before you had even dried yourself. On baking afternoons, the thermometer settled on 40°C – 100°F – with nights often hotter than the days. It is a common theme with prisoners and their guards, the same with the police and most men in uniform, they were all counting down time before they got out or got their pensions.

Autumn came with fresh figs and pomegranates. The inertia lifted and the men returned to their muscle-building exercises, press-ups and weightlifting. There was an open area called the patio, where Roberto spent his days playing volleyball. One day, he fell badly and gashed his knee on the rough surface. That evening, Keith paid him a visit and found Roberto in his cell with his leg bandaged and raised on a pile of pillows to bring down the swelling. They lit cigars and spoke in Spanglish.

'I'm going to get AIDS.'

'No you're not, mate, they cleaned the wound. You'll be fine. If they resurfaced the patio people wouldn't get injured.'

'¿Que?'

Keith went down on one knee and used his hand as a trowel …

'Necesitan una nueva …'

'Superficie.'

'Exactamente, my son.'

Keith thought no more about the conversation. A month passed and a crew of workmen appeared and resurfaced the patio. He watched for ten minutes, it was always a pleasure watching other people working, and when he got back to his cell, he found a box on the metal table. Pablo Escobar had paid for the resurfacing and sent every prisoner a television as an apology for the inconvenience caused during the work. Three months later, on 2 December 1993, Pablo was escaping from a safe house that wasn't as safe as he thought and was shot dead by the Search Bloc, a Colombian special operations unit backed by US Army Intelligence and the CIA.

···◆·●────·●◆···

Christmas in prison reminds you that you're in prison and the pressure to be joyful makes the atmosphere sadder and more poignant. Prisoners make decorations out of rubbish. Someone dresses up as Santa and at Albolote an old priest came to perform the mass. The blokes with their scars and tattoos crossed themselves and looked contrite as they lined up for a blessing. Spain is a land of kindness and cruelty, tears and laughter, extremes echoed in the weather, the summer heat like an open oven, the winters frosting the windows and freezing your toes.

One morning at the end of February, Keith was summoned to the Governor's office, where a Spanish magistrate was waiting. Keith dressed for the occasion in a suit, a red tie with thin yellow stripes and, as always, a silk handkerchief spilling from the breast pocket. The magistrate, dressed in black like an undertaker and heavy, black-framed glasses, stood and they shook hands. He then explained that Keith's extradition to the United States government had been granted. They sat and remained quiet for a few moments like mourners at a funeral.

Two weeks later, the Governor personally came to his cell to tell him that he would be leaving for America the following day. He spoke slowly and Keith felt a little ping of pride that after twelve months in Spanish jails he could *defend* himself in Spanish.

'*Aún puedes recurrir ante los juzgados de Madrid. El magistrado permitirá un retraso.*'

'*¿Un retraso?*'

'*Si, Señor.*'

The Governor explained that his transfer had been arranged, but the magistrate had the power to delay extradition, even at the last moment.

Keith was tempted. He had been thinking about this possibility for the last two weeks but, finally, he decided to get it over and done with. His lawyer, Leonard Levensen, had assured him that if he pleaded guilty in an American court, which he intended to do, there was no reason why he could not be repatriated to serve his time in Britain. The time he had spent on remand in Spain would be deducted from his sentence with summer days counted as double because of the excessive heat. He was also optimistic – his nature – that by accepting the extradition, it would count in his favour in some small way.

He shook hands with the Governor.

That night, the cooks served roast lamb English style with mint sauce and roast potatoes. Roberto Escobar and Jesús Gil made sure every man and every guard had a glass of Bodegas Robles red from the nearby winery in Granada. Keith stood. They fell silent and he threw up his hands.

'*Lamento tener que irme y espero volver pronto.*'

They laughed and cheered and spilled their drinks.

'I am sorry to be leaving and hope to be back soon.'

34. AMERICA

Keith wore his suit and carried a bag with his personal possessions. It is surprising how much we accumulate in life and prison teaches us how little we really need. He strolled along the corridor to the high double doors at the entrance with José, the Governor and two guards like old friends walking home from the pub. They shook hands and Keith turned to wave to the men pressed behind the rows of windows like small square portholes in the façade of the Albolote building.

Spring was in the air, fresh and clean with thoughts of new starts and regrets forgotten. The distant hillsides were quilts of cork oaks, ash and Aleppo pine. The sky was cornflower blue with flags of cloud like a Vermeer painting and the *levante* gusting across the Mediterranean from the east promised rain before nightfall. He gazed out at the panorama and took a deep breath.

It was 9 March 1993. After twelve months gathering evidence, this was the official handover of one of the FBI's most wanted from Spain to the government of the United States of America. The Governor signed forms gripped on a clipboard in triplicate and witnessed by one of the guards. A broad, square-shouldered Fed in a grey fedora creased lengthwise down the crown tucked the board under his arm. Job done. They'd got him.

Keith opened his box of Montecristos. José and the guards each took one and lit up, filling the air with pale blue smoke and the sweet sticky smell of leatherbound books and exotic spices.

The Governor blew ash from the tip and rolled the cigar between his thumb and fingers.

'*Muy bien.*'

'*Muy bien,*' the guards agreed.

The American waved away the smoke and transferred the clipboard from under one arm to the other.

'Time to go,' he said.

The Governor nodded. Keith pinched out the tip of his cigar, licked a finger and tamped down the warm end. They shook hands again and José's eyes roamed over the posse that had come to take his prisoner. There were six Americans in shades of black with nondescript ties and Ray-Ban sunglasses. They leaned against three darkened-glass vehicles variously posed: arms folded, hands in pockets, one guy with his hands on his hips, the straps of a shoulder holster showing on a striped shirt with a button-down collar. Four were US Marshals, two the FBI.

On the fringes, four on each side, were eight Guardia Civil in jackboots, gay red cravats and the pigskin hats that give those who wear them the appearance of torturers and inquisitors. They were armed with semi-automatics. Behind the civilian vehicles were two open trucks with machine guns mounted on the flatbeds and four motorcycle outriders astride their machines. Above, hovering, was a helicopter painted in Guardia Civil colours. The Governor looked back at Keith.

'Now it is goodbye. I hope you will be safe,' he said in Spanish.

'Don't worry. They'll look after me.'

One of the cops took Keith's bag and searched it while the marshal tapped him down, under the arms, down the legs. He introduced himself as Stanley Kaczmarek. He clipped handcuffs about his wrists and Keith climbed awkwardly into the rear of one of the vehicles. The door slammed and he saw nothing through the dark glass on the four-hour journey from Granada to the airport in Madrid.

The convoy streamed across the runway apron and he climbed the steps into an American Airlines civilian aircraft where they occupied first class. Keith sat, buckled up, and Big Stan removed the handcuffs.

America

'Thank you,' Keith said as Kaczmarek dropped down in the seat next to him across the aisle. 'I didn't know I was such a scary bloke.'

'What?'

'I was just thinking, I'm living proof that the pen is mightier than the sword.'

'What's that?'

'I just move numbers about with a fountain pen. If I'd run through a shopping centre with a machete, you wouldn't have brought out an army with machine guns.'

'What are you telling me? You wanna cut people up with a machete?'

'No, mate, it's a saying: the pen is mightier than the sword.'

'Not in Columbus, Ohio.'

'I suppose they don't speak much English there?'

'We speak American.'

Spain vanished as the plane took off into the Vermeer clouds and he felt in his optimistic way that at least after a year in suspended animation he was moving forward. Into what, he had no idea. After a reasonable lunch, no wine, Big Stan accompanied him to the loo.

'You know the windows don't open?' Keith said.

'Just do the business. Don't lock the door.'

Stan waited outside with fists clenched in case Keith had secretly arranged with international villains to have a gun taped behind the water tank and was planning to hijack the plane to Cuba. The security was overblown and it struck him that it was not that his crime had endangered lives, but that his attitude challenged authority, the status quo, that he always behaved courteously, never complained and never took his guards or jailers seriously. They were working stiffs earning a wage and their need to be officious stemmed from the realisation that Keith Cheeseman lived the life they would have liked to have lived themselves.

They landed at JFK at 5pm, just as rush hour was starting, and the Feds were in a rush to get their master criminal behind bars before nightfall. Three police cars with flashing lights, blasting horns and wailing sirens cut through the traffic like a wire through cheese and Keith watched the pedestrians flee from the sidewalk as they entered Manhattan and ran every red light.

Everything about America was terrifying, overpowering, oppressive. It was like the sky was lower and everyone felt the weight pushing down on their shoulders. The pressure to succeed whatever your business or profession was so great it put everyone on edge all of the time and gave the pharmaceutical industry the golden touch of Midas.

The Metropolitan Correctional Center, the MCC, was a brutish, blackened-walled tower block opposite the Empire State Building. They entered the administrative area on Park Row and Keith was transferred to the facility via a tunnel. He was locked into a cell on the high-security tenth floor among the serial killers, child abductors and mafiosi. Two cells away was John Gotti.

They met the next day on the exercise yard on the roof.

'So, you're the Big Cheese?' Gotti said. 'You know who I am?'

'You're the even Bigger Cheese.'

'That right?'

'Parmigiano Reggiano?'

Gotti stood motionless for a long time staring at him, weighing up the words. He had a wide, handsome face, glossy brushed-back hair and heavy eyebrows shadowing piercing dark eyes. Keith knew one of two things was going to happen: they were going to become mates, or three heavies would appear from nowhere and throw him off the roof.

'You did the Bank of England?'

Keith shrugged modestly. 'Well, I had a go, John. I rob banks as a public service, you know, because the banks rob everyone else.'

Gotti sniffed the air and looked from side to side before focusing again on Keith. 'You need something, you come to me. Some scumbag fucks with you, you come to me. You want to send the judge two fishes, you know where to come.'

As the head of the Gambino crime family in New York, John Joseph Gotti Jr. was one of the most powerful and dangerous

Mafia bosses in the United States. The news-reading public liked his flamboyant personality that had earned him the reputation as the Dapper Don and, later, the Teflon Don, when he walked free from three high-profile trials in the 1980s after widespread jury tampering and witness intimidation.

When Gotti's underboss, Salvatore 'Sammy the Bull' Gravano, learned that the outspoken head of the family had made disparaging remarks about him on an FBI wiretap, he turned state's evidence and in 1992 Gotti was convicted of five murders, conspiracy to commit murder, racketeering, obstruction of justice, tax evasion, illegal gambling, extortion and loansharking. He was in for life without parole, one of the last old-time gangsters who had grown up in poverty and made a fortune as the Godfather of a powerful crime network.

Anthony 'Gaspipe' Casso, the former underboss of the Lucchese crime family, said the jailing of John Gotti was 'the beginning of the end of Cosa Nostra'.

They ambled across the roof to join Victor Amuso, the Lucchese mob boss, who was staring up at the sky.

'Whatcha looking at?'

'There's activity up there.'

'You need new eyeglasses.' Gotti turned to Keith. 'You see anything?'

Keith was shaking his head as he looked up. 'We could have a spot of rain.'

'Aliens,' Amuso said. 'They're out there.'

'They're not out there, we've got one right here.' Gotti introduced them. 'Vic Amuso,' he said. 'Meet the Big Cheese, Keith Cheeseman. He's alright. He's English.'

Vic Amuso pointed a finger like a gun.

'You kidding me? You ever met the Queen?'

'No, but I used to have lunch with the Queen Mother.'

'Yeah? What's she like?'

'Well, you know, likes a gin and tonic. She's English.'

Knowing the Queen Mother was only a slight exaggeration. The last time he had lunch at Simpson's he was sharing a table with Georgie Best, and she did give them her little wave.

They strolled back across the roof and downstairs to the cells.

'Tell the chef you're Jewish,' Gotti advised. 'The kosher food's always better.'

Keith took his advice and shared a table that night with Gotti, Amuso and the Colombo crime family captain Joseph 'JoJo' Russo, three bosses from the Five Families that had controlled organised crime in New York since the bootlegging days of the 1920s. Outside, given the circumstances, they would have killed each other. Inside, what they had in common *was* each other.

Gotti carried a copy of *Time* magazine with his portrait on the cover. He slid it across the table to Keith.

'Here I am, imprisoned by the state, denied bail and my portrait hangs in the National Portrait Gallery in Washington. Pop gangster John Gotti. Immortalised by pop artist Andy Warhol,' he said. 'You wanna know how I feel about it? You wanna know how I feel? *Ambiguous*. Downright fucking ambiguous. I never asked for this crap. Wealthy people, high-class people, used to pay this guy Warhol to do their portraits. Mine, it gets done gratis.'

'It's a good likeness,' Keith said.

'Yeah, but what's it mean, Keith?' he asked and went on. 'Look, I'm wearing a black suit outlined in red, except the red outline is off, you know, misaligned, like the fucking printer was drunk or something. Who knows? The writer for *Time* says the colours are sombre and threatening because you can't use bright colours with Gotti. Shit, gimme a break. Some kid who went to Cornell or Berkeley who studied art told me it's off-centre because it's meant to symbolise – shit, I don't remember what. Society's misalignment?'

He folded the magazine and stuck it in his jacket. As they chatted, the three Mafia dons at the table looked, sounded and behaved like the characters from Francis Ford Coppola's *The Godfather* trilogy based on Mario Puzo's novels, and it was hard to know if they had imitated the gangsters or the gangsters had learned their swagger from Coppola. They were men with blood-steeped pasts who took killing and being killed as an occupational hazard. They had the freedom that comes to those with an absolute absence of fear, a passion to live for the moment and they took pleasure in life's little things like a good cigar, fine tailoring and suites in five-star hotels. Like Keith.

'He knows the Queen,' Amuso told JoJo.

'That right?'

'Actually, the Queen Mother. We always went to Simpson's in the Strand, great place for lunch.'

Amuso lit a cigarette and turned to Keith. 'You ever press the button on anyone?'

'No,' he replied. 'But I think I caused a few bankers to commit suicide.'

'That's enough to make you a made man.'

A bell rang. They stubbed out their cigarettes and walked up to their single cells on the tenth floor watched by wary guards armed with guns and clubs.

Next day, the yard was closed.

When they went out for exercise the day after, a steel mesh covering had been erected above the roof to prevent escapes by helicopter.

35. A CRIME AGAINST MONEY

In the spring of 1993, Keith was back in the tabloids with supersized numbers and embroidered versions of signing up George Best for Dunstable, the sado-masochistic sex wiles of the Dusky Maiden, the Duke of Manchester's fall from grace and Elaine Borg crying in her soup for the fraudster who broke her heart.

Reporters from London, red-eyed with jetlag and Johnnie Walker on expenses, filled the gallery with nods, winks and thumbs up. Up in the back, he was sure he caught a glimpse of David Strahan from Carlton, still on the trail like a bloodhound covering all the angles.

'How's it going, Keith?' the youngster from the *Express* called and an usher told him to 'Keep your mouth shut' as Judge Robert W. Sweet entered the United States federal court in Manhattan.

'All rise.'

The judge swept his black robe behind him as he sat. Feet shuffled and the sound of scraping chairs as they were pulled forward faded to an expectant silence. The prosecutor had remained standing. It was Wednesday, 11 March 1993. 'Keith Cheeseman, 50, of London, England,' was charged with six counts of criminal conspiracy to sell £292 million – *$550 million* – in stolen securities, including millions of pounds in bonds seized at knifepoint in the City of London in May 1990.

Rolling the digits over his tongue like good brandy, the Prosecutor described the robbery as 'the world's biggest mugging'. It was believed at first to be an attack by a small-time thief but, he said in a crisper tone, City of London detectives soon learned that, far from being a chance robbery by a lone mugger, the heist had been set up by an international fraud and money-laundering ring with organised crime links in the United States.

He paused for effect before explaining that the bonds had been fenced all over the world, and in the months after the robbery detectives tracked down all but £2 million of the £292 million stolen.

'They arrested 25 people but, as of today, only Mr Cheeseman has been prosecuted.'

Almost nothing said in court that day was accurate. The amount in bonds, the number allegedly recovered, and the work of City of London detectives was turned by the attorney into pulp fiction with the team at Operation Starling, always light years behind the curve, painted as a weird marriage between Sherlock Holmes and Miss Marple.

Pleading guilty to one charge, Keith admitted receiving and handling £16-million worth of stolen bonds. He told the court that he had not been involved in planning or executing the robbery. He had skipped bail, he said, because he was in fear for his life after the murder of Mark Lee Osborne. He requested that he serve his sentence in a British prison.

Then silence, except for the sound of pencil graphite breaking across the pages of spiral notebooks.

Judge Sweet drew breath. Keith held his own.

'You should not leave my court today without being fully aware that, due to the amount of money involved in the theft, you could be sentenced to up to 55 years in prison with a fine of $1.5 billion.'

Sentencing would take place the following month.

Keith let out his breath. His mouth dropped open. He gripped the rail in front of him and could hear his heart beating in his chest like a bird in a cage. The court rose. The judge swept through the exit door behind him and Keith walked on shaky legs back to the vehicle that would return him to prison.

...────•────•────...

He would rather have enjoyed a cold glass of white with his evening meal and Mafia amigos around the table but the regime was less liberal than he had grown used to in Spain. He thought that if he ever became a prison reformer a glass of wine with supper would be one of his first recommendations.

Gotti and the boys had an informant in court and knew before Keith returned to the MCC that he had been accused of ripping off half-a-billion bucks and was liable for more than a billion in fines as well as what amounted to a life sentence. He was the man. The numbers added to his celebrity and would ease his way through the prison system starting right there with dinner. Gotti had arranged with the kitchen to have a bowl of freshly cooked pasta brought to the table with anchovies melted off the base of a heated iron.

'Fabulous,' Keith said, and Amuso put his fork down.

'Judge Sweet. I know this guy. Sweet by name. Acid as a car battery.'

Gotti nodded his head as he listened to Amuso, then turned to Keith. 'I daresay putting your hands on $10,000 ain't no problem?'

Keith shrugged. He knew what was coming. 'That's doable,' he said.

Gotti snapped his fingers. 'You can make it all go away.'

'The thing is, John, judges are like London buses. There's always another one just round the corner.'

They laughed. 'I like this guy,' Russo remarked.

'Five hundred million greenbacks,' said Amuso and raised his tin mug.

The faceless cons rattling cutlery across the canteen couldn't stop themselves glancing at their table and Keith contemplated spending 55 years in prison among these men when there were murderers who came out with good behaviour in ten. Wife killers and dangerous drivers don't undermine the system. Taking on banks eats at the very foundations of the American Dream, the giant steel wheels of the economy, of capitalism. Every time you screw a bank you compete with bankers running scams to screw their clients.

Bank robbery was more prevalent in the United States with its hundreds of small banks and savings and loans. Bank robbers were legends – Jesse James, Machine Gun Kelly, Pretty Boy Floyd, Butch Cassidy and the Sundance Kid, John Dillinger, Bonnie Parker and Clyde Barrow. In the 1990s, more than 2,000 banks were robbed every year. Sixty per cent of robberies were successful, with an average taking of $10,000. A third of the robbers were never caught.

Now that he had appeared in court, Pia Linstedt, Keith's lady friend when he was living at Charlie Gray's apartment in Tenerife, contacted the Swedish Ambassador to the United Nations, and he made a personal visit to Keith at the prison block. The Ambassador added an impressive edge to Keith's case and lobbied US authorities to have him returned to the United Kingdom to serve his sentence. Kerry, who never took no for an answer, persuaded the new Home Secretary Kenneth Clarke to write to the US courts to support Keith's case.

Legal and personal calls took place on the fifth floor of the MCC, the demarcation between the men's cells above and the women's below. One time, when John Gotti had Liza Minnelli and James Caan visiting with his lawyer, he dropped a few twenties among the guards and took Keith along to meet them. The connection between Gotti and these massive celebrities was never made clear, except gangsters and stars both walk tightropes, albeit different ones, over the void and for both one false move ends in the abyss – prison or obscurity.

Liza Minnelli had just finished a tour with Frank Sinatra and Sammy Davis Jr. in *Frank, Liza & Sammy: The Ultimate Event*. James Caan had won an Academy Award playing Sonny Corleone in *The Godfather* and sounded pure New York Mafia as he gossiped with Gotti. Keith mentioned his exchange with Sinatra in Australia and they threw up their hands.

'That's Frank,' Liza said. 'He likes things his way. When he's nice he's the nicest guy in the room. When he's not, he's a monster.'

'You know, we made him?' Gotti said. 'He respected that.'

'I'll tell you a true story,' Liza continued. 'We were at a dinner party one night in Long Island and this gal comes up to Frank and says, "Hey, Mr Sinatra, you owe me $200. I bought a new dress to go to your show and it was cancelled." She was just being funny.' She paused. 'You know what Frank did? He took her arm and led her to the door where a couple of his gophers were standing. He told them to help the lady find her coat and put her in her car. She was going home.'

'No sense of humour,' Caan said.

'At least he didn't shoot her,' said Gotti.

'No,' Liza said. 'But he wanted to.'

On another occasion, Keith ran into Leona Helmsley. She knew who he was from prison gossip, but he felt out of touch after a year in Spain, and was unaware of the daily news stories of the New York businesswoman – known as the Queen of Mean – with a reputation for tyrannical behaviour. During her trial for tax evasion, a former housekeeper testified that Helmsley once said: 'We don't pay taxes; only the little people pay taxes.'

Those few words – a universal truth – were her doom. The sixteen-year sentence imposed on her in court – she served less than two – was welcomed by the public with mass approval.

People had grown to regard Leona Helmsley as a 1980s symbol of arrogance and greed – one more figure from a passing era, like John Joseph Gotti – and as he stared up at the cracks on his prison cell ceiling, Keith wondered if he should add his own name to that list. Eighties glam had been washed away by the electronic wave of home computers, the coming of car phones and cell phones, hip-hop, oversized jackets and baggy jeans. He was the last gentleman villain in a world where larceny was becoming corporatised and giant internet companies with billions beyond imagination would know your every move, thought and desire.

Keith had found Leona Helmsley charming and ruthless. On the day they chatted in the waiting area, she told him that at 9 that evening all the lights would go out on the Empire State Building in protest at her incarceration. His cell faced the building and, sure enough, at 9pm on the dot the building was in total darkness. The next day Keith learned from Leonard Levensen, his lawyer, that Leona Helmsley's husband owned the Empire State Building.

Sentencing day was 10 April 1993. He woke early. Gotti made sure there was a glass of fresh orange juice on the table for him in the canteen and the cook brought out two fried eggs, sunny-side up with buttered toast. It was hard not to think about the 55 years he was going to serve. He'd be 105 by the time he got out.

'See how the dice rolls,' Gotti said, and they shook hands.

'Been a pleasure, John.'

He dressed in his suit and stood, shoulders back, in the federal court before Judge Robert W. Sweet: face stern, unreadable; clipped moustache; Yale haircut, neat and boyish.

Keith had, he acknowledged, tried to evade justice by skipping bail and was 'well-known for his criminal past'. The judge reminded him that he had also been involved in another fraud scheme, in which 'he had seduced a supervisor at a financial services company. He rented her a luxury apartment and they conspired to transfer £8 million into an offshore account, before the two were arrested by the Fraud Squad.'

He did wonder where the figure came from. The *Sun* had thrown out £5 million. The *Independent* upped it to £15 million. Now, deflation, he assumed, it was down at £8 million. He gripped the rail.

He had pleaded guilty to one charge and, after a pause, Judge Sweet pronounced that he was sending Keith down for 'the maximum available term of six-and-a-half years'.

36. CON AIR

Keith breathed a sigh of relief and walked through the canteen shaking hands and punching shoulders in that way prisoners do when they're not sure what to say. He took a stroll with the Mafia dons beneath the iron grille on the roof.

'Six-and-a-half. You can live with that,' Amuso said. He leaned over the edge and peered up at the sky.

'Any aliens?' Gotti asked him.

'Nah. Too many clouds.'

'I just had a thought,' Keith said. 'You wouldn't be able to land a helicopter, but if you had a parachute, you could jump off the far corner.'

'What if it don't open?'

'Then it don't open.'

Gotti glanced at Amuso. 'He's right,' he said and turned back to Keith. 'You ever jumped?'

'Course I have. Back when I was in the army. I was going to join Special Forces, then they found out I couldn't swim.'

'A parachute,' Gotti repeated.

'In the war,' Keith continued. 'Against the Germans. A lot of officers were locked up in a place called Colditz Castle, and they built a glider under the roof.'

'Did they get away?'

'No, the war ended before they'd finished building it. But the thing is, you have to keep having ideas until one of them pays off.'

'When it does,' Gotti said, 'I'm coming to see you. I wanna have lunch with the Queen Mother. You know what I'm saying?'

'My treat.'

Next morning at breakfast, JoJo Russo carried a box that he gave to Keith. Inside was a pair of New Balance trainers, a gift that served as a metaphor. Later that day, he was run out of the MCC to begin a tour of America's prisons, crisscrossing the country every month or so and clocking up enough air miles to have made a trip around the world in first class.

The Justice Prisoner and Alien Transportation System (JPATS), Con Air to the cons, was operated by US Marshals in flak jackets and dark glasses chosen for their aggression and impatience. You were not allowed to talk to them, and they didn't talk to you. They barked like ravening dogs. 'Shift ass. You gonna suck my dick or shut the fuck up.'

There were no announcements. You were never entirely sure where you were going or how long you were going to stay. While you were in the hands of the marshals, you were outside the prison structure. With the help of the Home Office, Kerry continued to pressure for Keith's transfer to the UK and was told on several occasions when she tried to get in contact that he was 'lost' in the system.

In the first six months of internment, he saw the inside of prisons in Otisville, New York; Atlanta, Georgia; Lake Charles, Oakdale and Terre Haute, Louisiana; Houston, Texas; Estill, South Carolina; and a few times in Oklahoma, the marshals' hub, where Keith ate gourmet meals arranged in the kitchen by Gene Gotti, John's brother, who made sure he always got his morning eggs done the way he liked them.

Gene was inside for racketeering and drug smuggling. He served 29 years and came out in 2018. Keith got the news from Gene that after he was sentenced, John Gotti was moved from MCC to Marion, Illinois, the first Supermax prison, opened in 1963 to replace Alcatraz in San Francisco. He smoked himself to death, going from hospital with lung cancer into the grave in 2002.

Friends wrote letters and sent news cuttings that followed Keith one step behind from jail to jail. David Strahan finally pinned him down and he went on camera to talk guardedly about the bonds theft. He was interviewed at MCC by Michael Gillard for the *Observer*, who wrote an article under the heading 'My Role in the World's Biggest Bank Robbery'. It came out on Sunday, 11 April 1993. A week later, the *South Bedfordshire on Sunday* told its readers Keith Cheeseman 'languishes in Otisville prison', where one of his closest pals is the former lawyer of Godfather Mafia don John Gotti.

He recalled Oscar Wilde's quote: 'There is only one thing in the world worse than being talked about, and that is not being talked about.'

Two Brits from Scotland Yard turned up when he was in the Oakdale Federal Correctional Institution in Louisiana to ask what he knew about the villains involved in the Brink's-Mat bullion robbery. Apart from knowing Kenny Noye and Johnny 'Little Legs' Lloyd, he didn't know anything about their business and wouldn't have told the Old Bill anything even if he had.

'Johnny "Little Legs" Lloyd? There's a name you don't forget.'

'So, you do know Johnny Lloyd?'

'Very well, as it happens.'

Keith recalled his dealings with Lloyd and gave the two coppers an edited version. After the Brink's-Mat robbery, when Kenny Noye was nicked for handling the stolen bullion, 'Little Legs' wanted to get away sharpish and Keith agreed to buy his penthouse at the Barbican. The deal was arranged by a dodgy lawyer – always easy to find – with a cash deposit and a mortgage arranged through the Halifax Building Society

By the time Lloyd left for America, it was reckoned that he had already stashed more than £10 million from his involvement in most of the big crime capers that had gone down in the seventies and eighties. In the US, he had plastic surgery on his toes, disfigured since birth, and wore tailored shorts to flatter his spindly pins.

Lloyd's notoriety caught up with him when he was outed on the TV crime show *America's Most Wanted*, and he took the biggest gamble of his life. He returned to London and walked into Rochester Row police station with his brief to give himself up. The Crown Prosecution Service decided there was insufficient evidence for a successful prosecution on the Brink's-Mat job. In one of those twists that defy explanation, Little Legs walked free but he 'reluctantly' donated a five-figure sum to a consortium of insurance companies that had covered the Brink's-Mat gold.

On the evening before he left for the United States, Little Legs met Keith and his lawyer at the Sutton Arms, around the corner from the Barbican.

'Bloody nice place you're getting, Keith, I don't mind telling you. Fucking bargain as well.'

'Who knows, mate, maybe we'll do a switcheroo, and you'll buy it back again.' They drank to that. 'Not at the same price, mind you.'

Lloyd smiled. 'I've always fucking liked you, Keith. You're a bit of a cunt, but not one of those hairy cunts, if you see what I mean.'

'Nice of you to say so.'

Lloyd scarpered and Kenny Noye lived the good life until 1996 when he killed Stephen Cameron in a road rage incident and was given a life sentence for murder.

The two cops made notes, Keith couldn't understand why, but they were enjoying the freebie with a hotel in New Orleans and were in no hurry to return to the UK. Keith suggested they try the soft-shell crab po' boy and they liked the spicy baguette so much they brought one in for him the day they left to fly back to London. After six months in the United States, he was growing to appreciate the police and prison system at home.

The regular transfers in leg irons and chains from mesh-windowed vans smelling of piss and vomit to rattling aircraft in their last days of service was unsettling and intimidating. It prevented prisoners forming gangs, but also long-term relationships and maintaining family connections. In his particular case, Keith suspected the frequent moves were a game of cat and mouse with the UK government, in order to keep him in the US to appear before the grand jury hearing into Mark Osborne's death.

Only Mafia inmates with political and financial clout had any power over their place of imprisonment. During his stay at Otisville, upstate New York, Keith became friends with Michael Coiro, John Gotti's consigliere. When Michael, imprisoned on various obstruction of justice charges, moved to Nevada State Prison in Las Vegas, word reached Keith that he could join him at any time – an offer he refused because his transfer back to the UK was being discussed. In Otisville, he enjoyed his position of trust, working in the law library helping inmates appeal sentences and convictions, file writs of habeas corpus and make claims relating to their civil rights and the conditions of confinement, as guaranteed under the American Constitution.

At the time, he assumed he had got the job because he was one of the few inmates who could spell 'library'. On reflection it was more likely that he was one of the few who could spell 'law'.

Keith was shocked at the low level of education among prisoners. He studied and passed the American High Schools Diploma, which enabled him to give classes. A young black guy he taught, named Eli Johnson, had been inside since the age of eighteen. He had served eight years on a ten-year term for conspiracy. Two white teens had robbed a 7-Eleven store while he was a customer and he was accused of being an accomplice. He had not appealed because he couldn't read the paperwork.

The prisons were tribal: older blacks, young blacks, Hell's Angels, Cubans, Latinos, indigenous Americans, Mafia, members of the Ku Klux Klan (normally serving short spells for serious offences). Keith wasn't identified as a threat, more a curiosity they were unable to judge from his accent or appearance. He never met with any anti-British sentiment, on the contrary, there was always someone who wanted to take him under their wing.

Just as Vic Amuso had asked Keith if he had met the Queen, this was the most common question he heard in American jails. General knowledge and a vague sense of geography were non-existent, but everyone had an opinion on Michael Jackson being accused of 'fondling' boys at Neverland and the marriage problems between Princess Diana and Prince Charles.

One mafiosi who had been caught on the run told Keith that he owned an island off the coast of Puerto Rico.

'Why didn't you go there?'

'Don't have no passport.'

Only 4 per cent of US citizens had a passport at the time. Going on the run was flying from New York down to Florida or Las Vegas.

Keith was tutoring Eli Johnson on his General Education Development, GED exams, when the door to his cell swung open and the man with the leg chains appeared.

'Now where am I going?' said Keith.

'You talking to me?'

'Well, there's no one else here, is there, mate?'

'Shut the fuck up.'

Rattling van. Plane smelling like a dead rat. He arrived as the sun was setting in streaks of orange and pale green over Atlanta, Georgia, the journey from what seemed like a holiday camp to a prisoner-of-war camp. Atlanta was a big, stone-walled monstrosity built in 1899. With its 3,000 numbered, scarred and tattooed cons, the facility served as a detention centre for Cuban refugees from the Mariel boatlift who, for reasons never fully explained, were ineligible for release into American society.

In 1987, the Cubans rioted for eleven days and seized hostages later recaptured by gun-toting guards in helmets and bulletproof vests. One of the prisoners was killed. Dozens went to hospital with gunshot wounds. Before the riot was over, the Cubans set fire to the prison and the long, smoke-stained, unpainted passageways gave Keith the feeling he was on the highway to hell. All American prisons stewed with an undercurrent of violence. Stabbings were regular events. Murders meant lockdown and the demon fear slid silently from floor to floor up the iron stairways and along the walkways and gangways.

The cells in Atlanta comprised three plain stone walls and one open side with floor-to-ceiling iron bars like a sheriff's jail in a movie. The door was opened by a lever operated by a warden at one end of the corridor. Keith was told to sleep with his head beside the toilet recess, not next to the bars, as he could suffer a head injury by the door unexpectedly opening, and there was a risk of passing inmates slashing at your face with a homemade blade because that's how some blokes get their kicks.

In Atlanta Keith always felt that the prison was about to erupt. It didn't happen. That experience came along when he was transferred to Oakdale, Louisiana, where almost half the prison population were Latinos. Some of the men had been charged with illegal entry into the United States and had been stuck in the prison system for ten years. Others had been given six months for a misdemeanour like shoplifting a meat pie because they were hungry and kept on serving time because they'd been forgotten. Some of the prisons were privately managed, meaning the company was earning by keeping inmates in, not by re-educating them and letting them out.

These conditions were dehumanising. They led to anger, resentment and feelings of stress and hopelessness. When there is no light at the end of the tunnel and no tunnel where a light might have glowed, the authorities create the conditions for a riot. When it happened, for the first time Keith was in fear for his own life.

He was lying on his bunk reading a John le Carré novel when five armed guards stormed into the cell opposite and started yelling at Sancho, a Colombian drug peddler with whom he sometimes practised Spanish. He obviously didn't respond quickly enough, and Keith heard his head crack as the blast from a taser threw him back against the wall.

More guards appeared with clubs and guns. He stood, hands up to show he was not going to resist. He was turned to face the wall, wrists cuffed and legs chained. They moved on along the corridor and returned with a chain gang of about a dozen inmates. Keith was linked to the group, and they shuffled downstairs to a communal area where they witnessed the disturbance on the gangways and stairways opposite. Why they were directed to this area made no sense, unless there was a risk of a fire being started and they would have been trapped in their cells.

A group of Latinos had taken some guards hostage. Prisoners filled the gangways rattling tin plates against the ironwork, the noise like an orchestra plunging off a cliff. A knife appeared, flashing in the dim light as it circled a guard's throat, and his head was almost decapitated as he was flung down the stairs. There was blood everywhere like it had been thrown from a bucket and the sight and smell calmed everyone down.

Armed vehicles with wailing klaxons disgorged their loads of riot cops with heavy weapons. Keith was bundled out of prison with the chain gang, connected to a central bar in a prison bus and driven to the airfield. They were flown to El Reno, Oklahoma, and distributed to various prisons. Keith never got to finish the John le Carré and missed the mail that arrived the following day in Oakdale, Louisiana.

What the murder of a prison guard said to Keith was that it was time to get out of Dodge and it was a relief when he was finally transferred to Houston, Texas, to face the grand jury hearing into the death of Mark Lee Osborne. It was coming up to Christmas 1994.

The hearing was a bit like going to the opera with a panel of some 30 or 40 legal representatives on the balcony, the same number of lawyers in the stalls and Keith centre stage like the tenor starting a two-hour performance with short breaks outside the chamber to take legal advice.

'Should I take the Fifth?' he asked.

'No. You've got nothing to hide. You take the Fifth Amendment and you'll get three years for doing nothing.'

'Great legal system you got here.'

'Best in the world.'

He went back into the theatre, took his place and agreed that he was William Keith Cheeseman of London, England. The speaker had a good ole boy accent and reminded him of Billy Bob Ryder, the tall Texan with the young wife and a bank for sale.

'Did you murder, or cause to be murdered, or were you involved in the murder of Mark Lee Osborne?'

'No.'

'Do you know who did murder Mark Osborne?'
'No.'
'What do you know about Mark Osborne's business affairs?'
'He wanted to sell me an interest in a water purifying product called Aquatest.'
'Would you be prepared to take a lie detector test?'
'Yes, sir, I would.'

The hearing was adjourned and Keith, as he put it, 'had more wires attached to me than a patient on life support'.

The polygraph wires connect to sensors attached to the chest, on fingers, the temple and close to the heart. The machine measures heart rate, blood pressure, respiration, perspiration and skin conductivity. Beating the polygraph can be done with practice. Keith had been kicking around dirty prisons for two years and was desperate to get home. He would not have been able to beat the machine.

He was asked all the same questions again and gave the same replies. The meter never wavered.

The technician removed the wires.

'What are you going to try now? Not thumbscrews?'

'Shut the fuck up,' the technician said and gave Keith a backhanded slap on his bare arm. 'Put your shirt back on.'

He was driven back to the jailhouse.

Two weeks later, he stood again before the grand jury and a different image came to his mind. He felt as if he were in a Roman amphitheatre, a Christian martyr waiting for the wild beasts to be released. He wiped his brow with a handkerchief and took deep breaths as he glanced around at the grim faces. Silence fell and he was informed in that slow, Texan manner that, in regard to the murder of Mark Lee Osborne, he had nothing to answer for.

He collected some more Con Air miles being transferred to Estill, South Carolina – he had no idea why – then, after twelve months of travels, back to Manhattan where his journey had begun.

37. END GAME

It was a cold morning with rain in the air and he felt the old spring back in his step as he upped the pace across the tarmac at La Guardia in New York.

'Hold your horses, Keith. They aren't going to take off any quicker, you know.'

That was Graham, a few pounds overweight and the older of the two Scotland Yard coppers taking him back to England. He'd been signed over at the gate by four men in black, two marshals, two FBI, four weapons and a form in triplicate.

'Just getting the old ticker going, my son.'

He climbed the steps and was the first to board the scheduled American Airlines flight to Heathrow. No cuffs. No chains. No luggage. *New York Times* under his arm. His seat in first class was in the emergency row at the front with Graham Amos and Luke Duckworth – Scotland Yard – in the adjacent seats.

It seemed to take ages for the passengers to fill the aircraft. The lids snapped shut on the overhead lockers. They buckled up and he found a smile on his lips as the big Pratt & Whitney engines roared to life. Keith was watching the stewardess go through the safety procedures when a tall guy ten rows back left his seat and started waving his arms about.

'Let me out. Let me out. I want to get off.'

Two years in American prisons had taught Keith to keep sharp and be ready for anything. He quietly disengaged his seat belt.

Women were screaming and weeping.

'I can't take it anymore. I want to get off.'

The big American was still shouting as he pushed his way down the aisle to the emergency door. The stewardess who had done the demo tried to stop him as he swung back the lever. He grabbed her around the waist and dragged her towards the open door.

Keith bounced from his seat, pulled the girl from his grasp and eased her back behind him.

'Come on, son, you can't get out of a moving plane. You'll kill your bloody self.'

'I want to get out.'

'Don't worry, they'll let you out. I'm on your side, mate.'

The pilot appeared with his co-pilot, a young guy with muscles and a red-haired crew cut. He took the panicked man by the arm and twisted it up his back to the point where it didn't hurt if he didn't struggle. The two coppers from London were out of their seats and joined the entourage as the man was escorted from the plane. The captain relatched the open door.

Naturally, he knew he was carrying a prisoner back to the UK. He shook Keith's hand and said he would write a commendation to the Home Office. He was a man of his word. Graham Amos marched back, charged up on adrenaline.

'I'll tell you what I'm going to do,' he said. 'I'm going to write to the Governor at Wandsworth and tell him what you did.'

Keith's first-class supper was served with champagne and copious smiles from the stewardess. She refilled his glass and leaned over.

'I can't imagine why you were in prison,' she whispered.

'Nor can I. I only robbed a bank.'

Keith had been released from the American prison service thanks to pressure from home, but also from Bob Sweet, the judge who had sent him down. When he first arrived back in Manhattan, he received a call from Judge Sweet, who told him that he had tried from the start to get him transferred to the UK to serve his sentence.

'But you can't go against these people. My hands were tied.'
'What people, Bob?'
He lowered his voice. 'The FBI.'
'You mean they have power over the justice system.'
'Not exactly. They are just *very* persuasive.'

He arrived in Wandsworth where the story of his intervention on board the American Airlines flight had already circulated. He was given a job in the library with his own office and the authority to order new books. He started with *The Secret Pilgrim,* the John le Carré he'd left behind during the riot at Oakdale. Chained up. Bussed out. Flown off in a rainstorm. A chill ran down his spine.

He left the paperwork neatly on his desk and passed Paddy O'Hay, the Irish warden, as he walked back to his cell.

'Now is everything in the world in its right place, Keith?'
'All bright and dandy, Paddy.'
'That's good to hear. I'm going to make myself a cup of cocoa. Would you like me to bring you one?'
'Yeah, lovely. Best news I've had all day.'

It was less than 24 hours before Kerry was in the visiting room sitting across the steel table, legs crossed, her *I told you so* expression on her pink-painted lips. Her new hairstyle softened her face as it fell in two curves around her cheeks and she wore a Versace white suit with a long jacket, wide shoulders and tight skirt.

'So, he's back, is he?'
'Fresh as a daisy.' Keith folded his arms. 'If you don't mind my saying, you look good enough to eat.'
'Aren't they feeding you in here?'
'No, I mean it.'
'I've heard enough soft soap from you to start a laundry. How they treating you?'

'Like a bloody king, to be honest.'

'Kings don't end up in prison.'

'Course they don't. They make the laws.'

He was going to mention the French Revolution, but why bother? Sitting there with Kerry in Wandsworth made it feel as if life had been on pause and the start button had been pressed again. His journey from prison to prison across America seemed like a surreal movie and he looked back with cynicism and a touch of pride that he had travelled the highway to hell and come out the other side.

'I'll tell you something, I wouldn't want to go back,' he said.

'Then don't break the law, Keith.'

'I'll do my best.'

'If I had £5 for every time you've said that I'd be a bloody millionaire.'

'You are a millionaire.'

'That's not the point.' She lit a Rothmans. 'And that's not why I'm here. I had a talk with Ralph Haeems and he's put Anthony Mulrenan on the case.'

'Best news I've had. Who's paying?'

'Never mind about that. You'll see a bill when the time comes.'

Anthony had worked on getting Keith repatriated and now took charge of the judicial review. Another four months passed before Keith appeared at his appeal hearing at the Law Courts in the Strand. Mulrenan showed that, with parole and considering the two-days-for-one 'patio time' in hot Spanish prisons, Keith had already served beyond his time. He was released immediately.

They crossed the road to Simpson's for a late lunch where George, the maître d', gave them his best table and Keith remembered John Gotti's plan to jump jail and head for London. Gotti had killed people and had people killed. He was a showman, a narcissist, but Keith had a feeling that his brief friendship with the Godfather had made life for him in American prisons a lot easier than it could have been.

EPILOGUE

The table was covered in newspaper clippings and notes.

'Speaking of lunch, I'm bloody starving,' Keith said.

'You're always starving,' Sarah told him.

'Got to feed the inner man.'

'The inner man looks like he's already been fed.'

Sarah went to make lunch and Keith passed me a copy of the *Evening Standard* from Monday, 8 November 1993. On page three, under the London Voice column was an article with information gathered from, it said, two informants: Jeffrey Kershaw, now living in Cyprus, and a man named 'Dave' interviewed at Joe Allen's, the brasserie in Covent Garden.

I read through the article. 'Dave' was described as 'having a shock of white hair' and being 'a well-known fence – mainly dealing in art works'. Further down the column, it described Kershaw as Dave's former solicitor.

'Off the top of your head, who do you think this so-called Dave is?' Keith asked.

'Henry Nunn.'

'Ten out of ten. Now I'm going to tell you a story. You'd better bloody record it because I'm not going to say it twice.'

···◆—●———●—◆···

Henry sits in a leather armchair mulling his brandy with four friends at White's, or one of his other clubs in St James's. The group consists of one of the top dogs at the Bank of England. We'll call him A for Arthur. There's someone from the Met, a police commissioner, say, B for Bobby, and someone high up the ladder at MI6. Let's call him Christian, a good name for a spook. Finally, we have Symes, with stains on his pinstriped jacket. They have firm connections, a crisscross. Perhaps they all went to Gordonstoun or Oxbridge or are related by marriage. They are toffs, the elite. Friends of Prince Charles and the Duke of Edinburgh. This green and pleasant land belongs to them.

After taking a sip from his drink, Henry places the glass down on the table and makes a spire with his long pale fingers.

'Have you ever thought about taking a few samples home with you, Arthur?' he asks the banker.

'All the time, dear boy. Trouble is getting caught.'

Henry glances at Bobby. 'We have a scoundrel in our midst.'

'Only if he gets *collared*.'

They laugh. Henry continues.

'You must have devised a plan?'

Arthur lights a cigar and blows out an enormous cloud of smoke. 'As it happens, Henry, I have let it pass through my mind from time to time and, yes, I think there would be a way.'

He pauses. They are intrigued. Christian waves away the smoke.

'The best laid schemes o' mice an' men. Gang aft agley,' says the spook, quoting Robbie Burns.

'But we are not mice,' Henry reminds him. 'And we are not ordinary men.'

They nod in agreement.

'Indeed,' Arthur says. 'Couriers, as you are no doubt aware, trot around the City every day with millions of pounds in bearer bonds in leather satchels. If one were to be held up by a thief and a large sum were stolen, the police,' he paused to glance at Bobby, 'would be consumed with hunting down that money and getting it back.'

'And no doubt they would succeed,' says the commissioner.

'But if the satchel were registered as carrying, say £300 million, but someone had slipped in another £100 million, while the police

Epilogue

were tracing £300 million, the £100 million would be quietly passed through the banking system garnering 30 or 40 per cent.'

'Smoke and mirrors,' the spook remarks. 'You'd need the right person to do the actual mugging.'

'Young black man,' suggests Bobby. 'Fits the profile.'

'What if the thieves do sell off some of the stolen bonds?' the spook asks.

'Who cares?' says Henry. 'We need to get some underworld figures involved.'

'That's your department,' Symes pipes up.

Henry glances from face to face. Each man in turn nods his head. No words of encouragement. No handshakes. They are English. There is an understanding.

'Why did Henry set the whole thing up?' Keith asks, and then answers. 'Because he could. Because he wanted to. It was a game. Ray Ketteridge, Pat Thomas, Mark Osborne, me. We were just pieces on the chessboard. Henry knew he could have got chopped at any time – by the Irish, the London villains, the Colombians. That's what he thrived on. It was a sexual thing, in my opinion.'

'In what way?'

'Flirting with gangsters gave him a thrill. When it came to the bonds robbery, he was at the centre of everything.'

'Why did he bring you in, Keith?'

'A safety valve, maybe, a backup. He was going to make money out of the £135 million in bonds no one except his little group knew about. He knew I could pass 200 mil to Indonesia and that would have been a fuck-you double whammy, checkmate in five moves.'

'But why did he let you and John Bowman count the other, what was it, 135 bonds?'

'That's Henry, a risk taker. He liked stirring things up for his own amusement.' He turned in his chair and pointed a finger at me. 'Coyle,

Rooney and Dunne, the three Irishmen, they all walked. They had never *handled* the stolen bonds in British jurisdiction. Then Tommy Coyle has the balls to buy a racehorse and call it 77 Mill.'

He broke off. 'Ray Ketteridge gets nicked and it's not in the *public interest* to continue the case.'

'Why, exactly?'

'You know why. They didn't want anyone in court talking on the public record,' he said. 'MI6 has the power to manipulate the court in the UK, just as the FBI has that power in the United States.'

We sat back. The shifting clouds patterned the mountainside. It was warm still, but you could feel autumn in the air. Keith lit a Montecristo No. 4.

'Henry bloody Nunn. Where is he now?' He blew invisible dust from his palm. 'In a shallow grave in Bolney Wood? Down in the deeps with Davy Jones? A new name on a numbered account in the Caribbean and a new boat race courtesy of some surgeon in Harley Street. Me and Sarah have been searching for years and come up with nothing. Gone. Disappeared.'

He refilled the glasses and I watched the liquid turn misty.

'Now you're going to ask why me?' he says. 'Eighty people arrested, one goes to jail. Me. Why? I suppose it was to make Mr Dickinson and his 40 Starling agents look good. He was a nice fella, the Super, but he never had a clue what was going on. He went on record to say they had got back all but two of the bonds reported as stolen, two of the 292. That's cobblers. I tore three into tiny pieces myself.'

'What about the other two?'

'What other two?'

'Ray Ketteridge gave you five bonds that night in Henry's house.'

'Did he?'

'The two you kept hidden in a John le Carré book?'

'Me? I don't remember that.'

Clifford Thurlow
Turkey, 14 September 2023

ACKNOWLEDGEMENTS

Sincere thanks to Keith's wife, Sarah Hancock, who has patiently read and reread the manuscript for errors and inaccuracies; it would be hard to find a better editor. Also Iris Gioia for her suggestions and Nicholas Furst, a recent graduate from the University of Toronto, for his guidance on American phraseology. Our thanks to Peter York for reading an early draft of the manuscript and Mike Wallington for his inspirational comments. We are grateful to our agent Andrew Lownie, who has been with us every step on the long, often harrowing road that leads to a finished book, and also Connor Stait, Ellen Conlon, Steve Burdett and their brilliant team at Icon Books.